Bill:

En[illegible] as you continue your journey through life.

Green Ivy Publishing
1 Lincoln Centre
18W140 Butterfield Road
Suite 1500
Oakbrook Terrace IL 60181-4843
www.greenivybooks.com

ISBN: 978-1-943955-72-5

Small Business Owner's Desk Reference

Dick Larkin, M.B.A., Ed.D.

Table of Contents

Preface

This *Desk Reference,* written in a common sense manner, is designed to provide answers and direction to any person hoping to become a business owner, grow their existing small business, or work their way through a business decision when they are not sure where to turn for help. It is organized into easy-to-understand sections covering a wide range of topics from developing a business plan and financing a business idea, to performing daily operations, evaluating competition, creating marketing plans, maintaining inventory, developing pricing strategy, hiring the right employees with an affordable compensation package, etc.

The writing is based upon the author's personal experience as a small business owner, a corporate Planning Director, and as an independent management consultant. Topics addressed in the *Desk Reference* were selected by the author from experience as a counselor and mentor to small business owners. They are the most common challenges to individuals developing and operating their own independent companies.

The first two parts of the *Desk Reference* focus on helping a person transition from a business *idea* to a *ready-to-go* well-planned business. The early chapters provide suggestions on how to begin the planning process by sharing examples to help understand the role of an entrepreneur, think critically about their business idea and competition, develop a clear company vision or mission, and develop a practical business plan.

The last portion provides help with the daily operations of a small business by giving ideas on how to arranging a business interior, manage people, control inventory management, determine product prices, and several related topics.

In addition to the primary chapters, there are appendices dealing with personal financial statements, estimating startup or expansion expenses, cash flow projections, and a sample business plan.

Acknowledgments

This book is dedicated to the hundreds of co-workers, students, and SCORE clients I have had the privilege of associating with and learn from over several decades as a paid worker and as a volunteer. It is a testament to the concept of lifelong learning and is written with the hope of creating one more stepping stone for growth in the world of small business ownership.

In addition to my professional support, I want to thank my family and friends for putting up with me as I worked to create this *Desk Reference.*

Part One – Realities of Business Ownership

Chapter 1 Owning a Business

Is this how you picture yourself in your current position?

Is this what I will be doing for the rest of my life?

How can I find a job I will like? Can I create my own business?

How can I break loose from this boring routine?

Maybe I can become my own boss. Can I run a business?

If you are reading this and want to have more control of your own career, you are starting to look into what it takes to create and operate a successful business of your own.

This book will help you define a clear goal, build trust in your own capabilities, develop a thorough business plan, and help you achieve your dreams of business ownership.

This chapter provides some ideas about the challenges, commitment, and enjoyment of owning a small business. It is intended to support a person's desire to develop their own company, while sharing some of the realities that should be considered while they are thinking about creating their own business.

Introduction

Owning a business can satisfy a dream for many, provide a challenge for others, and at times present a burden for nearly every entrepreneur. Like raising a family, running a business can be the most satisfying experience in a person's life, while at the same time providing (hopefully brief) moments that might make a parent or manager wonder how they ever got themselves into such an awkward situation.

Each person is unique and every business is unique. The goal of every business owner should be to develop their dream business that fulfills and supports their unique interests, style, principles, and beliefs. Some people try creating a business because they want to make lots of money, be their own boss, control daily activities, be allowed to do things their own way, or they just want to provide a product or service they think or believe has no competitors. Whatever the reason for becoming a business owner, it is certain that each company is different from every other company because of the culture that emanates from the owner.

The company should fit the owner

"Choose a job you love, and you will never have to work a day in your life"

Confucius

No two jewelers, grocery stores, clothing stores, or dentists are quite the same. They may provide the same, or similar products or services as their competitors, but there will be some differences in their operational processes, employee relationships, and customer relationships. The differences will be in a large part due to the personality of the business owner and therefore the people they hire and train to support customers.

A business owner with a positive, can do, helpful attitude who sincerely cares about others, will develop a company with the same attitude. A business owner with a negative and confrontational personality will create a company with an aggressive or abrasive operating atmosphere. This *Desk Reference* is written for people with a positive, can-do attitude about their work and their work place.

A business owner with the right company fit should be able to *retire the first day they go to work. Retire* does not mean stop working and lounge at home every day. *Retire* in this case means a person should look forward to going to work each day. If going to work feels like a burden and a person spends a lot of time dreaming of the day they won't have to head into their place of business anymore, they are very likely not in the right company and they are almost certainly not suited to be the owner of that business.

A business owner with the right company should:

- Enjoy and take pride in their company, including the staff, the facility, and the product or service they provide

- Feel motivated by their daily tasks and let their motivation be contagious to others they interface with

- Never stop trying to improve the quality of their product or service and welcome comments or suggestions from customers and staff members

Realities of business ownership

Consider a few myths versus reality provided by the U.S. Small Business Administration (SBA) related to business ownership:

As an entrepreneur, you won't have to work so hard or put in such long hours.

> **Reality:** Most entrepreneurs work much longer hours than their employees, but they tend to enjoy it more because they are building something of their own.

My company product or service is unique. I do not have any competition.

> **Reality:** There is always competition, even if it begins after your company has started and builds off your idea. Competition may be in a different form, but you need to watch for it and improve your product, service, or customer relations to deal with it.

As a business owner, you won't have a boss.

Reality: You may not have a person designated as your boss, but your business will not survive if you don't satisfy the needs of your clients and customers.

Business owners get to do what they want to do.

Reality: Sort of. You will be able to do what you enjoy, but some of your time will be spent doing tasks you find difficult or boring.

Characteristics and behaviors of a business owner

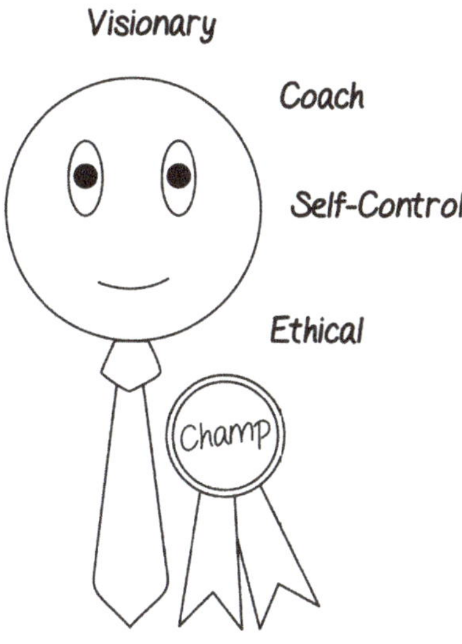

Most successful business owners and entrepreneurs have several characteristics in common. They tend to be confident in themselves and their ability; they are optimistic; they are self-starters and able to stay on their plan; and they are open to new ideas. In addition, they usually have the following characteristics:

Self-control:

They are able to concentrate on their objective and avoid being overly influenced by day-to-day distractions.

Willing to accept change:

They accept differences in operations, regulations, and processes as a learning experience, or business opportunity, rather than a setback. They are positive and accept the Deming Wheel model of continuous improvement (plan-do-check-act-plan again). They encourage and appreciate new ideas and suggestions.

Competitive:

They are vigilant about competition and continue to adapt where necessary to keep their company successful. They perform competitive actions with high ethical standards.

Coaching skills:

They are excellent communicators and motivators. They have a natural ability to motivate and celebrate the success of others. They are team oriented, rather than self-oriented.

Strong work ethic:

They tend to be the first person reporting to the work place and the last to leave. They don't wear themselves out to the point of ineffectiveness through long hours. They tend to love their work and never stop researching ways to make the business improve.

Listening skills:

> They know when to stop talking and concentrate on what others are saying. They are willing to hear opposing views without becoming defensive. They encourage opposing ideas in an open and non-confrontational manner.

Visionary:

> They are able to understand and strategize on a high level. They do not lose sight of the mission or purpose of the business while they are involved in day-to-day decisions.

So you have the right characteristics –

Can ***you*** run a whole company?

Responsibilities of a business owner

Even if a person has all of the right characteristics to be a business owner, they may not have all of the *skills* required to make the company function successfully. Most upper level managers have a variety of skills, which they need to perform their job, but very few people are experts in *all functions* (such as legal issues, accounting, engineering, production, and marketing).

There are several examples of excellent professional athletes that do not do well when they are promoted to coach, or coaches that are ineffective when they become General Manager of a sports team. In the business world, there are people with a very positive history as design engineers, medical doctors, journeyman machinists, sales associates, etc. who fail when they are promoted to top level management positions. The failure is because they are promoted to an area of responsibility they are not ready to accept. It is referred to as the Peter Principle. (1)

> Peter Principle
>
> In 1968, Laurence J. Peter, Ph.D., a Canadian born educator shared his belief about promotions within business and government bureaucracies, which stated simply, is . Dr. Peter argued that many people who do well in their position are rewarded by being promoted to a higher level of management until eventually, they are quite often promoted to a position requiring skills they did not learn in their work experience.
>
> A person can be a highly qualified and well-respected accountant and make an excellent high-level accounting manager, but not have the skills to run a production department. At the same time, a top-notch production manager might not be very good at running an accounting department.
>
> When discussing company promotions Dr. Peter said "The

cream rises until it sours."(2) The Peter Principle simply means people can be an expert in their field, but not necessarily effective as a manager. It means a good general manager, or business owner should recognize their limitations and hire the services of experts in areas where they need help such as legal matters, sales, or production.

Functions of a small business

A person planning to become a business owner should understand while they might be very knowledgeable as an employee or Department Manager, they need to understand all of the *job functions a business owner is charged with coordinating.*

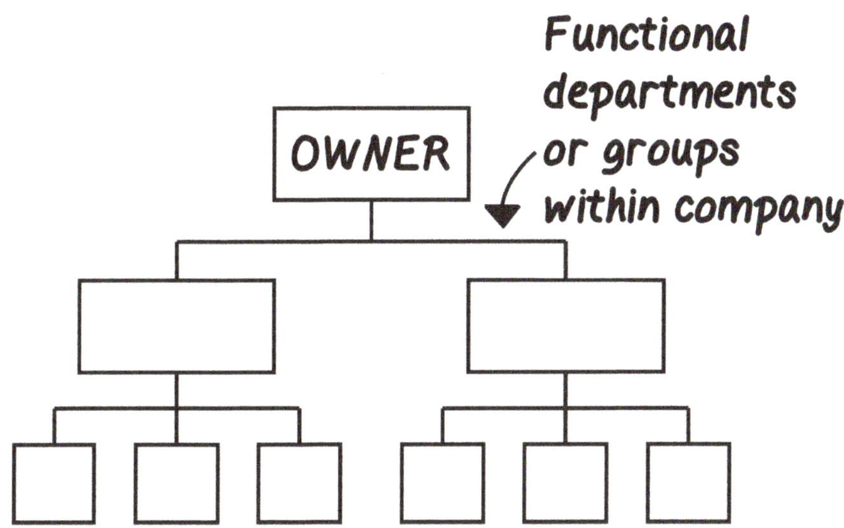

Administration

Office functions, paperwork, telephones, email, office systems, insurance

Accounting and Finances

Bookkeeping, taxes, recording sales, accounts receivable and payable

Human Resources

Managing employees, job descriptions, recruiting, hiring, training, employee compensation, employee safety

Marketing and Sales

Creating and promoting company products and services, advertising, public relations

Production and Operations

Producing the company product or performing the company service, coordinating supplier orders, managing inventory, and shipping

Information Technology

Selecting, purchasing, installing, and maintaining information systems, operating technology, and coordinating support services

Facilities (Plant and Equipment)

Selecting and maintaining business location, negotiating leases, coordinating cleaning and preventive maintenance activities.

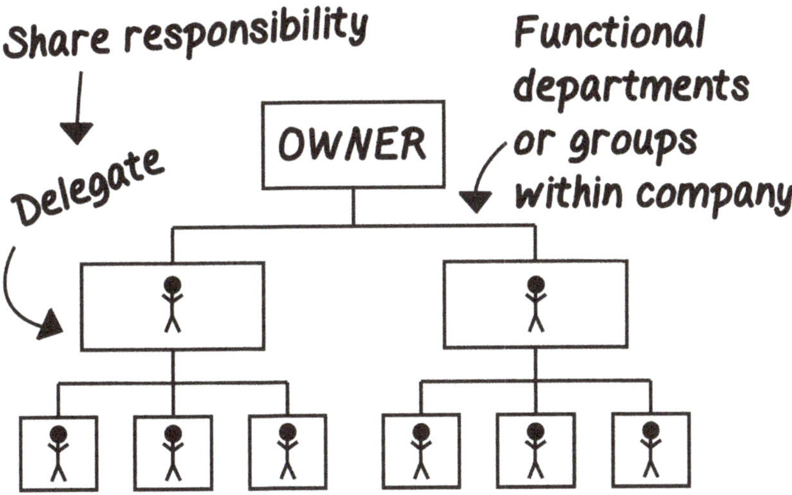

Delegating responsibilities

A small business owner is not expected to be able to have the skills necessary to do everything that is required to run a successful business. They ARE expected to know the limitations of their expertise and be willing to hire or reach out to others to help them in some specialty areas.

Having concerns about "total" responsibility should not scare a person away from following their dream of starting a business. It should just be an area to think through while they are developing their business plan, which is discussed in detail in Part 2 of this *Desk Reference*.

Questions to ask while considering the realities of business ownership include:

- As a potential business owner, do you have a weakness in any of the responsibilities listed above?
- Can you take a course to improve the area you consider a weakness?
- If there is an area that does not fit your skills, can you hire employees, or outsource the tasks?

"I'm a good chef – but I'm not a good accountant"

"I'm a good mechanic and planner – but I'm not good at sales"

"I'm good with my hands – but I don't like office work"

Even if a person is good at all areas of company ownership, as the business grows, they won't have time to do everything. When developing the staffing portion of their business plan, they should consider prioritizing tasks and responsibilities. They should identify which functions will be delegated to others either right away, or as the business grows.

Advantages of owning a business

In his book *The Three Boxes of Life, and How to Get Out of Them*, Richard Bolles(3) argues that our lives tend to be spent in three boxes:

- **education,** when our energy is consumed by learning,
- **work,** when our energy is consumed by producing and growing in our career, and
- **retirement,** when we attempt to devote our energy to enjoying leisure.

Experience shows that in our retirement years, many people are no longer physically able to do all of the things they have been dreaming about.

This writing will take advantage of Bolles' suggestion. "…leisure is not to be saved up until you are a senior citizen but it is to be indulged in, throughout your entire life."

Working should mean you are doing something that you enjoy doing. Work should NOT be drudgery.

If you find yourself in the position of owning your own business and fulfilling the dream of producing a product or providing a service you are really happy with, you should feel comfortable in a lifelong box of learning, working, and playing. If Bolles' did not already take advantage of it with the title of his book, this section might be changed to *Small business ownership, the ongoing experience of youth, young adult, and mid-life.*

Owning a small business should always be exciting, provide thought provoking challenges, and include the satisfaction of playing an active role in keeping a dream alive. Just as earlier in this chapter, business ownership can be compared to raising a family. It includes a lot of pride, a lot of challenges, but overall, an ongoing, long-term feeling of accomplishment.

Concerns about owning a business

Life is full of transitions and stressful events. They include school graduation, marriage, childbirth, kids leaving, career changes, health concerns, moving to a new home, etc. Each stressful event represents a major change in a person's life. Starting a new business would rank high as a life changing stressful event.

> In 1967, Psychiatrists Thomas Holmes and Richard Rahe examined the medical records of over 5,000 medical patients to determine whether stressful events might cause illnesses. Patients were asked to tally a list of 43 life events based on a relative score.
>
> Their results were published as the Social Readjustment Rating Scale (SRRS), known more commonly as the *Holmes and Rahe Stress Scale.* (4) Over several years the SRRS has been validated through related tests by the U.S. military, Cornell University, and other organizations. The scale has been studied over a diverse population of ethnicity and education.
>
> The SRRS is used to determine stress levels in adults by providing a score for "Life Change Units" they experience over a 12-month period. The total score provides a rough estimate of how stress affects health. Life change scores on the SRRS include a high of 100 for the death of a spouse, to 11 for a minor traffic violation. The total points, according to Holmes and Rahe indicate:

Score of 300+: High risk of illness

Score of 150-299: Moderate risk of illness

Score <150: Slight risk of illness

Job changes or starting a new business could cause increased stress to individuals according to the SRRS.

Dismissal from work = 47 points

Retirement = 45 points

Business readjustment = 39 points

Change to different line of work = 36 points

Change in responsibilities at work = 29 points

Based upon the research by Holmes and Rahe, it would be safe to assume starting a new small business can be stressful and the new owner should be careful to take care of their health during the transition period.

Despite the differences in each transition, every change creates stress for the individual because they are feeling the *loss of what was familiar* to them before the change. Sometimes the losses can appear to be overwhelming during the early stages of the transition.

The stress of creating a new business can be minimized it the new owner will remember that during any major change in their life they will miss the things they are losing, or giving up.

However, they cannot transition into a new situation without letting go of some familiarity. Think of a well-planned new business as an adventure and an opportunity to grow.

They may feel a *gap* in their life before they can begin to appreciate and feel comfortable with what is new.

Anticipating the gap or loss should help them maintain control of their life and new business venture during the early planning and opening stages.

A *transition* is a major reshaping of a person's day-to-day existence, a redefining of who they are and their role with others, and a reworking of how they conduct their life. Remember transitioning to a new business is changing a work habit, not a whole way of life. By starting a new business, they are NOT changing the principles that drive their behavior.

Suggestions to help:

- Remember change (transitioning) is about action. Don't be too impatient.
- Think about your own unique values and beliefs. Stay grounded in who you are and who you want to become. Don't let circumstances or the influence of other people pull you away from your principles.

- Develop a business plan to help you break your transition into small change components and tasks you can handle.

Work – family – life balance

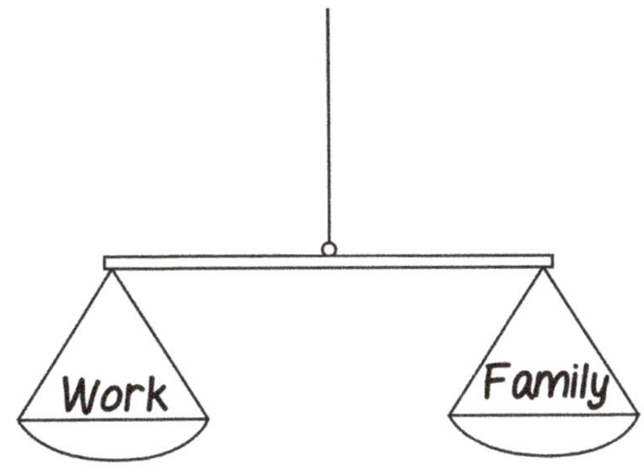

"I try to take one day at a time,

but sometimes several days attack me at once." Jennifer Yane

"There cannot be a stressful crisis next week.

My schedule is already full." Henry Kissinger

Starting and operating a business is stressful. It demands constant attention as problems requiring prompt and decisive action come from all directions – staff, customers, suppliers, regulators, twenty-four hours a day. A business owner cannot walk out the door and forget their work concerns until they return. They are expected to be available every day at every hour to solve problems as they arise.

Quoting Pete Carroll, Head Coach of the Seattle Seahawks in his book *Win Forever* (pg.167)(5)

"I will be the first to admit that the coaching profession is

> demanding and the pressure is real. However, this is the job and the life we coaches have chosen, so how we deal with it is up to us. We can live the experience any way we choose. My choice is to take on the challenges and all that accompanies coaching and find the enjoyment and the fun whenever possible."

If a new business owner can think of themselves as a coach, they can learn a lot by watching the leadership styles of coaches of winning sports teams. They need to think of their business position as a great job and they should feel fortunate to be in their position.

If a person can enjoy the positive aspects of business ownership, they can also celebrate the positives with their family, friends, and associates. Think of a business as a team and the owner as the head coach, and help everyone learn their role, take pride in their participation, and generate a winning business.

Summary

Owning and operating a business can be fun, rewarding, and a great source of self-esteem. It provides a person freedom to try things they have been unable to do under another person's direction. It can provide a feeling of accomplishment that can almost never be totally possible when working for another person or company.

It can also be a frustration and provide overwhelming challenges, which, if not corrected, can have a very adverse effect on a person's finances and personal relationships. A well-analyzed business plan will usually let a person know if they are ready to start their own business, and if they decide to begin a business, provide a roadmap to help them achieve success.

When thinking about starting a new business, or expanding an existing business, do the critical thinking during the planning process, not when the door is open and customers are demanding products or services beyond the scope of the company.

Chapter 2 Company Startup Decisions

This chapter provides some tools to help a potential business owner begin their business planning process by thinking critically about the business they would like to create and how they will manage it.

If a person knows what kind of business they want to start, they can probably bypass the first section of this chapter and go to "Describe the Business." "Comparison of starting new, purchasing existing, or franchising"

If they know they want to start a business of their own, but are not sure exactly what kind of business to create, this section is for them.

Deciding the *kind* of business

Begin by finding out what makes the potential new business owner happy.

Thinking about growing into a new career or creating a new business is a full-time job in itself. Developing a serious business plan should require as much time and effort as performing a full-time job. If a person is unemployed and thinking of starting a new business, then planning the business *IS THEIR JOB.*

If they are going to find the right fit between their interests and a new company, they need to establish clear occupational goals then develop a strategy on how to achieve the goals. Their personal goals and strategy should become a career *plan* and be incorporated into, or supported by, their business plan.

Without clear goals and a well thought out plan, the career or business idea is likely to be aimless, frustrating, ineffective, and put them right back into a job that makes them unhappy.

Hint:

> *The steps shown on the next few pages have been used by several people with a desire to start a business of their own, but who were uncertain what kind of business they would be happy with for a lifelong career. Follow the steps with an open, nonjudgmental) mind and the result might be surprising.*

A person should begin by finding out what interests them, what they like to do, and who they like to associate with.

For about 3 or 4 weeks, they can keep a journal or list of what they do when they are doing what THEY want to do. They should not analyze the journal as it is being written. Once or twice a day, they should think back over the past few hours and write these things in their journal:

- If they pick up a book they want to read (not a required book for a class), write down the title (or at least the topic).
- If they visit someone because THEY want to, write down the name of the person they visited. If they go with someone else and the person they are visiting would not have been their first choice, don't write their name. If they go with someone else and the person they are visiting would have been your first choice, write their name.
- If they go to a movie, sporting event, shopping, dining, or any form of relaxation and it would have been THEIR first choice. If they go somewhere with another person and, given the choice, they would have done something else, don't write it down.
- If they listen to music or watch home entertainment (TV), they should write what THEY enjoy, not what others select that they might not have chosen.
- If they read a newspaper or magazine, write down the types of article they read 1st, 2nd, or 3rd, and not the rest.

> They should NOT *list things they do, or people they associate with... if they would not be their first choice if they had a clear choice.*

Don't jump to conclusions

They should *not* analyze the journal or list while they are entering data and they should not share it with others. Analyzing the journal too soon before it has a large amount of data collected, can cause a person to jump to conclusions and misinterpret the information being gathered.

Remember, the journal is personal and private. It is designed to help an individual find out what interests them without someone else reading through the entries and influencing the person making their own entries. It is meant to help a person find out what they enjoy doing, so they can incorporate their interests in deciding what kind of business to create that will motivate them.

Look for a consistent theme

After three or four weeks, when there are a large number of journal entries, look over the data. Hopefully a theme will be developing. There should be some strong indicators showing what interests them, what they like to do, and who they like to associate with. This is the beginning of *identifying their interests* and starting to consider career goals and an ideal company to create.

Maybe they will find that they enjoy outdoor activities, or indoor activities. Maybe they are interested in the arts, dining out, dancing, knitting, physical labor, researching genealogy, or something else.

Maybe they like to be on the road a lot, or they like to stay close to home. Maybe they like solving complex problems, working on detailed plans, or thinking of the big picture and leaving delegating detail work to others.

Maybe they like to be alone, in small groups, or with large groups. Maybe they like doing things with their hands, have mental challenges, team oriented activities with structure, or independence with little or no formal structure. From the common theme, they should begin to get a mental picture of how they would like to spend their day and what kind of business they might enjoy creating.

Identify personal skills and abilities

Anyone planning to start a new business needs more than a dream of working for themselves. They need experience or abilities that will help them understand and run the business.

A person should not start a restaurant if they have never cooked.

A person should not start a trucking company if they don't understand the freight industry.

A person should not start an auto repair company if they have not worked on vehicles.

They don't have to be an expert in all areas of a business to be successful, but they do have to know their limitations and either delegate portions of the responsibility to people with specific skills, or obtain training in the area where they are less skilled.

A potential business owner can begin by developing an understanding of what they personally have to offer. They need to think about and understand what they will bring to the company to make it successful. What do they have to offer that will make their company stand out from their competitors?

Sometimes it helps to put skills and abilities into two categories: job specific, and self-management:

Job specific abilities

> Specific to a job or occupation, these are the skills and abilities that will apply directly to a job they are interested in. They include familiarity with a particular piece of equipment or software, experience working with certain tools or procedures, ability to manage inventory, maintain records and work with customers.

Self-Management abilities

> Sometimes referred to as personality traits, these are the skills or abilities they use each day to help them deal with other people. They make them unique and set them apart from other people. They include sincerity, tactfulness, flexibility, timeliness, and tolerance.

Review past experiences

- List the titles of jobs held, beginning with the most recent. I*nclude volunteer positions, clubs, and social activities.*
- Write a short description for each of the jobs listed.
- Think of the *skills required* to accomplish each of the jobs on the list.
- Write a list of those skills. Include Job Skills and Self-Management skills. Be sure to include machines and software.
- Highlight the skills considered most enjoyable.
- Compare the list of skills enjoyed with the personal interests developed during the self-analysis.

This should be starting to show what kind of company would be highly motivating and help understand whether a person has the right skills. It may also let a person see whether they might need to take part in some further education or training to learn specific skills.

Evaluate the *need* for a new company

Research the industry

Research through the local library, Internet, local Chamber of Commerce, or the U.S. Small Business Administration to determine:

- Growth trends – How fast can a new business in the industry expect to grow?
- Profitability – What kind of profit can be expected? What are the average profit margins for the industry?
- Trends – What current and future trends (demographic, economic, local, and global) are affecting the industry?

Define target market (potential customers)

Explain the need the new company's product or service will fill. What problem will it solve?

Think about potential competitors and answer the question, "What will this product or service provide that is not being met by competitors?"

Who are the potential competitors? Name them.

> Consider conducting a SWOT analysis to compare the planned company with competitors. The analysis will identify benefits and challenges related to starting a new company in the geographic region or industry.
>
> SWOT analysis is explained in Chapter 5 of this *Desk Reference.*

What is the *competitive advantage* of the new company?

A competitive advantage is what a company has in the form of management skills, facilities, location, quality, cost, or other criteria over competitors. It is an advantage that allows the company to generate more sales, and support more long-term customers than its competitors.

Develop a draft (*informal*) Marketing Plan

The formal Marketing Plan will be addressed in more detail later in this Desk Reference in a chapter devoted to marketing and advertising.

Answer these questions:

What will the new company do to attract and keep their target customers?

Who will the business serve? Narrow the marketing plan to fit a specific target.

Where is the potential market located? Are they retail customers, wholesalers, walk in or on-line customers, or other businesses?

What is the income level and potential for payment by customers?

What is the lifestyle of target customers? How do they spend their money?

What are the spending habits of potential customers?

Describe the business

There is more to a person becoming their own boss than putting out a sign and opening the front door. The first step is to develop a clear understanding of what kind of business they want to create.

Think about how a new owner might describe the business to somebody they are meeting for the first time – a potential investor, or maybe a realtor who will help them find a business location.

Without worrying about the structure or format of a written *business plan*, think through a few basic questions and write down ideas.

> The format at this stage is not important – just the thought process.
>
> Write notes to yourself. They are for your own use to help you later as you write your formal plan. Don't be concerned about formality or sharing them with anyone else.

The company description should include, where practical:

- A description of the industry, including an explanation of whether it is new, growing, or in a state of change
- The company goals and objectives
- The form of ownership (e.g. sole proprietorship, partnership, LLC, S corporation, or other
- Business philosophy of customer relations, employee relations, and quality
- Description of target market
- Additional factors which are expected to make the company succeed
- Franchise details, if applicable
- Strengths that the owner will personally bring to the business

Comparison of starting new, purchasing existing, or franchising

Starting a new business

Creating a new business from the ground up and making it profitable can be highly motivating for a new entrepreneur. It is a chance to prove their idea for a new product or service works and is marketable. It is exciting from start to finish, provided everything goes as planned – but it rarely does.

No matter how well researched and planned, every new business venture can expect to run into unexpected problems. There may be surprise announcements from competitors, unexpected zoning restrictions, infrastructure and facility concerns (heating, lighting, mold), financial changes (unplanned family emergency), problems with suppliers and product availability. These are not meant to be negative statements, just realistic statements.

Any new business should build extra time in their grand opening schedule and additional funds in their budget planning. It is referred to as contingency planning . Allow for and expect the unexpected, and hope it is not necessary to use the extra time or budget.

Developing a totally new company from a dream or a fresh idea is an exciting and fulfilling activity for anyone with the courage to develop a business plan and stay the course. The process will include many frustrations along the way, but if the individual following their dream is willing to work through the awkward moments, they will most likely have proven themselves able to run a small business successfully.

Purchasing an existing business

When thinking about creating a new business, it is worth considering the purchase of an existing company with the same, or similar products or services.

Benefits

The operating business will have worked out its processes and debugged system problems.

- It is likely to have established relationships with suppliers.
- It may have experienced staff willing to work with and support new ownership.
- Transferring staff might have good ideas for improved operations that they were unable to share with former owners.
- The business should have an established location.
- Housekeeping and maintenance processes will probably be established.
- Operating, or accounting systems should already be in place.
- New ownership should inherit the customer base, which will save advertising expenses.

Concerns

The first question that comes to mind is, "Why is the business being sold?"

- o If it is due to age (retirement) or illness of the owner, it is probably a reasonable reason to sell the business.
- o If it is due to poor profit, declining customer base, increased competition, changes in the surrounding neighborhood, or poor operating processes, the emphasis for a potential buyer should

be on whether they have the ability to convince customers to support new ownership.

Investigate the existing business

Business consultants highly recommend that potential buyers of a new business do as much investigating as possible before they approach the owner to negotiate an offer. These are suggested steps to learn about a business that is being offered for sale:

1. Contact the sales agent the owner has appointed to manage the sale of their business and express interest in a possible purchase. Do NOT approach the business owner until the sales agent schedules an appropriate meeting.

   The business owner is running their company and usually too busy to deal with a potential buyer until they are ready to make a firm offer.

2. Consider appointing an advisor or agent to represent your interests. In a complex negotiation, a lawyer or accountant may be a valuable agent to support the buyer.

3. Ask up front why the business is for sale. It may provide enough information for they buyer to decide whether to proceed with an offer. At the least, it will provide information to use during negotiations if their investigation does not support the reason for selling.

4. Talk with the local Chamber of Commerce, real estate agents, the Better Business Bureau, U.S. Small Business Administration SCORE counselors, suppliers, customers, and others to find out what they think about trends related to the existing company, the industry, the region, etc.

5. Observe the company at different times of the day and on different days of the week. Watch for customer volume at different times.

6. Act the part of, or send in a secret shopper. Learn from the experience of being a customer of the existing business. Try the same exercise with nearby competitors and compare the differences.

7. Consider conducting a Strength, Weakness, Opportunity, Threat (SWOT) analysis of the completion competition to determine whether the company is strong enough to succeed and grow with new ownership. (SWOT analysis is described in Chapter 5 of this *Desk Reference.)*

Before beginning *negotiations,* the buyer and seller will usually require three agreements:

The potential buyer will usually agree to not hire any of the seller's employees if the purchase does not work out.

The potential seller will usually agree to not conduct any sales discussions or activities with other potential buyers while the buyer is investigating and negotiating.

Both parties will usually sign a confidentiality agreement regarding information about the business sale, whether or not the sale is completed.

Due Diligence

Due diligence refers to evaluating a potential business decision by reviewing and considering applicable financial, legal, insurance, marketing, and general company records. In other words, due diligence allows one to make an educated business decision, rather than an emotional, shoot-from-the-hip decision.

This evaluation helps a potential buyer be certain:

- The business owns all of the property, equipment, vehicles, and intellectual property (patents, etc.) the owner claims to own.

- There are no pending lawsuits or any history of legal concerns that could limit company operation or expansion,

- What, if any, contracts are in effect with suppliers, customers, equipment maintenance, software or operating systems, etc. that will, or might transfer with the purchase? This will clarify the company obligations.

> *Helpful hint:*
>
> *There are several Due Diligence checklists available on the Internet to help a prospective business buyer know what to look for when investigating a business. Use search words like "legal advice" or "legal services," or visit the U. S. Small Business Association Administration (SBA)*(6)

Additional sources

Talk with current staff

- Find out their experience level.
- Compare their qualifications with competitors to know whether they could help introduce positive changes.
- Determine whether they are content with their current position and level of responsibility, or whether they would welcome and support a change.

Review financial records

Unless the potential buyer is experienced in financial analysis, it is usually a good idea to hire an accountant to audit the financial records of an existing business.

- Be sure the business is using proper accounting techniques for the company or industry.
- Look for trends that indicate market demand and profitability on a monthly and annual basis.
- Compare budget targets with actual accomplishments.
- Compare financial reports with others in the same industry.

Establishing a purchase price

Establishing the value of an operating business requires considering far more variables than purchasing a home where the price is nearly always limited to the age and condition of the building, the property, and the neighborhood. The price of a business can require an evaluation and comparison of net present value (property, equipment, inventory, etc.), current and forecast earnings, and comparisons within the industry.

It is usually a good business idea to bring in a legal and/or financial advisor to help establish a fair purchase price.

Negotiating payment

Purchasing an existing business does not usually require a full cash payment at the closing of the sale. The negotiations should include an agreement to pay over time, rent or lease the facilities and some assets from the seller. The buyer and seller can also consider a partnership or a partial merger.

There is no standard payment process for purchasing an existing business, so it is a good idea to discuss several alternatives.

Consider a franchise

A franchise is an established business that expands to new branches by selling a license to use its name, operating procedures, and support systems to provide *branded* products and services. The owner (seller) of the franchise brand is called the franchisor. They buyer of a franchise is referred to as a franchisee.

Advertising, operating procedures, facilities, and in some cases, staff uniforms, are controlled by the franchisor making each branch or outlet indistinguishable from the other locations in the franchise.

The purchaser (franchisee) usually buys the rights to a geographical region. Within the franchised region, the franchisee is expected to use the sellers name, signs, uniforms, suppliers, and operating procedures to sell products and services under the name of the franchise business.

The seller (franchisor) provides name recognition, large-scale advertising, reduced inventory costs through centralized purchasing, and training of the franchisee's staff and management.

In return, the franchisee pays an upfront or startup fee and, usually, a percentage of sales and, or monthly fee to the seller.

A person considering buying a franchise should think about why they want to start a business. If they want to be independent and free to try new processes or product lines, a franchise may be too restrictive for them. If on the other hand, they want to be their own boss but could use some help with advertising and operational training, a franchise might be a good business choice.

Helpful hints when considering a franchise

- *Consider talking with an attorney specializing in franchises for guidance.*
- *Be careful before spending a large upfront fee without receiving anything other than promises of things to come.*
- *Discuss and understand mandatory ongoing costs such as monthly advertising fee, monthly minimum inventory purchases required to buy from the franchisor, and training fees.*
- *Research the geographical region and investigate potential zoning changes or expansion by competitors.*
- *Visit other franchisees with the same company to learn about their typical day-to-day experiences.*
- *Attend franchise trade shows to compare similar franchises for similarities and differences.*

Legal structure

> *Disclaimer: The author is not an attorney and has no formal legal training other than limited business law courses and experience in the business community. This section is to share ideas, interpretations, and experiences but is NOT to provide any legal advice, either intentional or unintentional.*

A new business can be structured in several ways; each one has some benefits and some drawbacks. When the business plan is nearly complete and the company is getting ready to become a formal entity, the owner(s) need to decide on what type of structure they will set-up. Whether sole proprietor, partnership, corporation, or LLC, the structure, will determine their liability, define their rights, and affect taxes.

This section is provided to discuss options to consider when deciding on the company legal structure. *It is a top-level summary and not intended to take the place of legal counsel.*

Sole Proprietorship

Considered the simplest form of business ownership, there is no legally recognized separation between the business owner and their personal life. If a person starts a small business, no matter how small, and they sells goods or services as an individual, in the eyes of the law, they are a business. If they have not registered a different legal structure, they are considered a *sole proprietorship.*

Benefits

- There is no legal paperwork required to begin the business
- Overhead costs are generally low.
- Profit belongs to the individual owner and there is no need to share with partners or investors.
- No special tax paperwork is required because profit and loss are reported with individual or family tax return.

Concerns

- Owner is liable for all debts and liabilities of the company. Losses can be settled by taking family assets.
- Losses are absorbed (paid by) the owner from personal assets.
- It can be difficult to get financing due to personal liability of ownership.

General Partnership

When two or more people develop and operate a business together, it can begin with a formal agreement, though it is not necessary. If two or more people begin working together to produce goods or services, they are by default, a general partnership unless they have formally registered another business structure.

It offers very low start-up costs and an easy way to begin a business, but it does not provide any liability protection for any partner if the business fails or another partner becomes unable to work or makes poor financial decisions.

Benefits

- There is no need for a formal partnership agreement.
- No special tax forms or reporting is required for the business. Like a sole proprietorship, business income and losses are reported on the partners' individual tax forms.
- Partners can change operating policies and processes without investor approval.

Concerns

- Each partner is personally liable for all business expenses and operational problems.
- It is difficult to transfer partnership responsibilities if a partner leaves.
- It can be difficult to agree on a fair distribution of profits and losses.
- Problems can arise with relatives of a partner who becomes ill or unable to function within the partnership.

Limited Partnership

Unlike the general partnership, a limited partnership usually has to be registered with the state. It is owned by general partners and limited partners. The general partners run the business and, like the general partnership company, are personally liable for debts and operating problems of the business. Limited partners do not take part in running the business and they have no operating responsibility. Limited partners' liability is limited to the amount they invest in the business.

Benefits

- It is a fairly easy way for some companies to obtain operating capital.
- Like a sole proprietorship or general partnership, tax filings can be handled with each partner's personal tax reporting.

Concerns

- Due to the need to register with the State, it is a more complex business arrangement than a sole proprietorship or partnership.
- Limited partners have no say in the operation or management in the company.

C Corporation

State law considers a *corporation* to be a separate and distinct legal entity owned by its shareholders. Shareholders personal liability is limited to the amount of their investment. The corporation is taxed as a distinct entity *and* investors (shareholders) are taxed as individuals based upon any profit they are awarded by the company. Some consider this double taxation. C Corporations must be registered with the State.

Benefits

- Owners are only liable for the amount they invest in the company through the purchase of stock shares.
- Owners (shareholders) have the opportunity to participate in the selection of operating managers of the company.
- Ownership can be transferred though the sale of shares.

Concerns

- Forming a C Corporation can be complex, requiring legal coordination and registering it with the State.
- Obtaining policy or procedural agreements with all shareholders can be cumbersome.

S Corporation

A special IRS category referred to as *Subchapter S Corporations* was established to provide small companies (75 - 100 shareholders) with liability protection without the double taxation experienced by C Corporations. Company profits are passed directly through to shareholders who report them on individual tax forms.

Benefits

- No double taxation because investors are taxed directly and the company is not.
- Personal liability is limited to the amount invested by each shareholder.

Concerns

- Registration with the State is a complex process and the company must maintain corporate reporting forms.
- The corporation is limited to types of income (e.g. real estate, royalties, etc.) determined by IRS Code.

Limited Liability Company (LLC)

This business structure combines features found in corporations with those found in partnerships. It protects investor's personal assets by protecting them from company debts, with limited liability. There is no double taxation as company profits and losses are reported only one time on the investor's income tax forms._

Benefits

- Owners are not personally liable for company debts. Their personal (family) assets are protected although financers may require owners to use personal assets as collateral for business loans.
- Owners' personal property and family are protected against liabilities resulting from company operations.
- There is flexibility in management of the company and distribution of profits among investors.

Concerns

- Most states limit the types of business that can form an LLC.
- Transferring ownership can be complex, based upon the company forming (partnership agreement) documents.

- It must be registered with the State and follow applicable state regulations.

Summary

Starting a new business involves a wide range of emotions. Excitement, frustration, joy, anxiety, surprise, anger, trust, fear, etc. all come with the challenges and rewards of operating a business, from conception to grand opening. Like any major life event, the emotions can be controlled and the anxiety can be reduced by planning. Hopefully, this chapter provided some ideas and tools to help make the decision to develop a new business an exciting and lifelong rewarding venture.

Part Two – Planning a Business

Chapter 3 Purpose and Benefit of a Business Plan

"He who fails to plan, plans to fail."

(Author unknown)

Definition

A **business plan** is a written statement describing the purpose and values of a company, along with an explanation of its goals. The plan details how the business owners expect to reach those goals, has a clear statement describing their target market and how their product or service differs from their competitors. In usually includes distinct sections to address the business operations, marketing, and financial management.

Business plans are helpful when beginning a new business, expanding a business, or auditing the performance of an existing business.

Value of a business plan

According to the U.S. Small Business Administration:

"67 percent of new business are successful after just four years."(7)

A few do fail because they were not planned out properly, or the owners began with a business plan, but did not follow it.

The value in creating a strategic or operating business plan is that it provides a *structured process* to review, research, and think about a total business. Like most structured research, the *process* of analyzing a total business, is more useful than the written *plan*.

There is almost no limit to the number of articles and statements by professional business planners and consultants telling readers and listeners:

"The real value is not the document itself; it is the *process of developing it…*"

(Multiple sources)

When to plan

Nearly everyone involved in creating a new business will advise someone to develop a *business plan* as a starting point. Planning itself is part of everyday life for many people, so why are some individuals confused about planning for business?

- Everyday planning in life includes:

- Developing a shopping list
- Making reservations and packing for travel
- Deciding on furniture for a home
- Thinking about what to wear for a day, evening, or special event
- Working out an exercise schedule
- Picking an appropriate route to work or to some other destination
- Scheduling activities for family activities

There is nothing magic about a business plan. It is just a structured way of thinking about creating or expanding and managing a new business adventure. It is the last step of a process of thinking through all of the elements involved in getting from an idea to a finished product or service.

Developing a business plan should NOT be a one-time activity that a company goes you go through to obtain financing and open your doors for the first time. The business plan should be a living document which you refer to often and if your business situation changes, it should be modified to fit the new environment.

In addition to developing a business plan before a company opens, they you and your key staff members should go through the planning process whenever they you are considering developing a new product, moving to a different location, or phasing out an existing product line.

The business plan should not be written, approved, and filed away on a shelf to gather dust. As a living document, it should be reviewed by key staff members in a group setting at least annually to help people remember what the business was established for and to keep everyone on track to accomplish their goals.

Who does the planning?

Developing a business plan is NOT a one-person show. It should involve everyone who has, or will have responsibility for ensuring compliance with company goals and objectives and making sure that every member of the organization understands the company values. Business *planning* should be a team-oriented process.

If a business plan is written by one individual, the result will be limited to the sole perspective of that individual. It will not include varied ideas or concerns of a wide range of potential customers, employees, or other people associated with the business. Even with a sole proprietorship, the business plan should address the demographic mix of a target market without being limited to only the owner's ideas.

> Definition: *Demographic mix* in a business plan refers to the differences between individuals' expectations which can result from differences in age, race, religion, gender, family size, income, and education.

The team responsible for creating a business plan can be as small as two people, such as a married couple or two partners, or it can be a larger group with varied functional skills such as administration, production, finance, marketing, etc. An ideal problem solving team has 5 to 7 members. Even a couple trying to plan a new business can usually add to their business planning team by including support from an expert such as an accountant, or a legal advisor.

> Team size: A problem-solving group with less than 5 members tends to have a limited perspective, often with a built in bias affecting decisions. A team with over 7 members can get unruly

and break into smaller groups which defeats the purpose of having all members work together as a single decision-making group.

Helpful hint: The U.S. Small Business Association has a branch known as SCORE which offers free one-on-one counseling and mentorship to small business owners, and potential owners trying to prepare business plans.(8)

Benefits of team planning

In their book *Teambuilding that Gets Results,(9)* Linda Eve and Harriet Diamond state that "most business owners see themselves as 'the business.' (pg. 7) They point out that an owner that does not include other members of the company in the business planning process can limit themselves to a very narrow range of ideas and problem solving options.

In addition to a narrow focus, business owners who exclude others from the planning process will over time, demotivate staff members and employees because they will not feel their opinions are accepted or encouraged. Preventing other members of the company from participating can cause a business to stagnate in its growth and eventually lose customers to their competitors.

Include a varied selection of members on a business planning team to:

- create a team atmosphere and culture in the company by allowing people from different functional areas to work together.
- take advantage of *synergy;* the whole (resulting plan) is better than the sum of the individual parts (suggestions). Sharing ideas will result in a far more comprehensive plan than a single individual (owner) could develop.
- develop *consensus,* or acceptance and support of the final plan by team

members who were involved in creating the plan.

- create active support from all employees who feel their concerns were addressed by a planning team member supporting their interests.
- reduce the rumor mill by sharing knowledge and providing a common vision and goals for all company staff and employees.

Possibly the most important reason to have a business planning team is that as a company grows it will eventually reach beyond the capability of the owner to make all of the operational decisions AND plan for future expansion. As your company grows, you will gradually have to hire employees or contract workers with specialized expertise to share the load (e.g. accountants, sales people, production people, etc.).

Generating ideas

There are several techniques to help a person or team generate ideas. This section will address two of them: *mind mapping* and *brainstorming*.

Mind mapping

Mind maps are a tool to generate creative thinking. They help people come up with ideas and solutions that they might normally overlook. Mind mapping takes some people out of their comfort zone and helps them refocus their efforts.

Mind maps can:

- improve the way a person takes notes
- support creative thinking

- encourage non-linear thinking
- identify and illustrate a problem

There is no set format for mind mapping. It is a *free flowing* exercise to generate ideas. Do NOT follow a closely monitored set of rules.

Example of a mind map developing ideas to *increase sales*

Near the center of a page, write the problem being addressed and draw a border around it. For example:

From the central bubble, let ideas flow in any direction like branches.

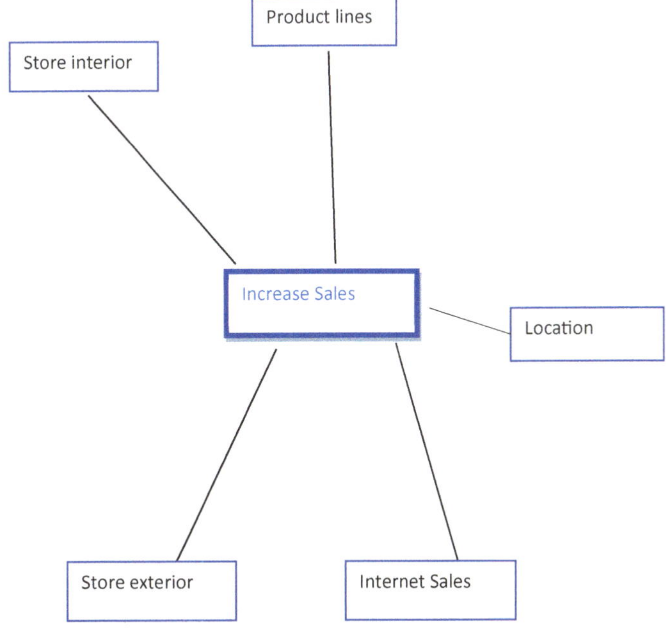

- Look at each branch one at a time. Think about ideas related to the branch. Draw spokes out from the branches as ideas come to mind.

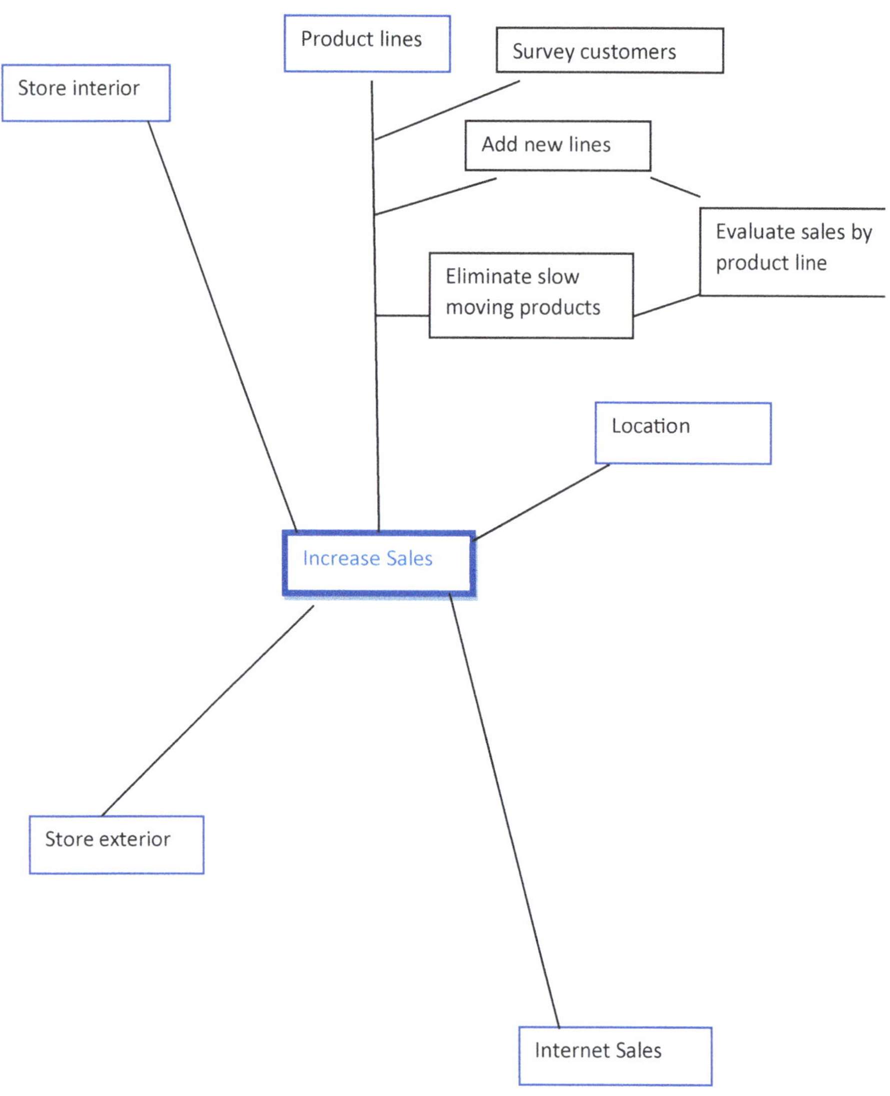

Work with each spoke independently and draw branches identifying subheadings.

Continue developing layers or tiers of subheadings until there is enough detail to develop specific plans to solve problems or concerns.

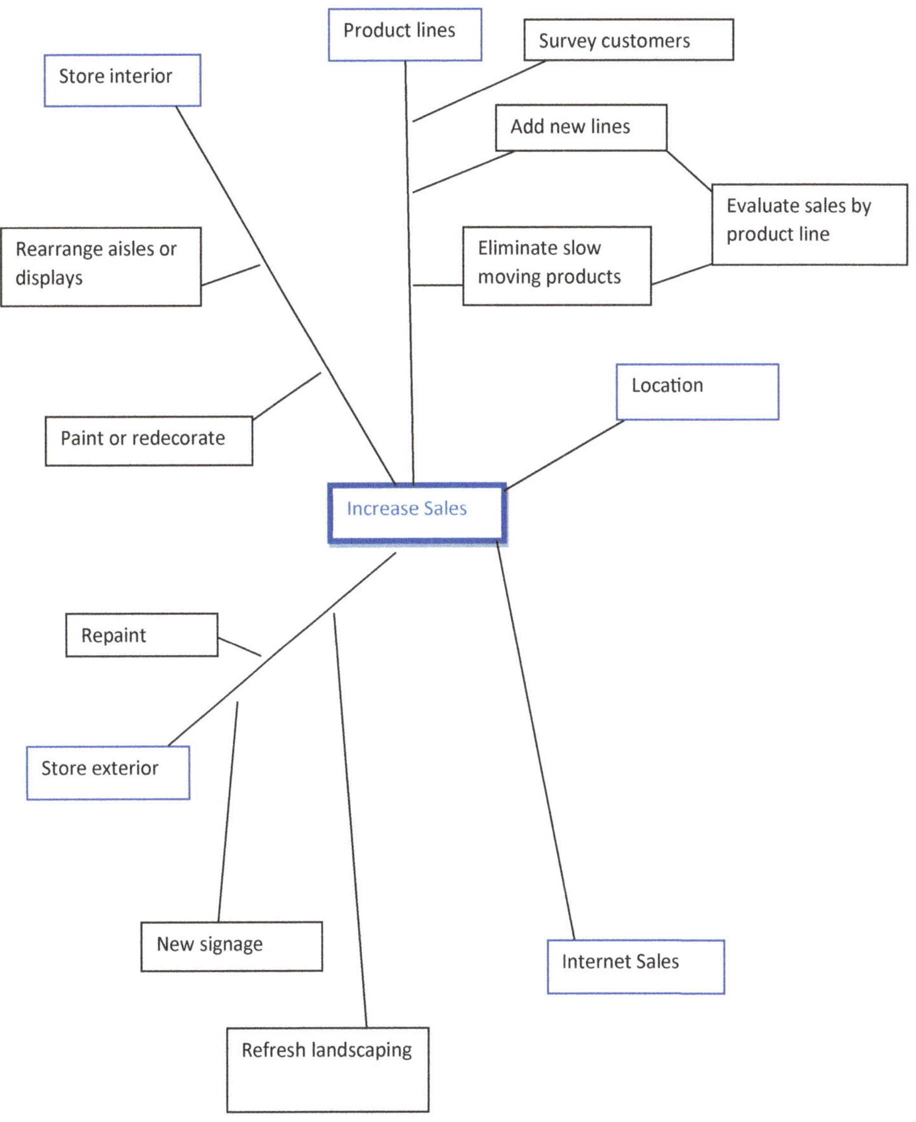

Mind mapping does not have to be complicated. It is simply a method to help people generate new ideas without getting over burdened with a wide range of interfering thoughts.

> Many young people grew up using a form of mind mapping when they played football in the neighborhood park.

> As their team got into a huddle and drew plays in the sand with their fingers, they were mind mapping – *generating ideas.*

Brainstorming

This idea generating process is designed to help *teams* solve problems. It can be used with small groups, or large groups up to about 30 members.

Brainstorming had the advantage of involving all members of a group. If there are some members who are a little too shy to share their ideas in a group setting, brainstorming helps them open up without being intimidated. If some group members tend to be assertive and known for pushing their ideas forward at the expense of the shy people, brainstorming lets them participate but in a respectful manner.

The brainstorming process:

Materials needed

- Large white board or large poster paper pads that can be mounted to a large surface
- Enough white board (dry erase) marking pens for at least ½ of the problem-solving participants

Process

Generating ideas

1. The team leader explains the problem and makes sure all participants understand and agree to address ONLY THE PROBLEM THAT HAS BEEN EXPLAINED.

2. Beginning with one person, the leader asks the individual for ONE idea that might solve the problem.

    a. Even if a person has several solutions in mind, they can only suggest ONE when asked.

    b. If they have additional ideas, they must wait until the team leader asks them again for a single idea.

    c. If they have no suggestion, the person says, "Pass."

3. The team leader writes the suggestion on the board or poster paper.

    a. There cannot be any discussion related to the suggestion at this time.

4. The team leader asks the second person in line for ONE idea that might solve the problem.

    a. Like the first person, they either give ONE idea or say, "Pass."

    b. If they provided a possible solution, it is written on the board or poster paper.

    c. The ideas written on the board should not be in rows or columns. They should eventually cover the board or poster paper surface with NO systematic order.

5. The team leader moves to the next person and continues writing suggestions on the board, one at a time for each team member.

    a. When every member has been asked for a suggestion, the team leader starts the process over again with the first person who, again will give a single idea or say, "Pass."

b. If a person passes they will be asked again for a suggestion when the team leader gets back to them.

c. The reason for one idea at a time is to let everyone hear a wide variety of solutions that might cause them to think of a solution they had not thought of earlier. This is why the process is referred to as *brainstorming.*

6. The process continues repeating around the group until every participant says "pass" which indicates all of the solutions they have are listed on the board or poster paper.

Narrowing solutions

Gaining consensus on the final solution requires narrowing the board full if ideas to one everyone can agree on, or at least support. The final idea selection can be done through *multi-voting.*

1. The team leader asks every participant to look at the list of ideas, or problem solutions, and be sure they understand each one.

    Anyone who does not understand an idea on the board can ask the person who submitted the idea to explain it.

    No idea can be criticized. That might keep the person who submitted the idea from participating in a future problem-solving team and it could limit the likelihood of all good ideas being discussed.

2. hen everyone understands the meaning of each idea on the board, they all come forward and using dry ink markers, they put 10 check marks on the board next to the ideas, or solutions they prefer.

    If they like only one idea, they can put all 10 votes next to it.

    If they like only two ideas, they can put 5 next to each of them.

    They can spread their check marks, or votes, however they want to but they ARE LIMITED TO 10 TOTAL CHECK MARKS.

3. When everyone has placed their 10 check marks, the team leader counts the votes for each idea on the board.

The idea with the most votes is the most acceptable solution to the entire problem-solving group.

If there is a tie vote, all ideas with the high vote number are considered potential winners and treated equally.

4. The group discusses the advantages, concerns, and general thoughts about the winning idea(s) then develops a plan to implement the solution and solve the problem that was addressed at the beginning of the exercise.

Avoid planning mistakes

"About the only person who does not need a business plan is someone who is not going into business. A person does not need a *plan* to start a hobby or to do occasional small jobs outside their regular work. But anyone beginning or extending a venture that will consume significant resources of money, energy or time, who expects a profit, should take the time to draft (write) some kind of plan." (Tim Berry) (10)

Poor planning, or lack of planning *can be catastrophic* to a company.

The company can fail to attract customers, or lose existing customers because they *assume* they know what customers want rather than listening to them, and planning to provide products and services that are desired.

Money can run short. A company can be forced into bankruptcy because they were not realistic in estimating start-up and operating costs.

Management becomes overwhelmed with the day-to-day decision processes because they did not take the time to develop a company mission, and then create a *total business plan* to support their mission.

The company has no focus or direction because it was developed from an undefined dream and a belief in entrepreneurial skills without thought to the elements it requires to operate a successful business.

Self-Audit of a Business Plan

The following suggestions are provided as a *check list* to help develop and review a business plan and avoid the most common mistakes.

- Remember the value of a business plan is the *planning process*, not just the written document.
- Develop the parts of the *plan* that are considered the most important to the company first. Then work on other sections as the planning process becomes comfortable. Do not skip sections of a business plan. Even if a standard section does not seem to apply to the business, include it with a notation like, "This section does not apply at this time." It shows a potential investor that the section was considered, not forgotten.
- Be as accurate as possible with cost and income estimates, and inventory needs. It is usually a good idea to make a positive (almost a dream) financial estimate, a negative (if everything goes bad) estimate, and a (most likely) conservative estimate in between the positive and negative. Plan revenue and credit limits using the negative estimates, but try to develop realistic marketing and operating plans to achieve the most likely estimates.

- Remember the *business plan* is considered a living document. Don't develop it, write it, and file it away. Keep it available to anyone with a role to play in support of the plan (investors, key staff members, financial and legal advisors, etc.). It should be reviewed by a planning team at least once a quarter during the first year of operations, and then at least annually as the company matures.

- Review and modify the plan whenever the company is considering expansion, consolidation, relocation and product or service modification.

Summary

The *process* of planning is more important than the Plan itself. Think of the planning process for business in the same way a person plans a birthday party for children, obtains reservations for a trip, paints a house, or selects a home.

It (nearly) always starts with a dream, a vision, or a goal. Then the person with the dream begins to think their way through all of the steps and details that have to be accomplished to make the birthday, trip, painting, or home selection successful. A business is no different. Start with the dream, then consider the details to make it work, and write the plan. Believe in the process, the plan, and the team. It will work!

When the excitement settles, the operation becomes routine, and everyone involved acknowledges their role – a culture has formed.

Culture is NOT just a part of the company business plan. Culture IS the plan.

No company will be successful for the long term without all members of the organization fitting comfortably in the culture and supporting their position in the plan.

Chapter 4 Writing a Business Plan

How do we start writing?

Are we ready, or capable?

What should it look like when it is finished?

Every company ends up somewhere, but it helps to have a good idea of where that somewhere will be.

Introduction

There is no printed script or design for a written business plan. There are no mandatory formats for a written business plan. There are examples available in stores and online, but you, the business owner should feel free to create your own business plan in whatever style or format you are comfortable with. The plan The format an owner decides to use will become your their own tool to help them you think through your business ideas and consider the problems or concerns they you can expect to experience as the business transforms from a dream to a reality. The plan is intended to help the owner and you and your staff be ready for business problems by having solutions in advance of a crisis situation.

Even business plan formats taught in college or written in textbooks are not intended to fit the exact needs of every small business owner. They provide ideas on how to write and present a plan rather than dictate a set of forms to that MUST be completed.

The written document called a *business plan* should be designed by you, the business owner and your support team in a format you are comfortable using in your company. Most business plans include specific sections but none of the sections are mandatory to call the finished product a business plan.

Business Plan Audience

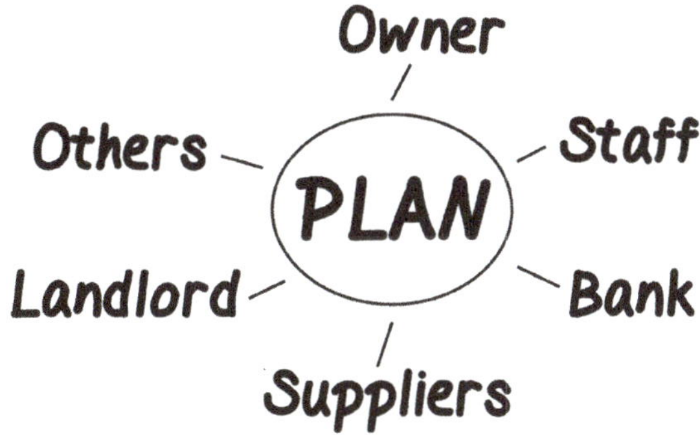

A reasonable idea to keep in mind while preparing and writing a business plan is to constantly think about the person or persons who will be reading and using the plan.

If it is going to be submitted to an investor or potential lender, the business owner should ask the lender which sections of a business plan they consider essential, helpful, and not necessary, then design the plan to fit their needs.

If it is going to be provided to potential business partners or key staff members, it should be written in a way that they will find helpful to let them know where their skills will fit into the company.

If it is to provide the sole owner with a plan to review regularly and keep the company on track, then it should be designed to provide quick reference to the owner for specific areas of concern, as well as include an easy to monitor schedule of goals.

> Ken Blanchard, in the book *One Minute Management,* suggests helping employees work on only a few goals at a time instead of trying to solve all of their problems at once. (11)
>
> **The same approach can apply to a business owner keeping track of their own goals. To prevent becoming overwhelmed, develop a *short list* of primary goals in the *business plan* that can be monitored regularly. Keep working toward the planned outcome, to avoid straying off track in daily operations.**
>
> **Some might refer to it as KISS: Keep it Simple S....**
>
> **Don't make the *business plan* complicated. Design it to be reasonable and workable.**

Sections of a Business Plan

While there is no mandatory structure to a Business Plan, there are some sections that should be in the plan. The sections shown below are *typical*, not required. They are listed to help a person preparing a business plan think about what each *possible* section addresses, then decide for themselves whether they want it in their own plan, or whether a potential user of their plan might want it.

Cover sheet, or Company Identification page

The top sheet of a business plan contains the company name, company logo, the title (Business Plan), company address and contact information, and the date the plan was published.

EXAMPLE OF A BUSINESS PLAN COVER SHEET USING AN IMAGINARY RESORT, THE SUN SPOT

The Sun Spot Resort

Business Plan – January 8, 2015

Owners: **Sam and Martha Washburn**

Address: Magic Island, South Pacific

Telephone: 1-18-234-993-2994

Fax: 1-18-234-993-3339

Email: Sunspot@nowhere.com

Executive Summary

This section should be the first written page of the *Business Plan* after the cover page, and it *should be the LAST part of the plan that is written.*

The Executive Summary is an abstract of the information that will be covered in detail inside the Business Plan. It should be limited to two pages and be written in a way that an individual can read it and understand what the business is (what products or services it provides), how it is organized, where it is located, how it fits within its competitive marketplace, and what the company hopes to accomplish in the future. It should be enthusiastic, professional, complete and concise.

It is similar to the paper flap on a book jacket, or the back cover of a paperback in that it explains the book premise without providing any of detail. It is also like an abstract found at the beginning of a story for a business journal, such as the *Harvard Business Review,* which explains what is in the article without providing any of the detail.

Write the Executive Summary LAST, because until the entire plan has been researched and recorded, it would be an incomplete summary.

General Description of Company

This section provides a detailed description of the business, its products, it services, and where it will fit in the industry. In other words, this is where the plan will tell potential investors *what kind of business it is, or will be and why it is different from its competitors.* It describes in some detail what makes the company unique.

It should include the goals and objectives you are trying to achieve by starting a business, including all critical elements *really important and unique* to your business.

The company description should include, where practical:

- Industry description and the industry stage (new, growing, changing)
- Company goals and objectives
- Ownership form (e.g. sole proprietorship, partnership, LLC, S corporation)
- Business philosophy (e.g. customer relations, employee relations, quality)
- Target market
- Additional success factors, if applicable
- Owner strengths

Products and Services offered by Company

Provide a detailed description of products and services the company provides, or will provide, including brand name information, trademarks, and proprietary features.

This section should not give away detailed information which could be considered a competitive advantage. It should be a high-level discussion of factors that show the company is supporting a definite customer need.

If the company owns patent rights to a process that allows them to support a unique market, the business plan should mention the patent but not include specific detail that could inappropriately be used by competitors.

Note: Do NOT include technical specifications, drawings, photos, or sales brochures. They should be included in an appendix.

Management Team

Explain who will manage the business on a day-to-day basis. Does the manager have any special or distinctive competencies related to the business? How does their background and experience qualify them to run this type of a business?

Provide a high-level biographical description of the owner(s) and key management individuals employed by the company as well as their functional role within the company. It is not a section for detailed resumes, but instead it is a place to identify the skills and special talents that people will bring to the company to help it achieve its goals.

This is an appropriate location in the *business plan* to include an organization chart.

EXAMPLE OF A MANAGEMENT TEAM SECTION OF A BUSINESS PLAN USING AN IMAGINARY RESORT CALLED THE SUN SPOT

The owner's Sam and Martha Washburn, are the primary operators (General Managers) of the resort. They share functional responsibility. Sam spends most of his time with the guest rooms, marina, and grounds and Martha is actively in charge of the restaurant and gift shop.

There are only two positions other than Sam and Martha that could be considered management:

Kitchen Chef, Pierre de Sol

Pierre began as a dishwasher in a Los Angeles cafeteria, where he watched cooks prepare numerous delicacies over his 5 year tenure in the position. Later he moved on to the *Hardened Artery* restaurant in Baconsville where he earned the coveted Trans Fat award from the community. He left the *Hardened Artery* and moved to the *Sun Spot Resort* when the *Hardened Artery* had to close due to its diminished customer base.

Maintenance Manager, Ole Dole

The head maintenance person has responsibility for all resort infrastructures (gardening, plumbing, electrical, etc.). Ole began learning his trade as a store greeter for a big box home repair center talking with contractors and do-it-yourself homeowners. He was with the big box store for 12 years before moving on to a landscaping job on Wisteria Lane. After some awkward moments with the residents of Wisteria Lane, he moved to the South Seas to accept his position with the *Sun Spot Resort.*

If there is an apparent lack of critical skill in some area of the business, the *business plan* should include an explanation of recruiting and hiring plans to fill the vacancy.

Operating Plan

This section explains the daily operations of the business. It should include the following topics:

Production

How and where will the company produce your products and, or services?

The production section should address technology, quality control, inventory control, transportation and delivery of products, customer service, product development, and variations in demand.

Location

Describe the physical location of company facilities and whether they are owned or leased. Discuss the type of construction (brick, wood, stand alone, strip mall), the number of floors, square footage and zoning considerations. Include the company business hours and a description of access to company buildings (for customers, employees, shipping, receiving, and parking).

If the location is not yet determined, discuss the characteristics of the desired location.

If possible, include a drawing, or layout of the proposed facility as an appendix to the business plan.

Staffing (Personnel)

Include statements covering the following:

Number of employees: current, future, seasonal, part-time, full time

Type of labor: skilled, unskilled, professional, independent contractors

Union affiliations

Inventory management and control

Explain how inventory will be managed to keep costs down, while avoiding outages. Include a discussion of seasonal requirements and distribution channels and supplier history/reliability.

If the company has established critical supplier relationships during the early planning stages of preparing to start a business, it should be mentioned briefly in this section to let potential lenders or business associates know the ground work is in place to support production requirements.

Pricing strategy

This section of the business plan does not need to go into detail about markup policies and sales margins. However, it should establish the baseline for the company to create a pricing plan. Pricing strategy for the company should reflect the company vision and approach to customer relations.

If the company intends to provide high volume, low price products, then the pricing strategy should reflect it.

If the company expects to be a direct competitor with other companies in quality and pricing, the pricing should indicate this.

If the company expects to provide high end, high quality products with lower (less frequent) sales, the pricing strategy should make this clear.

Marketing strategy

When a Business Plan is being developed and written for an existing business rather than a new business, the Marketing Strategy becomes one of the most important sections.

A marketing plan, like a business plan, is developed by reviewing several elements of competition, advertising options, sales forecasts, etc. It is quite often required by potential lenders when reviewing a company asking for funds to expand their business.

This section of the business plan addresses a marketing plan, but it does not *present* a fully documented approach to the company sales and marketing.

The marketing plan section of a business plan should remain at a very high level and not get into specific studies, evaluations, or advertising ideas. It should mention:

- the state of the industry and projections of future changes
- estimate of demand to support a new or growing company in the region
- target customers (customer niche) demographics and buying habits
- competitor profiles and potential vulnerabilities
- high-level company advertising plans (e.g. social media, newspaper advertising, personal solicitation, etc.)

Credit Policies

Explain what payment method the company plans to use for payment transactions: case, debit or credit card. What credit card associations will be established (e.g. Visa, Master Charge, Discover, etc.)? Will they provide in-house lay away options, or time payment plans?

This is the section to include statement(s) about the company return policy or warranty coverage. Will the company accept returns? Will they repair damaged merchandise, or will the customer have to work with the manufacturer for warranty coverage?

Financial Estimates

Personal finances (opening day balance sheet)

The business plan should include personal financial statements for the owner(s) in the form of a balance sheet indicating their personal assets and liabilities outside the business, and their net worth. Identify and explain any apparent concerns related to the owner(s) financial condition, and provide a plan to address them.

Startup or expansion estimated expenses

The business plan should include a contingency allowance, often referred to as *management reserve*. It is a built in budget amount to help the company be financially prepared for unknown, or unexpected costs. It can be built into estimated startup and operating expenses by padding a little extra on each budget line in the financial statements, or by adding a separate budget line called *Contingencies* or *Management Reserve*. The written business plan should include a statement explaining how contingencies are covered in the budget estimate.

Hint: Estimates for startup or expansion expenses can be developed by talking with other businesses in the industry, or simply by adding a fixed amount (at least 20%) over the total of all known startup expenses.

Cash flow projections

The cash flow projection is usually made up of a 12 month profit and loss projection and a 4 year profit and loss projection. It should start with the opening day balance sheet, and then project potential income and expenses for each month.

Hint: Dependent upon the product or service being offered, the monthly projections usually vary by season. For example, customer interactions can expect to differ between summer and winter, vacation season and holiday season.

Financial plans, like sales projections, should be based upon best guess estimates, as well as worst case and most likely estimates. In other words, do the financial estimates in three versions to see how well the business could do, how poorly it might do, and what it should do somewhere between.

Examples of financial statements are in Appendix A of this *Desk Reference.*

A sample business plan is in Appendix D of this Desk Reference.

Chapter 5 – Sales, Marketing, and Pricing

Marketing has many definitions, but in simple terms:

> **Attracting customers and providing the right product or service on time, in the right quantity, and at a reasonable price while making a profit for the company.**

Marketing to a small business owner means staying aware of every aspect of the company and never forgetting to improve the customer's experience. It involves all company operations including customer research, product planning, pricing, selling, and delivery.

Six Marketing Ps

Marketing textbooks and manuals refer to the *Six Ps*:

Providing the right	**P**roduct
In the right	**P**lace
For the right	**P**rice
Using the right	**P**romotion
With the right	**P**eople
Following the right	**P**rocesses

Product

Product refers to the goods and services offered by the business. It includes not only the physical product, but also the warranty and service that follow a sale.

Place

Place refers to where the business is located and how customers find it and buy products. It includes business locations, sales channels (on-line, telephone, walk-in, etc.), as well as transportation and parking variables for suppliers and customers.

Price

Price refers the company pricing policy, such as discounts for quantity purchases, military personnel or seniors, and credit policies.

Promotion

Promotion refers to how the company contacts, attracts, and retains customers. It includes one-on-one sales, advertising, customer referrals, sales promotions, news releases, etc.

People

As one of the 6 Ps of Marketing, 'people' refers to all members of the company staff and management. In marketing, 'people' includes the combined product or service knowledge, experience, skills, and attitude or teamwork of everyone employed by the customer.

Processes

Processes refers to daily operations and functions of the company and more specifically, their effect on the customer's perception of the company and its products or services. It includes product quality, ongoing improvement, sales follow-up, warranty coverage, and any other activity involved in maintaining positive customer relations.

Market Research

Understanding industry trends, customer desires, and potential regulatory changes should be an ongoing part of managing any business, whether small, mid-sized, or large. Technology is in a constant state of transition, just as customer trends and expectations are constantly changing. A product or service that was supported by customers in the past, even very recent past, can become thought of as out-of-date or less than trendy very quickly.

In order to maintain an ongoing operation and hopefully, grow in the future, it is very important for a company to keep up with market trends and adapt in ways that will provide them with an edge over their competitors.

> Would a person drive across the country without looking at map to compare possible routes, considering weather conditions, and checking the condition of the vehicle?
>
> Do people purchase a home without ever entering the premises or comparing other homes for condition, price and neighborhood?
>
> Should a person always select goods in a store based solely upon price, or would they make a more informed choice if they also considered quality and functionality?

These are fairly simple scenarios, but they are examples of research which people do regularly before deciding to take action. The same reasoning applies to a company considering introducing a new product, changing a product line, or purchasing advertising space in a local newspaper. Start with the *research*, and then make the right plan.

Benefits of Market Research

Market research, if it is done correctly, will provide information to:

- understand current and potential customers' buying habits for the products or services the company provides.

- decide what, if any, adjustments or modifications to make to current products or services to keep its market niche.
- know what changes are expected in the community or region it serves so it can make appropriate adjustments to the product line or services.
- modify its company business plan to adapt to anticipated changes.

Describe marketing concerns

Using the same approach as the start to any research project, the first step is usually to define the purpose, or objective of the research. Agree on what the research is intended to do in fairly narrow terms.

Examples:

- Are customers satisfied with current products or services?
- What modifications if any, would they like to see?
- Are they satisfied with the pricing?
- How do they think the company compares with competitors?

If the company is trying to identify possible customers, they could consider these demographics: age, family home size, average number and age of children, income level and education level.

Develop research objectives

When the research question, or problem has been defined, the research methods can be selected to reach formal and specific objectives, which are clearly stated.

Examples: To develop an estimate of how many potential customers can be expected to pass by the building entrance on a daily basis.

To determine a price range that would be expected and accepted by potential customers for the product or service.

To determine whether there is an adequate market for the product or service to support a new or expanding business in the area.

To evaluate customer perception of new packaging on a product.

Determine the research methods

Think about the specific objectives of the research and develop a plan of action which could involve surveys, interviews, random sampling, library research, Internet research, or secret shopper exercises. Consider timing, sample size, using outside consultants, and other areas when developing the specific methods of research.

Suggestion: If a person is not sure where to go to find information to support their research, it is usually helpful to visit the local library and talk to the Research Librarian. They can offer some good pointers on how to conduct nearly any market study.

Investigating market potential for a new business, expanding a business, or possible product changes is done with either primary research or secondary research.

Secondary research

Usually the least expensive research method, secondary research reviews data from studies performed by others: government agencies, chambers of commerce, professional organizations, universities and others. It is relatively easy to locate at a library, in professional journals, and online.

Secondary research can be limited because it is designed to provide information to a large audience, rather than a specific company. The data available from secondary research can provide helpful information from a large sample (e.g. age group, income class, etc.), but it will not always have the detail a business owner needs to make a decision related to a specific store location.

Primary research

It can be more expensive than secondary research, but depending upon the problem decision to be made, it is sometimes worth the cost. Primary research is designed and managed to fit a specific concern of an individual company or situation. It is conducted by surveys, interviews, tabulating coupon response, and observing specific criteria or behavior.

When designed correctly, primary research sampling a very small population can provide information representing a fairly large market. For example, in the political arena, small voter polls are used to indicate early election results.

The recommended approach to market research for a small business owner is to begin with secondary research (online or with a library) and follow up with primary research (talk with potential customers to find out if they agree with the results of the secondary research).

Surveys

Surveys can be conducted by visiting competitors with a check list of items and conditions to observe.

Examples:

- the arrangement of aisles and display cases
- prices
- number of staff available to help customers
- customer shopping patterns.

They can also be done through personal contact with current or potential customers. Prepare a checklist of questions for face-to-face contact, or prepare surveys to be handed out or mailed. If a company is going to use surveys of any kind, they need to consider the demographics* of the participants.

*Demographics: a definition of a particular segment of a population (customers or potential customers) grouped by age, gender, income level, occupation, housing type, etc.

The demographics are important to business owners as they develop marketing plans based upon:

- Leisure activities suggest or determine what kind of products or services customers might be interested in.
- Age ranges predict customer expectations.
- Family status influences buying patterns.
- Transportation and traffic patterns in the area (automobiles, bicycles, walking, or buses) can affect customer ability to carry products.

Demographic data to help small business owners is available online from the U.S. Census Bureau: http://www.census.gov/. The site offers information about population characteristics of any state or county, and most cities in the United States.

Always test a survey with a small group of individuals before sending it out to a large group of people. It is best to test a survey or questionnaire with people who do not work with the company. They will be more objective.

Note to consider when designing a survey:

The author of this *Reference Manual* has been involved in the design of surveys for primary research. At first glance, they might appear to be fairly simple to design, but experience shows for them to be effective, they have to be well thought out. A survey needs to interest and motivate a potential respondent to take the time to complete and return the questionnaire. The collected data needs to be easy to tabulate, and the form (on-line or on paper) cannot be too lengthy. Anyone planning to design a survey would be well advised to go beyond the Internet for design ideas and look through a book like *Internet, Phone, Mail, and Mixed Mode Surveys: The Tailored Design Method,* by Don Dillman, Jolene Smyth, and Leah Christian. (12)

Analyze the data

When the results of a survey have arrived, it is time to review the responses and make some realistic business decisions. Keep these points in mind when analyzing survey responses.

- Keep an open mind. Try not to let a preconceived response override an actual response.

- If a question is written poorly, it will receive a poor or unclear response.
- If the response shows the new business, product, or business expansion would probably fail, believe it and accept the outcome or start a new set of plans.
- If the response shows the business change might do well with some suggested modifications to the marketing plan, consider making the modifications.
- Don't be defensive if the survey results do not match expectations.

Strengths, Weaknesses, Opportunities, Threats (SWOT) Analysis

SWOT stands for **S**trengths, **W**eaknesses, **O**pportunities, **T**hreats. SWOT analysis is recognized as a simple, yet effective means of carrying out an analysis of a company, a marketing plan, an information system, or nearly any other business process. In this case, SWOT analysis is suggested to compare a small business with its competitors and to determine what must be done to gain, or maintain a competitive advantage*.

> *Competitive advantage: An advantage in quality, service, price, name familiarization, skills, or other area that a company has over its competitors which allows it to generate higher sales and/or retain more customers than its competition.

It is usually helpful to do a SWOT Analysis with a small group of key people from the company who understand the skills and abilities of the company, as well as their competitors. Taking one topic at a time, the group should list what they feel their company has to offer or needs. Potential questions for each category are shown below to get the analysis started.

Strengths

- What is the company good at, or best at?
- What skills or experience does the company have that makes them feel they can compete successfully with other companies?
- What does the company consider their specialty area, or area of expertise?
- What does the company have to offer that a competitor does not have?

Weaknesses

- Is the company likely to commit to something they will not be able to complete without a lot of trial and error?
- Are they about to try something their workers are not trained or qualified to do?
- Is the company short of resources they will need to try their new idea or expansion program?

Opportunities

- Are there other people or resources available to them from outside the company that could help them perform the task better or more efficiently at a reasonable cost?
- As a company, what do they think they have going for them to help their new product development or expansion succeed? Some examples are consulting support, employee enthusiasm or a slow period in the company business cycle.

Threats

- What will happen to their company if they do not proceed with their new product development or expansion plans?
- Are competitors implementing similar changes that could be

operational earlier than the company?

- Are some employees resisting the new plans?

SWOT Analysis is a helpful exercise for any small business to use as a tool as they review their own strengths and weaknesses and monitor their competition and the industry they are involved in. They should continue to build on the strengths that can make them successful while trying equally hard to correct weaknesses and minimize threats.

Pricing Strategy

$$$$$$$$$$$$$

How much should we charge? How much do we need to stay in business?

What do customers expect to pay?

How much do competitors charge?

What if we charge too much?

What if we do not charge enough?

Establish prices early. Before opening the doors of a new business, the owner needs to decide what they are going to charge for the products and services they will offer and how they will collect payments from customers. Pricing should be within industry standards to attract and retain customers. It should also represent the true value of products and services the company is providing.

Establishing prices is critical to a business. Prices cannot be too high yet they need to be adequate to cover business expenses and generating a reasonable profit.

Pricing considerations

- Does the selling price include all costs involved in producing the product or service?
- Is the selling price about the same as prices charged by competitors?
- Does the selling price support customer expectations for the value they expect?

  - Too low a price, customers might expect poor quality.
  - Too high a price, customers might avoid buying.

Pricing strategy and customer expectation is similar to the children's story about three bears who found food and determined some was TOO HOT, some was TOO COLD, and some was JUST RIGHT.

Establishing a fair price

If a company is going to advertise "quality merchandise at a fair price" then, what is a fair price?

> There is no single definition. Fair price is determined by considering how much the retailer paid for the merchandise (including parts, labor for assembly, stocking, etc.), the pricing policy of suppliers, and what competitors charge.

Pricing products or services is one of the most important decisions to be made by a business owner. The expected selling price of products or services produced by the company directly affects profit and the ability to continue operating. Pricing should allow a reasonable profit margin, while being low enough to keep products affordable to the target market and be competitive with other companies.

Establishing a fair price will require not only reviewing the costs of acquiring inventory and comparing competitor pricing. It should reflect the company vision, or mission which is defined in the Company Business Plan.

> If the company mission is to provide high volume, low price products, then the pricing policy should reflect it.

If the company expects to be a direct competitor with other companies in quality and pricing, the pricing policy should reflect it.

If the company mission is to provide high end, high quality products with lower (less frequent) sales, the pricing policy should reflect this.

Markup

Some business people think:

Selling Price = Purchase Price + Markup

Not quite true – but it would be an easy formula.

There is no universal rule for pricing merchandise, though it is generally considered reasonable to use a 50% markup as a *starting point*.

Note:

A 50% "markup" does NOT mean selling products at cost plus 50%.

It DOES mean purchasing products for 1/2, or 50% of what they are sold for.

Sound confusing? Here is an explanation:

Markup is a *percentage of the sales price.*

> If an item costs $1.00 to purchase after adding overhead charges like shipping, storage, inventory management, etc. to the purchase price,
>
> and the selling price is $2.00, the purchase price is ½, or 50% of the sales price.

The real interpretation:

> The definition of markup as a *% of the selling price is used to soften customer perception* that prices are doubled, even though both selling prices would be the same.

If a company announces sales of $500 million with an earned net profit of 4%, many consumers would conclude the company marks up (sells) its products at 4% over their purchase price. In reality, net profit is the amount remaining after overhead expenses (salaries, inventory, facilities, taxes, etc.) have been subtracted from gross profit (total sales, less the cost of merchandise).

MSRP, also known as Vendor Pricing

The acronym MSRP is common in automobile advertising. MSRP stands for Manufacturers Suggested Retail Price. In theory it is the price set by the retailer. In actual practice, MSRP can be applied in several ways.

- The retailer sells at the price suggested by the manufacturer.
- The retailer advertises a 'sale' and sells merchandise at a price below what the manufacturer suggests.
- The retailer lists merchandise for a price higher than suggested by the manufacturer, then encourages the buyer to negotiate for a lower price. The customer tries to make a good deal. The final price might be as low as the MSRP, but in many cases is higher.

Competitive Pricing

Pricing below competitors may attract customers, but the business will usually have to purchase large quantities from their distributor to bring their own purchase price down or develop an extremely efficient operating system to minimize overhead costs.

Pricing above competitors is usually only justifiable if the retail business is located in a hard to reach area, off a "beaten path" for consumers, or offering unusually good customer service.

Psychological Pricing

This form of pricing is used to work with a consumers' perception. Prices ending in an odd figure like $8.95, or $5.99 will often be seen as $8 or $5 by the potential buyer instead of $9 or $6. It is related to gasoline pumps ending in 9/10 of a cent. It is pretty hard to work out the correct change for 1/10 of a cent.

Business expenses in pricing strategy

Many retailers with low inventory costs have gone out of business because they did not include, or even consider other expenses when they developed their pricing strategy.

ALL business expenses MUST be included in any pricing strategy.

Income and costs to include when developing pricing strategy:

Revenue	Money earned from the sale of products or services. This is sometimes referred to as Sales.
Cost of Goods Sold	The price paid by the company for supplies, raw material, parts, etc.

	needed to develop the product. In the case of a restaurant, this includes the cost of food, beverages, and spices.
Gross Profit	The difference between revenue received from sales and the cost of goods or products sold.
Expenses	The cost of products or services used to operate the business, for example, accounting fee, utilities, and building maintenance.

<u>Expense categories:</u>

Variable Expenses	Costs that change based upon the number of customers that visit the business: the number of sales people on staff during peak time versus slow times, or the number of table settings needed at different times in a restaurant.
Fixed Expenses	Costs that do NOT change as the number of customers changes: advertising, administrative services, or maintenance and cleaning among others.
Occupancy Cost	Costs associated with occupying the physical structure of the business: rent or mortgage and interests, taxes, and depreciation.
Operating Expenses	Costs incurred during the operation of a business: salaries and wages, employee benefits, advertising, utilities, repairs and maintenance.

Operating Income	Total gross profit minus total expenses. This is the owner's income *before* interest and income tax is paid, and before paying any return or dividend to investors.

Suggestion: Many business owners have found it helps to have an accountant set up their bookkeeping and tax reporting system before they begin operating.

Pricing Ideas to ponder

- Prices *must* reflect what a customer expects and is likely to accept.
- Establish prices that represent the customer's *perceived* value, based upon market research.
- Be aware of the weather. In heavy rain, keep umbrella prices up. In hot weather, charge more for sunscreen. If the weather is uncertain consider a sale of weather related items to bring customers in the door.
- Not sure how to count customers when catering a buffet? Stack serving plates in stacks of ten and charge based upon the number of plates used for the banquet.
- Give customers a reason to justify the price.
    - Winner J.D. Power and Associates (13)
    - Rated #1 by the local newspaper
    - Best in the city
    - Or to share a familiar phrase from borrow from a well-known restaurant chain: "finger lickin' good" (Kentucky Chicken) (14)
- Be careful discounting prices for a grand opening. Customers may expect the same prices later or not return.
- Consider semi-annual sales with clear statements about when the

prices will return to normal.

- Think about customer demographics and consider small discounts for seniors, military, students, etc. on certain days or for specific operating hours.

- Send news releases to local news media, particularly newspapers, about the new or expanding company. Include pictures.

- Remember to review pricing regularly. Be aware that if prices increase, there may be a slight drop in customers.

Selling Solutions

- Know the target market. Understand the customers and potential customers and be sure all planning and operations are directed toward attracting, helping, and satisfying them.

- The product or service will not sell itself. Reach out through signs, displays, contact and media. Consider a web page and other social media exposure.

- Quite often it is better to use professional advertising firms than to develop advertising material from inside the company.

- Be wary of sending out quick advertising literature. – Watch for mistakes.

- Consider using:
    - Business cards
    - Printed forms and company stationary
    - Mailing labels with the company name
    - Professionally designed brochures

- Sales promotions:

Rebates	They might promote sales, but can be copied by competitors. Customers

	might delay future purchases while they are waiting for new rebates.
Samples	Introduces new products, but does not ensure sales and it can be an unnecessary expense.
	Contests Interesting to customers but full of legal loopholes.
Coupons	They can increase some sales while providing inaccurate source of information to indicate customer preferences.
Reward cards	A small reward for multiple purchases, such as "10 punches earns free coffee" can create customer loyalty over time and usually at very little cost to the company.

Marketing Plan

As discussed in chapter 3 of this *Desk Reference*, the Business Plan is a "… written statement describing the purpose and values of a company, along with an explanation of their goals, how they expect to reach those goals, and a clear statement describing their target market and how their product or service differs from their competitors."

A Marketing Plan may appear to be similar to the business plan, but it is focused on attracting and establishing positive relationships with customers. It is a plan that is designed to inform existing and potential customers about what the company offers and how it differs from competitors. It is based on in depth market research which defines the company market niche and creates clear objectives a clear focus for future decision making.

The following section descriptions are typically included in a marketing plan, although they not necessarily required.

Executive Summary

The executive summary for a marketing plan is similar to the same section of a business plan. It is a brief description of what is in the more detailed sections of the marketing plan. It is the *last section to be written* since the plan cannot be summarizes until the details are included.

SWOT Analysis

It is not important whether the section is labeled SWOT Analysis. What is important early in a marketing plan is to compare what the company has to offer when measured against competitors.

Marketing Objectives

Objectives are the road map of what the company is trying to accomplish with their marketing plan. This section should be specific in its goals so everyone involved can understand their role and what is expected of them to help support the objectives.

Marketing Strategies

This can be a very proprietary section and should be treated carefully. This section should identify the target market and include *big picture* plans stating how the company hopes to reach and support their target customers.

Financial projections

Estimates and budget allowances should explain how much it will cost to activate the marketing plan and how it will be financed by the company.

Plan Schedule

An implementation schedule should include the how and when for each person who will be expected to participate in the marketing plan.

Attracting Customers

Search Engine Optimization (SEO) Strategy

Any business planning to attract customers through a company website should include an SEO strategy that fits with the Marketing Plan. A well-designed SEO strategy will help potential customers locate the company webpage and help them find the right information to contact the company and hopefully, conduct business.

Unless the business owner or Marketing Manager is well versed in web design and attracting customers through social networks, they should consider finding an SEO Strategy expert to help them with their online presence.

Business Signage

Many communities have restrictive zoning requirements for signs on buildings and surrounding property. It is a good idea to check on signage restrictions with local authorities or a sign making company before investing in a sign that will have to be removed.

Typical examples of sign regulations:

Storefront	Primary storefront signs are permitted on each building. They shall be against the wall of the building projecting no more than 12 inches from the building surface.
Supplementary	A business with an exterior wall can, in addition to their storefront wall, install a supplementary wall sign on a wall facing a parking area that is not in front of the business.

Sign regulations are often very specific about size, illumination, type of lettering, colors, and materials used to make the signs.

Final thought:

Change promotional displays monthly!

Keep them fresh so customers will notice them.

Chapter 6 Financial Planning

Financial start-up considerations

When estimating the cost to start a small business, start with *expenses* and *assets.*

> Expenses include rent, salaries, inventory, licensing, advertising, etc.
>
> Assets include the value of owned buildings and equipment, incoming payments (accounts receivable), profit earned, etc.

While it is important to estimate start-up costs and develop income projections from (hopefully) early sales, it is also important to think about personal finances, which should be separate from the business. This portion of the *Desk Reference* is written to help a person decide whether they are financially ready and able to open a new business.

Whether a person is going to continue with an existing job and bring in household income while the new business gets going or they are going to leave a job and start out full time with the new company, they should have enough in personal income or savings to support their household and family needs for a period of six to nine months without counting on any profit from the new business to support their family needs.

A new business will usually require a few months to begin attracting customers, making sales, and generating a profit. When planning a budget for a new business venture, it is important to remember that the cost of living (food, mortgage, utilities, etc.) continue even if there is no income being generated. Include an allowance in the start-up budget for personal and family expenses.

Small Business Loans

General Overview

The bad news:

The U.S. Small Business Administration (SBA) does NOT provide free money, government grants, or no-interest loans. The SBA does not even lend funds directly to business owners. (14)

The good news:

All SBA financial aid is based upon a relationship between the business owner and a loan officer at a bank, credit union, or nonprofit financial intermediary. The SBA guarantees repayment of a portion of an SBA loan to an SBA approved creditor in the event of default.

After a business has developed a relationship with an SBA approved loan officer, there are several avenues to capital to start or expand a small business.

> Note: The Service Corps of Retired Executives (SCORE), an affiliate of the SBA, offers free one-on-one counseling and mentoring for small business owners. SCORE representatives can provide the name of an SBA approved loan officer. (15)

Definition of a Small Business

The SBA defines a small business as one that is independently owned and operated, is organized for profit, and is not dominant in its field. In addition, a small business requesting SBA financial support must fall within the following criteria dependent upon the industry.

Industry	Maximum employees	
Manufacturing	500 to 1500	depending upon the product manufactured
Wholesaling	100 to 500	depending upon the product provided

Industry	Maximum annual sales	
Services	\$2.5 to \$21.5 million	depending upon service
Retail	\$5 to \$21 million	depending upon product
General, Heavy Construction	\$13.5 to \$17 million	depending on construction
Special Trade Construction	\$7 million	
Agriculture	\$0.5 to \$9 million	depending on crop

Typical uses for Small Business Loans

The following list is comes from Community Capital Development, affiliated with the SBA of Seattle, Washington:

- **Equipment, furniture, and inventory**
- **Manufacturing or technology-based production needs**
- **Working capital** for business operations
- **Commercial or mixed-use real estate** purchase, renovation, refinance, or other project
- **Franchise** start-up or purchase
- **Contract financing** for goods or services, from payroll to equipment or supplies
- **Construction or contractor receivables** prime or sub-prime contractors with public sector agencies
- **Cash flow debt restructuring**

Qualifying for SBA loan

A company requesting a small business loan or grant must fit within the U.S. Small Business Administration (SBA) definition of a small business.

SBA's programs include financial and federal contract procurement assistance, management assistance, and specialized outreach to women, minorities and armed forces veterans. SBA also provides loans to victims of natural disasters and specialized advice and assistance in international trade.

With the possible exception of a grant, organizations offering to provide a loan to a small business have to be convinced the company will be able to pay back the loan. Lenders usually want two sources of repayment, proven cash flow from the business and collateral.

If a business has been in operation long enough to show a consistent profit, lenders are likely to offer funds to support expansion plans. A new, or startup business would be expected to provide a more detailed and comprehensive business plan to a lender.

Credit rating

If a loan applicant has a poor credit rating resulting from a divorce, illness, or some other life changing event, but had stable credit ratings before the event, a lender is more likely to grant a loan than they would for an applicant with a poor credit rating and no major extenuating circumstances.

Collateral

The U.S. Small Business Administration (SBA) and financial institutions working with the SBA want to be assured that the money they loan will be paid back. In order to have that assurance, a lender will generally require collateral, or assets, that can be used to generate cash for repayment of a loan if the borrower defaults. The loan value of collateral is not determined by market value. It is the discounted value generated after expenses of a forced liquidation.

Typical loan values provided by the SBA:

Type of collateral	Acceptability for SBA loan guarantee
House	Market value x 0.80, less mortgage balance

Car	Not usually acceptable as collateral
Truck & Heavy Equipment	Depreciated value x 0.50
Office Equipment	Not usually acceptable as collateral
Furniture and Fixtures	Depreciated value x 0.50
Inventory: Perishables	Not usually acceptable as collateral
Jewelry	Not usually acceptable as collateral
Other assets	10% to 50% of market value
Receivables	Under 90 days x 0.50
Stocks and Bonds	50% - 90%
Mutual Funds	Not usually acceptable as collateral
Individual Retirement Accounts (IRA)	Not usually acceptable as collateral
Certificate of Deposit (CD)	100%

Management Experience

Lenders review management experience and education in an applicable field critically since poor management is one of the most common reasons for business failures.

Franchises

SBA loans can be used for franchises provided the franchisee (borrower) retains the right to profit from efforts "*...commensurate with ownership.*" A franchise will not considered for an SBA loan if the franchiser "*...retains power to control operations to such an extent as to equate to an employment contract.*"

Change in ownership

SBA loans can be obtained for a change of ownership "*...if the change is seen as promoting the development of the business or, in some cases preserving its existence.*"

SBA Loan Program Comparison

For *Profit* companies with good credit rating

7(a) loans

Maximum	$5 million
% of Guarantee by SBA	85% to $150,000 75 over $150,000
Required use of proceeds	Expansion, renovation, new construction, land or buildings, equipment, fixtures or working capital.
Qualification Requirements	A for-profit business, that meets SBA size standards. The borrower must show good character, *good credit management history*, and ability to repay.

504 loans

Maximum	$5.5 million
% of Guarantee by SBA	40%
Required use of proceeds	Long-term fixed asset loans
Qualification Requirements	For-profit business that does not exceed $15 million in tangible net worth.

Community Advantage (Sometimes referred to as Micro-Loans)

Loans and grants available through an SBA certified community development financial institution. They provide access to capital and business assistance to low-income women and minority entrepreneurs and small businesses *in distressed and underserved communities.* (16)

These loans which are guaranteed by the SBA, are controlled by strict community-based criteria and require attendance in training sessions to develop a business plan.

The loans typically range from $5,000 to $100,000, while an SBA guaranteed loan can be up to $250.000.

Note: It may be advantageous to work with a SCORE Counselor/Mentor before contacting a Community Advantage organization. They prefer to work with business owners that have a Business Plan prepared in advance.

Like SCORE, they are affiliated with the SBA. Their mission is to provide micro loans and grants to individuals trying to develop a new business, or expand an existing small business.

They are prepared to support the needs of individuals with a less than perfect credit history.

They work with clients one-on-one in a two-phase process.

Phase one	The client works with a business consultant to make their business plan functionally ready to submit for a financial loan.
Phase two	The client works directly with a loan advisor to determine their financing options. The loan advisor works with them throughout the loan process.

A business owner applying for a loan for a *start-up company* needs to begin with a completed *business plan.*

A business owner applying for a loan to expand an *existing company* needs to begin with a *marketing plan.*

Five C's of Loan Financing

Micro loan and grant applications are evaluated with the five C's of financing.

Character	Owner's business character as reflected on a personal credit report
Capacity	Owner's ability to be successful with the business as proven by a pristine business plan, thought-out business model, experience in the industry, and solid financial statements
Capital	Owner's contribution of at least 20% of the requested financing amount
Collateral	Acceptable collateral to back the loan in case of default
Cash flow	Sufficient operating cash to pay the owner and employees, and service the debt

Loan application checklist (material required for loan processing)

Completed and signed *Loan Application*

a. Loan need

Explain why the loan is needed. Be as specific as possible. Include the amount of cash needed to cover three to six months of operating expenses, an itemized list of starting inventory (with cost), furniture, fixtures, equipment, advertising, and marketing materials.

Note: It may be helpful to include pictures of the business (building) and equipment or supplies you are trying to finance to help the lender understand more detail about how the money will be used. In the case of a loan for advertising, consider including sketches of possible advertisements or signs.

b. Collateral

List all personal and business assets *that are available to secure the loan request.* Include all business assets at cost and personal assets at market value. If real estate will be used as collateral, include the latest appraised value.

1. Completed business plan (for a start-up) or Marketing plan (for an existing business).
2. Projected financial statements
    a. Cash flow: Month-by-month projections for 12 months of operation
    b. Balance sheet: Current and/or start-up balance sheet which includes the use of the loan proceeds and the loan amount.
    c. Income statement: A 12 month statement which reflects the months addressed in the cash flow projection.
    d. Key assumptions: A complete description of all issues that affect the financial projections.
3. Business financial statements: If available, provide at least 3 years of fiscal statements including a balance sheet, income statement, and the most current interim statements within 45 to 60 days of date of application. *All documents MUST be signed and dated.*
4. Business Tax Returns: If available, provide for the past 3 years.
5. Completed and signed Personal Financial Statement for each person

with 20% or more ownership in the business.

6. Personal Tax Returns: Provide 3 years of complete personal tax returns for each person with 20% or more ownership, signed and dated, including all supporting schedules.

7. Resume: Describe the owner's ability as the loan applicant to successfully operate the business. Include a description of business skills acquired from previous work experience, training and education for each person owning 20% or more of the business.

8. Licenses: Provide a copy of state and city business licenses, if in business, and copies of professional licenses. Include a copy of an unsigned lease agreement if appropriate.

9. Corporate, partnership, or LLC operating agreements.

Government Grants

Definition:

> An award of financial assistance in the form of money by the federal government to an eligible grantee with no expectation that the funds will be paid back.
>
> The term does not include technical assistance which provides services instead of money, or other assistance in the form of revenue sharing, loans, loan guarantees, interest subsidies, insurance, or direct appropriations.

The Small Business Innovation Research (SBIR) office is a government agency that gives grants. The SBIR specializes in small businesses looking for funding for high-risk technologies.

> The catch: The technology *must* meet the research and development needs of the federal government.

> Founded in 1982, the SBIR recently awarded $1.5 billion to startups, with grants going to software, biotechnology, health-care and defense companies. So if a business owner is planning on opening a pizzeria, they might have trouble getting a grant from this organization.

But there are federal grants awarded to food and nutrition companies. For instance, a pizzeria that caters to children and specializes in serving nutritious, healthy pizzas may be able to win a grant. It might be helpful to check with state or local government to see what is available. Start by visiting the local or state Chamber of Commerce.

Crowd Funding

> Definition:
>
> The act of fundraising by using the Internet or a similar network to solicit funds from a large pool of potential donors.

The author has done extensive research into the use of *crowdfunding* to finance a small business. This document only mentions *crowdfunding* as an option to consider WITH CAUTION. The author suggests getting the support of legal experts and financial consultants to understand what *crowdfunding is* and how it works before using this option. The primary concern for a small business using *crowdfunding* are the very strict rules which are enforced by the Securities and Exchange Commission.(17)

Angel Investors

Some individuals with an idea for a new business who are unable to qualify for an SBA loan will try borrowing from their friends and relatives. When they run out of friends and relatives willing to loan money or co-sign a loan, they may look for Angel Investors.

Angel Investors are people willing to invest in what they consider promising start-up business ideas. They will usually become part owners of the new business and maintain a strong voice in major operating decisions.

Angel Investors tend to be careful with their money and they are likely to do a very thorough investigation of the potential management backgrounds, the industry, the market potential, and details of the business plan.

Angel investors can sometimes be located by inquiring through trade associations, industry associations, and local centers similar to a Chamber of Commerce.

Humanitarian Financial Help

Organizations like Mercy Corps http://www.mercycorps.org (19) receive lending and operating capital from the Small Business Administration and personal donations. Like with other lenders, an application for a loan requires a business plan, although a major consideration is the applicant's motivation and commitment. They are sometimes more forgiving of a poor credit rating if the applicant can express integrity, a strong work ethic, and other qualitative characteristics.

Startup Costs

Every business, no matter how exciting and innovative it will be when it is fully operational and generating a profit, needs money (capital) to get going. Owners need money for rent, furniture and equipment, inventory, and reserve funds for personal and family expenses until the (hopefully) profits begin to arrive.

Possible deductions

Before listing categories that can be considered *startup costs*, there is another factor to consider. It is not only important to estimate startup costs to have adequate operating capital when the new business doors open, but it is important to keep good financial records for potential Internal Revenue Service (IRS) deductions.

IRS Publication 535, Chapter 8 Amortization, explains how to deduct the cost of starting a business. According to the publication, "…you can deduct a limited amount of start-up and organizational costs. The costs that are not deducted currently can be amortized ratably over a 180-month period."(20)

Qualifying cost, according to the IRS:

- a cost you paid or incurred to operate an existing trade or business in the same field as the one you entered, and
- a cost you paid or incurred before the day your active trade or business begins

Start-up costs, according to the IRS:

- An analysis or survey of potential markets, products, labor supply, transportation facilities, etc. (Review the Market Research section of this *Desk Reference* for more ideas.)
- Advertisements for the opening of the business
- Salaries and wages for employees who are being trained and their instructors
- Travel and other necessary costs for securing prospective distributors, suppliers, or customers
- Salaries and fees for executives and consultants, or other professional services

Examples of startup costs

Costs that arise before a business opens its doors:

Fixtures and equipment

Installation of fixtures and equipment

Decorating, remodeling

Beginning inventory

Utility deposits

Licenses and permits

Professional fees

Advertising

Signs

Leasehold improvements

Land

Staff salaries

Cash on hand

Cash in the bank

Insurance

And others

Operating expenses

Before any income can be considered *profit*, all financial obligations must be satisfied – hopefully using income generated by sales of products or services.

Examples of regular operating costs:

Salaries

Utilities

Rent or purchase payment

Stationary and printing

Insurance

Advertising and promotion

Building & equipment maintenance

Taxes

Inventory purchases

and others

Part Three – Daily Operations

Chapter 7 – Owner's Role and Responsibilities

Introduction

Potential customers in a fine restaurant cannot enjoy a meal if nobody unlocks the door, hires a chef, pays the utility bill to heat the stove, or develops a menu.

Hairdressers will not have many return customers if the salon does not have comfortable chairs or sharp scissors.

A delivery service or taxi service will not generate much profit if they do not service their vehicles regularly and they break down.

And so it goes. Operating a successful small business does not just *happen.* It needs to be planned, coordinated, and maintained. It needs to have an owner who is familiar with and is active in the role of *Manager.* It begins with an understanding of why the company exists and what it needs to do to attract and retain customers.

This chapter will address the daily activities of a small business owner, specifically each of the recognized functions of a manager which are *plan, lead, organize, and control,* and what it means to be a manager,

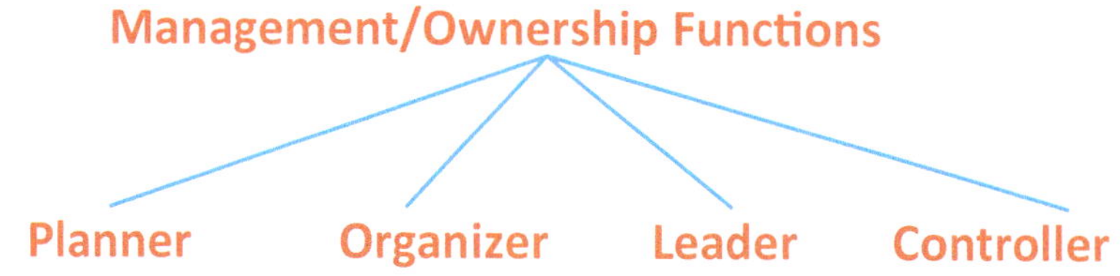

Manager/Owner as a Planner

A business owner as a planner has to wear many hats, as the saying goes. They have to be long range, or strategic planners always thinking about where they business will be in a few years and what they have to do to be sure the company stays on a course for consistent growth. They also have to be operational planners making sure the day-to-day functions are well thought out and the company is staffed to support daily production or operational needs.

Reacting vs. Planning

Many business owners will say they are too busy "putting out fires" and reacting to daily problems to take the time to plan. However, experience has shown many successful business owners that taking the *time to plan* can, if done properly, reduce the need to put out fires or reacting to daily problems. Planning may be seen as a luxury which the owner does not have time for but without taking the time to plan properly, many daily tasks will be uncoordinated or incomplete.

Planning is necessary to establish and stay within budgets, forecast inventory requirements, make hiring decisions and know how to provide customers with accurate schedule and cost estimates. It is not a scary thing or extra management burden; it is an important part of owning and managing a business.

Plans develop forecasts

The process of *planning* involves coordinating documents and ideas to keep track of the hundreds of details required to operate a business throughout the day. Written plans can be in the form of a drawing, a checklist, a series of sketches or written descriptions. Plans can also be locked in a person's mind.

Working with plans is not a new activity to most people. Individuals use plans when they build a piece of furniture from a kit, prepare themselves to attend a movie, take a vacation, cook a meal, or coordinate a meal. The concept of planning is not difficult, though the words "develop a plan" can intimidate some people if they get too caught up in the format.

From a business perspective, the end result of a company plan is an estimate of resources or actions required to get the company from where it is at the present time to where it wants to be. It is a forecast, or best (educated) guess at what must be done to reach a goal, repair a piece of equipment, satisfy a customer, etc. A finalized plan should be the best alternative for a situation than other choices.

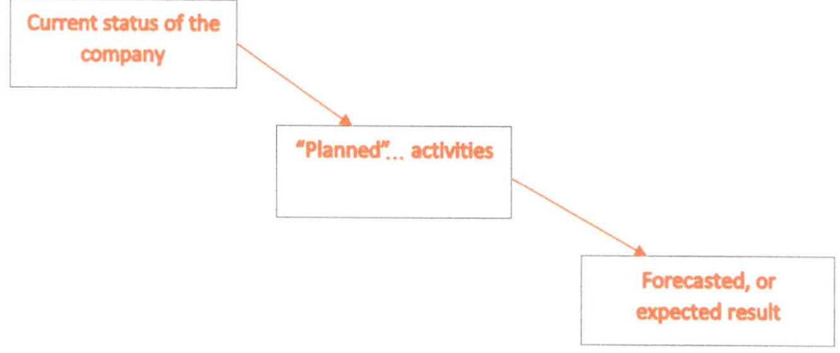

Things to keep in mind when developing a forecast:

1. *Forecasts are almost never perfect.* They are a best guess based upon the information available at the time the forecast was created. Economic and weather forecasts seem to prove this statement, though when they are created and presented, the forecasters are usually trying to be very accurate.

2. *Planning and the resulting forecasts are based upon unknown factors.* They are reasonable estimates of what to expect, based upon past experience and whatever limited data or information is available.

3. *Forecasts are more accurate in the short term than the long term.* For example, it would be easier to forecast the sales potential for a particular product for the next two weeks than to estimate detailed sales potential for the same product in 4 years.

Strategic vs. Operational Planning

Strategic Planning
Long range, top level, somewhat general

Operational Planning
Short to mid-range, mid-level to working level
Very specific goals and objectives providing direction to staff and management for day-to-day functions
Supports long range strategic goals

Strategic planning (long term)

Long term plans are future oriented and address the big picture, not day-to-day problems. Strategic planning concentrates on the growth and expectations of the company over the long term so that it can respond to changes in the market and stakeholder desires.

Examples of strategic thinking, long-range planning statements:

> The company will expand to a newer and/or larger location in approximately 4 years.
>
> The company plans to offer a new line of products in 3 years and is currently engaged in market research and potential supplier negotiations.
>
> The company is investigating a possible consolidation of administrative offices from five to two within 3 years.
>
> The company intends to stay in its current location and improve processes to increase production capability over the next 4 years.

Operational planning (day-to-day)

Short term plans address daily concerns and provide staff and management with directions for assigned duties, staffing, facilities, work stations, equipment and supplies and other resources that will be required. It includes the requirement to organize specialized training and associated human relations concerns.

Operational planning usually covers the current period to about 2 or 3 years into the future. All activities and events included in operational planning should support the company in the long term.

Examples of operational thinking, or short-term planning statements:

The company will not purchase additional equipment or new systems that do not fit into the strategic growth plans.

The company will develop a training program for all employees on the new product line as it becomes available for sale.

The company will not hire replacements for administrative staff that leaves to avoid layoffs during the consolidation phase.

The company will encourage employee suggestions for improving production processes.

Manager/Owner as an organizer

There is no perfect way to organize an office, a production facility, a retail store, a consulting business, or any other type of company. There are a wide variety of models and ideas to choose from when deciding on company departments, furniture and equipment arrangement, and personal work space. Even though there are a lot of experts around to give business owners suggestions, each company eventually organizes itself to fit its unique culture, goals, and customer expectations.

The ideas provided in this section are just that, ideas. They are not necessarily the best or the worst; but they reflect situations the author of this *Reference Manual* has experienced over many years of working with a wide variety of small businesses.

Departmentalization

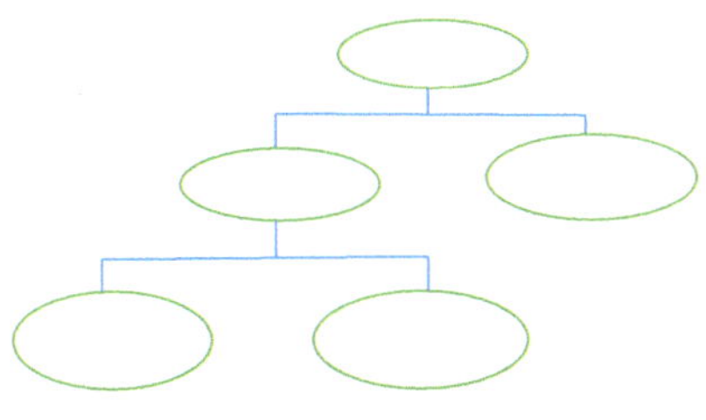

Departmentalization refers to grouping jobs by units, section, division, region, etc. according to a logical arrangement that fits the needs of the company and its customers. Grouping of individuals can take several forms.

Formal	Provide structure to job standardization, training, and growth potential.
Centralized	Provide control and direct management of decision-making.
Vertical	Provide levels of authority through a hierarchical structure.
Horizontal	Provide grouping by specialization or related skills and abilities. Horizontal groups can be divided into: Function (e.g. administration, finance, production, sales) Process (e.g. baking, kitchen prep., men's wear, ladies' wear, mill, lathes) Location (e.g. geographical region, district, shopping center) Product/Service (e.g. automobile: domestic, foreign, full size, mid-size; supermarket: delicatessen, bakery, produce) Customer (e.g. wholesale, retail, youth, senior citizen)

When to departmentalize

As companies grow and add more employees, they eventually reach a size where they need better communication channels, consistent work rules, control of decision-making, standardized training, and employee advancement pathways.

Some companies organize by mixing types of departmentalization. For example, a company may have both regional offices and branches, and each type can have an office, production area, and sales section. This is referred to as hybrid organization structure.

Organizing the workplace

Is this the picture of an orderly and productive work space?

Some people say they are happy working in disorganization with papers stacked in several piles, unusable chairs full of materials, and files in disarray. Others say everything must be in perfect order or they cannot perform their job functions efficiently. Is one right and the other wrong?

Not necessarily. Both workers may be effective with their own style of work area management. Are both extremes good for the company?

Probably not. When it comes to running a company and working with a wide variety of people, a small business owner needs an organizational middle ground.

Everything in the company that relates to making the business run should be stored or filed in a way that everyone, with a need to know, can access easily. It is especially important for a small business to limit access to company material and information to a few employees in case something happens to a worker and they are not at work.

People should be allowed to exercise reasonable control over the physical arrangement of their work place, while making sure that company information is accessible to appropriate co-workers and management.

Workplace data housekeeping suggestions

Dump outdated material regularly	Toss out whatever is out of date, no longer of any value, or can be found easily in other nearby locations. Consider taking a set portion of every other week (perhaps Friday afternoon) to review/ purge files. Leave a marker or flag showing where the files have been cleaned and start at the marker again in two weeks.
Consider storing files on the Cloud	There are several Cloud storage locations available on the Internet to store and retrieve files without using office space for paper copies of all company information.
Unsubscribe to junk email	Emails can get overwhelming. Unsubscribe or block any that

have no value to the operation of the company.

Manager/Owner as a leader

As a company grows, the owner with his or her entrepreneurial spirit will have to let go of some responsibilities and decision-making tasks that they have managed since the beginning. Most small business owners are comfortable directly managing up to six, or possibly eight people, but as the company brings on more employees, it becomes difficult to train and directly supervise a large group of people. The answer to the dilemma is through *delegation.*

> *Delegation:* Assigning groups or individuals the responsibility and authority to make decisions related to a specific category of skills, customers, production processes, or other defined area or function.

Delegating tasks and responsibilities sounds easy to some people, but it is not easy and it should not be taken lightly. By delegating, the business owner is releasing some of their ownership. It requires a great deal of trust on the part of the owner to transfer functional responsibility to another individual. In the end the owner will remember that he or she, not the individual delegated to, has the ultimate responsibility for success or failure of the business.

The U.S. Small Business Administration recommends the following guidelines for delegating: (21)

- Do it slowly; phase the changes in over time.
- Give adequate facts to the chosen individual(s).
- Share information to help the individual(s) make appropriate decisions.

- Be sure to give authority along with responsibility.
- Accept a few mistakes while the person is absorbing their new authority.

Leadership style

The owner of a small business is always watched by employees, suppliers, and customers.

The audience may be anyone in or around the place of business, but wherever an owner is, people will be aware of their presence.

People watch owners and managers' body language to determine their mood, attentiveness, and general approachability. It is up to each owner and/or manager, as well each individual to know their own personality style and how they project it to others.

In the case of a small business owner, it is important to project a positive attitude, to demonstrate knowledge of the company product, service, and organizational processes, and to appear welcoming to customers and employees.

Business owners would be wise to consider a quote from Henry Ford:

"Whether you think you can or think you can't – you are right."

Or a quote from Yogi Berra in the book *When you Come to a Fork in The Road, Take It:* (22)

"If you don't know where you are going, you might not get there."

It is important for a small business owner to circulate, be seen, and pay attention to employees, as well as customers. Don't get caught in a set routine, or pattern of walking to and from an office. Walk through at different times and with different routes. People will get used to the owner's presence and not disrupt their work whenever he or she appears.

An owner should be seen. Visit people in their work place, chat with them, make suggestions, offer assistance, but don't overwhelm them.

A suggestion shared with the author of this *Desk Reference* by Alan Mulally, former President of the Boeing Commercial Airplane Company and later CEO of the Ford Motor Company: (23)

> **"Whenever you leave a meeting with anyone, whether it is a formal meeting or social gathering, or it is a casual passing in a public area – the last thing you should consider doing as you are leaving them is look into their eyes and see if you have made them feel a little better for having spent time with you."**

Manager/Owner as a controller

Controlling within a small business refers to understanding company processes and monitoring to see that they are done within the owner's expectations. In their role as a controller, the owner or manager sets standards related to production quantity, quality, schedule, sales projections, etc. and makes sure employees understand the standards.

Production can be monitored directly or by a reporting system. If standards are not met, the owner/manager determines corrective action and coordinates implementation of the corrections.

Summary

When developing the policies and procedures for daily operations, a small business owner should begin by deciding the core values of the company which are the driving force behind all decisions.

> Is the company driven by product quality or production schedules?
>
> Does the company want to move customers through quickly (as in a fast food restaurant), or provide more service (as in a fine dining establishment)?
>
> Does the company profit through high volume production, or smaller customized output?
>
> Is the company structured to support high flexibility or limited flexibility production output?

Chapter 8 Staffing (Human Relations)

Studies have shown that companies who treat some employees as participating members of the team, or "in-group," and others as outsiders. the company will not be able to achieve, or maintain greatness. Every person in the company should be treated with equal respect and recognized for the skills and talent they bring to the organization.

Introduction

Any business with more than one person, is made up of a mix of personalities, talents, and interests with all hoping to get along while maintaining their own individuality. The workers of today are far more diverse than any previous generation in terms of age, ethnicity, physical ability, marital status, education, and personal values.

Bringing a group of strangers together to produce a product or service can be very challenging for a small business owner. When coupled with a seemingly never ending array of government regulations related to employee safety, salary, and anti-discrimination, it can be overwhelming to hire and manage employees.

This chapter addresses a wide variety of topics related to human resource (personnel) planning, recruiting and training, salary and compensation, employee motivation, and labor contracts. It includes suggestions to help a small business owner understand the regulations affecting their employees, in an easy-to-understand format.

Greiner Growth Model

In 1972, LEE Greiner wrote in the *Harvard Business Review* (Issue 50, 4, pgs. 37-46) about Evolution and Revolution as organizations grow. His writing became the basis for a business model referred to as the *Greiner Growth Model* (reference: *Five Stages of Growth*, by Scott M. and Bruce R., in *Long Range Planning* (20, 3, pg. 45, 1987). (24)

The premise of the Greiner Growth Model is that nearly all companies begin with a creative phase where the founder or owner is excited and motivated to produce new products and services that will create value for customers. Innovation is natural and the people creating the new business will work long hours doing whatever needs to be done to make the company succeed.

According to Greiner, as the company grows and demand for their products or services increases they will eventually have to hire people or contract work out to satisfy their customers. If they do not add staff to support their needs, the company will stagnate, customers will leave, and it will become impossible for the organization to grow.

This chapter is about deciding when to hire people, how to recruit them, how to train them, and how to keep the company growing with the right talent pool. Without *people,* there will be no product or service and eventually, there will be no company.

Job Analysis and Work Design

Any business with more than a sole owner has at least two people, and a byproduct of two or more people in a company is a division of responsibilities.

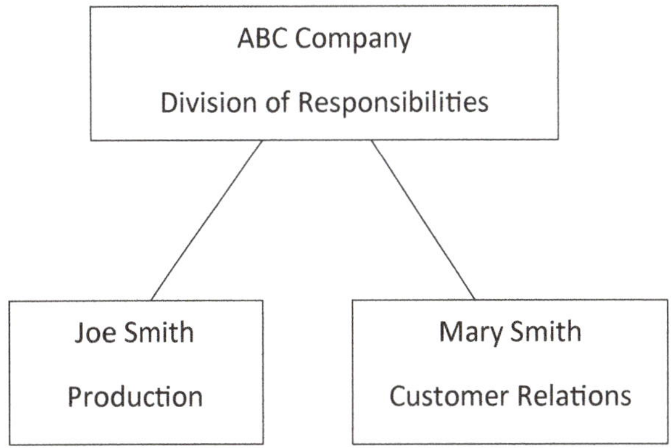

As a company grows and the need to add staff becomes obvious, the owner can reach out to friends and family to hire people. But they will not necessarily be the right people. It is far better to develop a *plan* add the right people at the right time.

Designing jobs, hiring staff, building a business involves planning how the work will be done, and by whom. People (usually) don't just appear on the scene and begin working. They need to be recruited, selected, trained, and compensated. The job and work design process can be fairly complex, but to be done effectively, it has to follow a fairly straight forward process.

When hiring, consider the answers to these questions:

What skills are needed for the business to operate?

Where will they find (or recruit) people with the needed skills?

How will they narrow a field of candidates and select the best employees?

How will they train people to perform the operational tasks in the company?

How should they compensate (or pay) people?

In order to comply with Equal Employment Opportunities Commission (EEOC) and other regulatory agency guidelines, the first step in any hiring process should be to conduct a JOB ANALYSIS.

Job Analysis - purpose

Job Analysis can be defined as *the process of studying jobs (not people) to develop an understanding of major job functions, worker skill requirements, and organizational reporting relationships.*

In simpler terms:

> *Job Analysis is process used to define a job's duties, responsibilities, and accountabilities.*

Job analysis is considered one of the most important functions of human resource management because it provides the foundation for:

- job descriptions – activities and responsibilities
- job specifications – skills and abilities required to perform job tasks
- personnel recruiting and selection
- employee/management orientation and training
- performance evaluation and compensation (salary) planning
- labor relations

The job analysis process involves describing what happens in a job by accurately and precisely identifying the knowledge and skills necessary to perform the tasks, the tools equipment and supplies required for the job, and the conditions under which the job is performed.

Job Analysis process

Using a form similar to the one shown on the next page, the first step is to interview workers, observe people doing the work and writing down the observations on the form.

IMPORTANT – Job Analysis is for evaluating the position,

NOT an individual worker.

Job Analysis Interview/Check Sheet

Name of observer: ______________________ Date: __________

Position (job title) being observed: ______________________________

Dept.: ______________________ Location: __________________

Job tasks

1. *Provide a short summary of major job responsibilities*
2. *List the primary tasks performed in job*

(Enter most time consuming task first):

Task	*Brief explanation*	*Estimated % of total job*

Include additional sheets if necessary to list all appropriate tasks

Tools and Equipment

3. List tools and/or equipment required to perform the job:

(List primary tools/equipment tools first)

Tool/Equipment	Skill level required Low Moderate High	Estimated hours used per week

4. List specialized software and operating systems required to perform the job (include specialized robotics in this section)

Skill level required Estimated hours used per week

Knowledge, Skills, Abilities Required

5. *Indicate the level of* ***education*** *required to perform the job*

No formal education required ___ 2 year college degree ___

Less than high school ___ 4 year college degree ___

High school or equivalent ___ Graduate level degree ___

Technical school cert. ___

Professional license (specify) ______________________________

6. Describe the primary knowledge areas required to perform the job functions

(e.g. customer service, clerical functions, computers, mathematics, counseling, English, foreign language, communication media, etc.):

7. Describe the primary skills required to perform the job functions:

Examples of Job Skills:

- *Communication, written or verbal*
- *Listening*
- *Analysis*
- *Planning and organizing*

Examples of desirable skills in candidates

- *Takes Initiative*
- *Exercises good judgment*
- *Detail oriented*
- *Independent*
- *Safety consciousness*
- *Risk taker*
- *Reliable*
- *Flexible and adaptable*
- *Innovative*
- *Service oriented*
- *Team oriented*
- *Creative*
- *Dependable*
- *Tactful*
- *Ethical*

8. *Describe the primary physical* ***abilities*** *required to perform the job functions (e.g. ability to lift 50 pounds, endurance, depth perception, vision correctable to 20/20, physical coordination, reaction time.):*

Environmental Conditions

9. *Describe the frequency and degree to which the employee should expect to encounter adverse working conditions (e.g. noise, vibration, cramped quarters, poor ventilation, excessive movement):*

Records and Reports

10. *What records and/or reports are prepared during performance of the job?*

Working Conditions

11. *Describe situations in which the job is involved in data interpretation, providing ideas/suggestions, committing company resources (e.g. deciding on room assignments, suggesting menu items, negotiating sale prices, etc.)*

12. *Explain whether the job is performed with little, or no direct supervision – or – whether it requires close supervision and instruction.*

13. *Explain whether the job is considered repetitive work, or it involves a variety of duties, often changing from one task to another of a different nature.*

14. *If the job is considered stressful (e.g. emergency response, dangerous, critical to company success, etc.), explain why.*

Other

15. *Include any additional comments about the job that would help a Workforce Planner understand the position.*

When the Job Analysis questionnaire is completed, it will be the source document for the following tasks:

Write job descriptions

Determine job classification and salary

Develop recruiting and employee selection process

Develop employee training

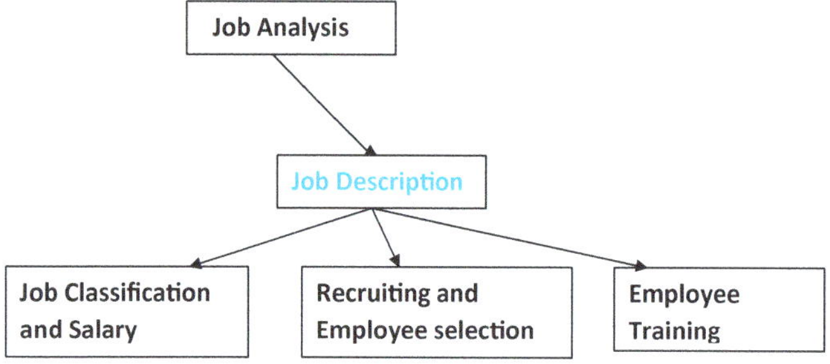

Job Descriptions

After a job position has been studied using Job Analysis, the responsibilities and tasks for each position in the company should be written in a *job description.* In addition to the responsibilities and tasks, a *job description* should clearly state the skills and experience required for a person to perform the position tasks.

A well written *Job Description*, when used as the basis for recruiting, hiring, training, developing salary plans, and classifying employee's (hourly or salary) will go a long way toward keeping small business owner in compliance with governmental rules and regulations.
A *Job Description* used properly, will help a manager focus on the work and not on the individual worker, which in turn will help prevent a biased or discriminatory workplace.

There are several job description templates available on the Internet, some for a fee, some free. There is no mandatory format, or writing style for a job description, but it should include the following:

- job title
- department, section, or work group
- job title of direct report (the individual the candidate will report to)
- summary of the job purpose
- primary duties and responsibilities of the job
- minimum qualifications required to perform the job

Job Description EXAMPLE

Sun Spot Resort

Job Title	Lead Maintenance Engineer
Department	Maintenance Department
Reports to	General Manager
Job Summary	Responsible for maintenance of all resort infrastructure. Duties include gardening, plumbing, and electrical repair and installation. This is a lead position with responsibility for training and assigning tasks to other employees in the Maintenance Department.

Primary Duties

1. Establish and maintain preventative maintenance schedule for all equipment in the resort gardens, hotel, and restaurant.
2. Perform preventive maintenance on resort equipment as scheduled.
3. Repair defective resort equipment including, but not limited to air conditioning, lighting, landscape tools.
4. Schedule and provide 24 hour maintenance support for all resort employee and guests.

Minimum Qualifications

- Working knowledge of resort equipment typically found in hotels, restaurants, and family recreation areas (swimming pool, jogging track, etc.).
- Ability to climb ladders, operate resort equipment, lift 85 pounds, and work in inclement weather.
- Certification as a qualified air conditioning maintenance technician.
- Experience hiring and supervising maintenance employees.

End of Job Description example

Bona fide occupational qualification (BFOQ)

Bona fide occupational qualification (BFOQ) is a legal term for the qualifications a person must have in order to perform a specific job function.

If an employer requires a job applicant to have certain abilities to be hired, the *abilities or qualifications* the employer is looking for MUST be an actual requirement of the job.

Examples:

If the job description example for a maintenance worker requires *an ability to climb ladders, operate resort equipment, lift 85 pounds, etc.,* the employer (business owner) MUST be able to prove a person who does not have these abilities could not do the job. If an applicant could only lift 75 pounds and it could be proven that a maintenance worker never has to lift 85 pounds, then the requirement to lift 85 pounds could be considered discriminatory.

Job requirements for age, religion, race, or gender, may be violating the law *unless* it the owner can prove those requirements are necessary to perform the job.

When advertising to fill a job opening or when screening job applicants, it is essential that any selection criteria be a true requirement to perform the job. BUSINESS OWNERS CAN AVOID VIOLATING ANTI-DISCRIMINATION REGULATIONS IF THEY USE JOB ANALYSIS TO DEVELOP WRITTEN SKILL REQUIREMENTS FOR A JOB DESCRIPTION AND RECRUITING ACTIVITIES.

Exempt and Non-exempt Employee Classification

These categories are also referred to as *salaried* and *hourly* employees.

Note: The author of this *Desk Reference* is NOT an attorney and has not had legal training other than independent seminars and several business law courses during the study of business.

This section contains information a small business owner should know, but it should not be considered a substitute for legal advice from an Attorney at Law.

Fair Labor Standards Act (FLSA) (25)

Minimum Wage

The U.S. Department of Labor, under authority of the FLSA, regulates and controls the Federal minimum wage through the Wage and Hour Division of the Employment Standards Administration.

FLSA rules require nonexempt (hourly) workers to be paid one and one-half times their regular salary when they work overtime.

The Federal (FLSA) minimum wage applies in any state with a state minimum wage which is lower than Federal minimum wage.

In a state, or city with a higher minimum wage than the Federal FLSA amount, the highest state minimum wage applies.

If a state has no minimum wage, the FLSA minimum wage applies.

Age restrictions

In addition to establishing the Federal minimum wage, the FLSA:

- restricts hours that children under age 16 can work for nonagricultural operations
- prohibits employment of children under age 16 for agricultural operations during school hours
- forbids employment of children under age 18 in certain jobs which are considered too dangerous

Some industries such as movie theaters and most agriculture are not controlled by FLSA overtime rules. In addition, jobs which are controlled by some other specific federal labor law are excluded from FLSA rules. Most notably, railroad workers are bound by the Railway Labor Act, and many truck drivers are bound by the Motor Carriers Act, instead of the FLSA.

Exempt or nonexempt

Employees with jobs monitored by the FLSA are considered either exempt or nonexempt. Nonexempt employees, sometimes referred to as salaried workers are paid a flat amount every pay period no matter how many hours they work, and they are not entitled to overtime pay.

The U.S. Department of Labor specifically designates certain classes of workers as exempt. (26)

Examples of exempt jobs: executives, administrative personnel, outside salespeople, highly skilled technical employees and licensed professionals, such as doctors, lawyers, architects, engineers and certified public accountants

In addition, managers who hire and fire employees and who spend less than half their time performing the same duties as their employees are typically also exempt employees.

In general, the more responsibility and independence or discretion an employee has, the more likely the employee is to be considered exempt.

Examples of nonexempt jobs: bank teller, bookkeeper, retail cashier, shipping-receiving clerk, janitorial and restaurant employees

Typical features of Hourly and Salaried work

Note: The table shown below shows examples of work features. It does NOT show a legal requirement or commitment.

Hourly (non-exempt)	**Salaried (exempt)**
Time reporting (e.g. clocks)	Usually no time reporting
Pay docking for missing work time	Pay docking is rare;—but poor attendance can result in termination.
Daily overtime for extra time worked	No daily overtime
Call-in pay (e.g. working from home)	No call-in pay
Piece rates sometimes in place of hourly wages	No piece rates; bonuses sometimes paid
End of shift clean up time	No extra pay for cleanup time
Formal paid rest periods	Paid rest periods common but not guaranteed
Sick time, personal time and vacation time earned during work year	Not always limited to a specific number of sick, personal, or vacation days.
Cumbersome work rules	Few work rules

The primary difference between exempt and nonexempt employees is overtime eligibility. Not knowing the difference between these categories could cost a company a lot of money in fines.

Nonexempt overtime violations to avoid:

- Treating all employees being paid a straight salary as exempt employees.
- Paying non-exempt employees commission only.
- Offering employees a choice between overtime pay or a higher pay rate.
- Excluding certain incentives or bonuses from the overtime calculation.
- Saving extra hours worked one week to be paid the next week as straight time.

Example of a potential problem:

The manager of a small company notices that the clerks in one department are working a lot of overtime. In an attempt to reduce costs, the manager changes the clerk's job positions from nonexempt to an exempt classification and offers a raise to the clerks salary while avoiding high overtime pay.

The result could be a serious wage and hour violation.

The federal Fair Labor Standards Act (FLSA) and the laws of the 50 states regulate what constitutes overtime. (27)

The federal jurisdiction applies to employees who:

- regularly use the mail or telephone for interstate

communication

- work for employers who contract clerical, custodial, or other work for businesses engaged in interstate commerce
- work for any company involved in the handling or production of goods in interstate commerce

Additional information

To obtain additional information related to minimum wage requirements or exempt and nonexempt job classifications, visit the Federal Wage and Hour Division Website: http://www.wagehour.dol.gov and/or call the FLSA toll-free information and helpline, available 8 a.m. to 5 p.m. in your time zone, 1-866-4USWAGE (1-866-487-9243).[(28)]

Recruiting and Hiring

This section is very brief because recruiting sources are changing as quickly as technology and social networking. The recruiting process for any small business should be adapted to the industry, the geographic region, and the skill base available in the local labor pool.

Some recruitment sources:

- Local colleges and universities usually have a pool of students looking for internship positions that can bring valuable knowledge into a small business.

Take advantage of social media networking to reach let people know about potential openings.

- Advertise through window signs (help wanted) or post openings on the internal company bulletin board

- Ask friends, company employees, and other social contacts to suggest potential job candidates.
- Advertise in local newspapers.
- Contact employment agencies.
- Encourage people to stop by and complete an application.
- Maintain a file of prior applicants.

Screening Applicants

Candidate Selection

Different types of positions require different selection techniques. It is generally a good idea to use more than one selection technique to narrow the candidate pool.

> An application form and personal interview might apply to a non-management position, while a supervisory position might also require reference checks.
>
> In some positions testing for physical abilities, drug use, or technical ability might be appropriate, but not in all cases.

Selection techniques to consider:

Structured interview

Assessing a candidate through a series of job related questions to gain knowledge of their work history and applicable experience. Structured interview questions do not have to follow the same order; but in order to prove objectivity and equal treatment of candidates, each candidate should be asked the same questions during the interview process. Interviews can be done by individuals, one-on-one, by a group, where several employees interview one candidate at the same time, or by several people in sequential one-on-one interviews.

Work samples

Have candidates perform some exercises they would be likely to experience in the work environment if they were hired to the position.

> Have a cook prepare a meal. Ask a carpenter to build a simple structure, or a tire installer change a tire.
>
> In an office environment, have the applicant prepare a memo, analyze a report, or demonstrate computer skills.

Peer assessment

Ask candidate's colleagues to observe a candidate in the work environment and provide feedback on what they saw.

Physical tests

Include job appropriate tests. Some examples are color blindness tests for electricians, lifting demonstration for delivery people, and other tests supporting BFOQ.

Consider Interns

Most colleges and universities require students to work as interns with a company or government agency before they graduate. The purpose is to help students apply new skills they are learning in their college studies to real life work situations. It also provides students with opportunities to network, become active team members, and add experience to their resume.

For the small business, interns can be a valuable resource. They are not full time workers, but they can help a business grow by sharing new skills and interest in areas the new company might be lacking. It is also an effective way to evaluate potential employees while they are performing as interns.

Employee Orientation

New employees to a company are typically excited to be hired, and sometimes a bit nervous because they do not know exactly what to expect, or what is expected of them. The first few days with a company (or in a new job within the company) can be stressful to a new person.

> Changing companies or jobs has been compared to standing on a platform high up in a circus tent and stepping into the air to grab a swinging trapeze. The person knows the trapeze will be there; but for a moment time they will be floating with nothing to hold except their belief in a better future.
>
> This compares to a person leaving a comfortable, established routine and moving into a new position. Inside they believe they will succeed and improve, but there is always a little anxiety during the transition period.

It is very important for a small business owner or department supervisor to make sure any new employee receives some formal orientation as soon as they arrive in their new position. The first few days are the baseline where the new employee will develop a positive or negative attitude toward their immediate supervisor, the company, and their job.

The owner or manager should greet and welcome the new employee, let them know the company is looking forward to having them on the team, and introduce them to their supervisor in a large organization, or co-workers in a small company.

Orientation is the term used to introduce the new employee to the company history, its policies about work times, vacation and sick leave, insurance, pay periods, and other topics covering all employees.

Training, sometimes confused with orientation is different. Training which is covered in the next section of this Reference Guide is the term used to teach a person how to perform their specific job functions.

New Hires

Rule #1 for a small business owner when they hire a new employee

> *Demonstrate care. Introduce oneself to the new hire, be sure their manager is available to them, monitor their progress during their first week of employment.*

Consider assigning a buddy for the new hire. Introduce them right away to an experienced employee they can go to with questions about break time, finding supplies and equipment. Let the buddy help them understand their new work culture and feel welcome.

Think about setting up lunch for them with other team members each day during their first week.

Give the new employee a project right away. Try to select a project that is a little bit challenging and able to be completed the first week to help them feel like they accomplished something.

Remember, any new employee is a little stressed by their changing situation, so cut some slack if their performance takes off slowly.

Employee Handbook

In order to prevent potential discrimination, a company should prepare an employee handbook for every member of the organization. The *handbook* should be given to each person on their first day with the company, during orientation, and be carefully explained.

Definition:

> An employee handbook is *a written document describing the benefits and responsibilities of the employment/company relationship*.

In the author's opinion is it better to think of the employee handbook as *a practical tool to help communicate consistent company policies between management and employees.*

Generally Recognized purposes of an employee handbook

- *Communication*

  It provides basic information related to compensation, benefits, work hours, and some historical, as well as organizational details to help a new employee jump start their understanding of the company.

- *Consistency*

  It helps prevent misunderstandings by ensuring all employees and managers receive the same information.

- *Legal protection*

  It can be considered a binding contract between the company and employees by clarifying policies such as harassment, smoking, attendance, and termination rights.

An employee handbook should be written in general terms, without getting into specific details such as pay scales or day-to-day operating instructions for a particular job.

Format of an employee handbook

There is no formal requirement for the design or size of an employee handbook. Depending upon the company, the handbook can be very short, very large, printed in a booklet form, or on typed sheets. The format is not as important as the consistency. The handbook should be the same for all employees in a particular pay grade (e.g. salaried, part-time, management).

Possible design of an *employee handbook*

Welcoming statement

A short statement from the owner or General Manager to let the new employee know they are happy to have them join the organization – along with a suggestion that they read through the rest of the *handbook* to help them understand how the company functions.

Short history of the company

Use this portion to provide some information about the company's background, history, and culture.

> Example:
>
> *The Sun Spot* is a mid-sized resort is considered a comfortable location where middle class couples and families can visit, stay a short time, and spend a relaxing time together. The *target* customers range from couples with small children to retired

couples visiting without their grown kids. The resort tries to provide an environment that will keep customers returning year after year – and so far, it has been successful.

Bulletin board

Include a statement letting employees where to find postings about work laws, company events, organization charts, and such.

Hiring Policy

- Equal opportunity statement

Work hours

- Shift hours
- Overtime policy for part-time and full-time employees
- Meal and break times

Pay policies

- Pay period, payday, pay advances, method (issue check, direct deposit), overtime policy (pay rate)
- Shift premiums (additional pay for night shift schedule)

Employee benefits

- Use of company property (vehicles, telephones, and other key assets)
- IT policy (computer use)
- Leave and time off policy (vacation, sick leave, and paid time off, family and medical leave, military, jury duty, and other unique situations

Performance

- Job performance expectations (This is related to the purpose statement. A sample statement: Customer service is a top priority; sales staff must return customer calls within four hours.)

- Job performance review schedule and method

Workplace behavior

- Professional conduct
- Punctuality and attendance
- Dress code, grooming, personal hygiene
- Policy statement regarding alcohol, drugs, smoking, and firearms

Health and safety

- How to report concerns related to safety and security
- What to do in an emergency

Ending employment

- Final paycheck and exit interview process
- Continuing health coverage

Handbook acknowledgment form

- Signed record showing employee received the *handbook*

Job Training

Effective employee training should be a very important part of any small business. Not only for new employees, but for anyone affected by a new process or technology (new telephone or point-of-sale system, etc.) that will alter job functions and require people to learn new skills

Studies have shown nearly 83% of company conversions to new or upgraded processing systems do *not* meet stakeholder expectations. One of the primary reasons for the poor return on investment in new systems is a lack of adequate training for users and support personnel. According to the Center for Effective Performance, "…business owners often fail to understand that the investment they are making is not just in new equipment or technology, but in what their employees must be able to do with this technology."

Remember – Employee training should be designed to help the trainee (employee) relax and be comfortable with their work. If they are poorly trained, it can lead to frustration and poor productivity in the work place.

Types of training sessions

This section applies to companies with a fairly large number of employees, but may be of use to small businesses as they grow and their processes become more complex.

The first thing to consider when designing an effective training program is whether the training will be offered on-site (on company premises), or outside (away from the company).

Training Option	**Explanation**
Tutorial	One person is taught at one time by another person
Classroom Course	Several people are taught together at the same time
Computer-aided instruction	One person is taught at one time by a computer system
Interactive training manuals	Combination of tutorials and computer-aided instruction
Resident expert	Individual familiar with the new process or system is on-call to assist as needed
Software help components	Built-in system components designed to train and troubleshoot problems
Training consultants	Vendors and training professionals provide tutorials, courses, and other training activities

When hiring a training consultant, training plans are compared on the following points:

- course description, content, objectives, and outline
- time devoted to each subject
- cost
- appropriateness of the course to the company and worker skill requirements

Developing a training plan

Suggestions to consider:

- Establish good communication between people who designed the new process or system and the employees who will have to learn the new process. Encourage information sharing between departments that will be affected by the change(s) so everyone involved will understand the needs of each functional area. Open communication helps people know about changes in other departments that may affect them.

- Train people on new processes and technology to support their immediate needs. Don't train everyone to work with all of the bells and whistles (features) of a new system or process when they are first introduced to it. New systems and processes can be overwhelming to some people, so phase in the training by helping them understand the features that apply directly to their current work assignments. Then as they become comfortable with the changes, introduce new portions of the system.

- Combine practice and feedback. Allow time for people to

try different features of the revised process on their own time. Consider isolated training stations for complex changes. Let them practice and share concerns with managers and trainers until they feel they are ready to work with the new process in their daily work. Adjust training if necessary to incorporate changes they have suggested from their practice sessions.

- Require learners to demonstrate competence in each job task they are being taught. Test them on each function before going on to more complex functions. Tests can be self-test exercises built into the training sessions.

- Provide on-the-job support tools. Give students handbooks, information sheets, or other support tools to help them remember new processes and procedures when they return to their work assignments.

Compensation (Salary Planning)

Salary planning is a very important part of any financial record keeping or budgeting process for a small business. It is usually not a good idea to establish a salary based only on what competitors pay. The salary and compensation package for a business should reflect company values.

- Companies seeking long-term employees who will gain experience and support customer needs over several years, should consider providing slightly higher than average compensation.
- Companies expecting short-term employees with frequent turnover usually provide low or average compensation.
- Companies such as agriculture, fishing, or landscaping are tied to seasonal fluctuations, and should provide a compensation package that would attract short-time workers when the demand for help is high. They typically lay off workers when their high production season declines.

This section explains some common approaches used by companies to determine how much to pay employees.

Compensation should be the equivalent of how much employees are valued.

Definitions

Employee compensation	All work-related pay or rewards that go to employees. It includes direct financial payments in the form of wages, salaries, incentives, commissions, and bonuses, as well as indirect payments in the form of fringe benefits such as time off for vacation or sick-leave, commute vouchers, and employer-paid insurance.
Financial incentive	Financial reward that is contingent on performance, such as sales commissions or profit-sharing.

Hourly Wage

A fixed amount paid for each hour a person works. Common for production and maintenance employees, also known as blue-collar workers.

Salary

A weekly, monthly, or annual rate of pay, based upon a pay period, rather than hours worked. Common for clerical, professional, sales, and management, also known as white-collar workers.

Job Evaluation

The systematic determination of the relative worth of specific jobs in a company.

Job Factors

Key elements considered to be of value to the organization, such as responsibility, skill, effort, and working conditions.

Comparable Worth

Value to the organization

Non-Monetary Compensation

Any benefit an employee receives from an employer or job that does not involve tangible value

Direct Compensation

A base wage, which can be an annual salary or hourly wage *and* any performance-based pay that an employee receives

Indirect Compensation

A broad category including everything from legally required public protection programs such as Social Security to health insurance, retirement programs, paid leave, childcare or moving expenses.

Employee Benefits

In addition to salary, employee compensation packages usually include some employee benefits that are unique to the company. Some employee benefits are required by law and regulations, while others are selected and offered by the company as a part of the culture used to attract, thank and retain employees.

Mandatory or required benefits

- Social Security taxes (Every employer must pay Social Security taxes at the same rate paid by their employees.)

- Unemployment insurance, according to state regulations and limits

- Workers compensation, according to state regulations and limits

- Disability insurance, required by some, but not all states

- Leave benefits for holiday, vacations, jury duty, personal leave, sick leave, and funeral/bereavement (These are required by most states but not by the federal government.)

Federal law requires 12 weeks of job-protected, but unpaid leave during any 12 month period for any of the following reasons:

1. Birth and care of eligible employee's child, or placement from adoption or foster care

2. Care of an immediate family member (spouse, child, parent) who has a serious health condition

3. Care of the employee's own serious health condition

Required benefits in some jurisdictions

(Check with local authorities and, or a legal adviser)

- Holiday pay
- Paid vacation, sick leave, personal time
- Dental care
- Paid funeral time
- Long term disability
- Paid military leave
- Paid jury duty

Unpaid benefit examples, generally not required

(Check with local authorities and, or a legal adviser)

- Retirement contribution plan
- Life insurance
- Non-production bonus pay
- Wellness programs
- Dependent care
- Financial planning
- Childcare subsidy
- Subsidized commuting
- Stock options
- Company car and or equipment (computer, cell phone,..)
- Gym membership
- Assigned parking
- Free coffee/snacks
- Physical workout area
- Company picnic or gatherings
- Non-cash awards

Cafeteria Plans

Cafeteria plans, sometimes referred to as flexible spending plans are designed to allow employees to have benefit plans that fit their lifestyle. An employee with young children might choose benefits that help with child care, or unusual medical expenses, while an employee with grown children may choose to put more of their compensation into a retirement fund. Others might select college tuition reimbursement or additional life insurance.

By using the cafeteria system, the benefit selection can be tailored to meet individual employee needs, while at the same time, reduce their gross income by allowing them to set aside non-taxable funds from their total salary.

Sometimes referred to as IRS Section 125 plans, an IRS FAQ bulletin dated January 6, 2015 states: (28)

> "A cafeteria plan is a separate written plan maintained by an employer for employees that meets the specific requirements of and regulations of section 125 of the Internal Revenue Code. It provides participants an opportunity to receive certain benefits on a pretax basis. Participants in a cafeteria plan must be permitted to choose among at least one taxable benefit (such as cash) and one qualified benefit."
>
> "A qualified benefit is a benefit that does not defer compensation and is excludable from an employee's gross income under a specific provision of the Code, without being subject to the principles of constructive receipt. Qualified benefits include the following:
>
> - Accident and health benefits (but not long-term care insurance)

- Adoption assistance
- Dependent care assistance
- Group-term life insurance coverage
- Health savings accounts, including distributions to pay long-term care services

Cafeteria plans may make benefits available to employees, their spouses, and dependents. It may also include coverage for former employees, but it cannot exist primarily for them.

Compensation package requirements

Any compensation, or pay system should include:

- Fair pay for each position when compared with the pay of others in the company
- Compensation which is equal, or related to other companies in the same industry or regional area
- Company ability to pay the planned (or committed) employee compensation
- A clear understanding by all employees about whether pay increases are based on performance, length of service, or both
- Clear and consistent compensation policy covering topics such as pay frequency and the lower and upper dollar limits assigned to a pay grade

Job Evaluation (Establishing Salary)

Relationship of Job Analysis, Job Descriptions, Job Evaluation

Job Analysis

Systematic investigation of jobs to identify their essential characteristics

Job Descriptions

Written summary of the basic tasks to be performed in individual jobs

Job Evaluation

Procedure for determining the relative worth of jobs within an organization

Job evaluation or classification looks at what a position (job) does and what is required to perform in that position.

Job evaluation does NOT evaluate the work of an individual on their personal performance in a position.

Job evaluation produces an objective examination and rating of positions according to job content and requirements, without reference to the current classification of any individual or the performance of a job incumbent.

Job evaluation concentrates on the *content* of the work – *not the amount* of work. It should be used as the basis for developing to compensation, or reward system.

For instance, an increase in the workload of a position will NOT necessarily result in a change to the job classification or rate of pay for a person performing the job.

Job Evaluation Methods

Ranking

One of the easiest methods to use, jobs are compared to each other based on the overall worth of the job to the organization. The worth of a job is usually based on judgments of skill, effort (mental and physical), responsibility (supervisory and fiscal), and working conditions.

Advantages

- simple
- very effective when there are less than 30 jobs

Disadvantages

- difficult to use as the number of jobs increases
- rank judgments are subjective
- new jobs have to be compared with existing jobs to determine rank

Repeat the *ranking process each time a new job is added.*

Method

- Place job titles on 3x5 index cards then place them in order of importance to the organization.
- Weigh the importance of each to find paired comparisons.

Grouping

- After ranking, the jobs should be grouped to determine appropriate salary levels.

Classification

Jobs are classified into an existing grade/category structure or hierarchy. Each level in the grade/category structure has a description and associated job titles. Each job is assigned to the grade/category providing the closest match to the job.

The classification of a job is decided by comparing the whole job with the appropriate job grading standard. To ensure equity in job grading and wage rates, a common set of job grading standards and instructions are used. Because of differences in duties, skills, knowledge, and other aspects of trades and labor jobs, job grading standards are developed mainly along occupational lines.

The standards will not describe every work assignment of every position, but should identify key characteristics significant for different levels of work in order to assign the appropriate grade level to all positions in the occupation to which the standards apply.

Advantages

- Simple
- The grade/category structure exists independent of jobs so new jobs can

be classified easily.

Disadvantages

- Classification judgments are subjective.
- The standard used for comparison may have built in biases that would affect certain groups of employees such as women or minorities.
- Some jobs may appear to fit within more than one grade/category.

Factor Comparison

A set of compensable factors are identified as determining the worth of jobs. Typically the number of compensable factors is small (4 or 5). Examples of compensable factors are:

1. skill
2. responsibilities
3. effort
4. working conditions

Next, benchmarking jobs are identified. Benchmark jobs should have certain characteristics:

1. equitable pay (not underpaid or overpaid)
2. range of the factors, low end to high

The jobs are then priced and the total pay for each job is divided into pay for each factor.

Note: The table shown below was developed in the late 1990's so the dollar amounts are probably very low, but the concept has not changed.

Example of Factor Comparison:

The hourly rate is divided into pay for each of the following factors:

Job	Hourly Rate	Pay for Skill	Pay for Effort	Pay for Responsibility	Pay for Working Conditions
Secretary	$16.00	$6.50	$4.50	$3.50	$1.50
Adm. Asst.	$21.00	$7.50	$6.00	$5.50	$2.00
Supervisor	$38.50	$18.00	$8.00	$9.00	$3.50
Manager	$51.00	$25.00	$9.00	$12.00	$5.00

This process establishes the rate of pay for each factor for each rated job. Slight adjustments may be made to the matrix to ensure equitable dollar weighting of the factors.

The other jobs in the organization are then compared with the rated jobs and pay for each factor is summed to determine the rates of pay for each of the other related jobs.

Advantages

- The value of the job is expressed in monetary terms.
- Can be applied to a wide range of jobs.
- Can be applied to newly created jobs.

Disadvantages

- The pay for each factor is based upon judgments that are subjective.

- The standard used for determining the pay for each factor may have built in biases that would affect certain groups of employees such as women or minorities.

Point Method

A set of compensable factors determine the worth of jobs. Typically the compensable factors include these major categories:

1. Skill
2. Responsibilities
3. Effort
4. Working conditions

These factors are then further defined:

1. Skill
    a. Experience
    b. Education
    c. Ability
2. Responsibilities
    a. Fiscal
    b. Supervisory
3. Effort
    a. Mental
    b. Physical
4. Working Conditions
    a. Location
    b. Hazards
    c. Extremes in Environment

The *Point Method* is an extension of the *factor comparison* method.

Each factor is then divided into levels or degrees which are then assigned points. Each job is rated by total points to develop a total score for the job.

Jobs are then grouped by total point scores and assigned to wage/salary grades so that similarly rated jobs would be placed in the same wage/salary grade.

Advantages

- The value of the job is expressed in monetary terms.
- Can be applied to a wide variety of jobs.
- Can be applied to newly created jobs.

Disadvantages

- The pay for each factor is based on judgments that are subjective.
- The standard used for determining the pay for each factor may have built in biases that would affect certain groups such as women or minorities. .

Additional factors to consider when developing compensation ranges include:

1. Education and experience

    What level of formal education is required for the job?

    Once the formal education has been gained, how much pertinent, practical experience is needed to perform the job?

2. Scope of activities

   How varied are the activities coordinated by the position?

3. Interpersonal skills

   How demanding is the job in terms of contacting, negotiating, and gaining the cooperation of others inside and outside the organization?

4. Kinds of problems

   What type of analytical and creative ability is required for the position?

5. Instruction received

   How much independence does the position holder have?

6. Influence on results

   How important is the position to the overall results of the organization?

   What ability does this position have to bring about a change in the organization?

7. Size of group

   How large is the department or unit being evaluated?

8. Personnel supervised

   How many people does this position supervise?

9. Subordination level

   Where is the position placed in the organization hierarchy?

Chapter 9 – Motivation and Leadership

"While a good leader sustains momentum, a great leader increases it." John C. Maxwell (30)

"Earn your leadership every day." Michael Jordan

Defining leadership

Leadership is one of the least understood concepts within the human race. Unlike *management* (people in formally assigned upper level positions), *leadership*, or the ability to lead others is a complex quality that arises from deep within a person.

Former President Eisenhower said:

> "Leadership is the art of getting someone else to do something you want done because he or she wants to do it." (Stogdil, pg. 14) (31)

In the broadest terms,

> A *manager* who is not a true *leader* does not totally trust their staff to make the right decisions or do the right thing. So they make decisions for them, give specific directions on how to perform tasks, closely monitor results, and limit opportunities for sharing ideas. Some people refer to this as micro managing.
>
> A *leader* trusts their staff to make the right decisions and do the right thing. They explain an assignment or business concern then allow each individual the freedom to perform the task without interfering. A *leader* is available for consultation, but they do NOT micro-manage workers.

A small business owner will, by his or her role at the top of the organization chart, be recognized as the company manager. A successful small business owner should want to go beyond being recognized as a manager and be known as a *leader.*

The *Handbook of Leadership* says "there are almost as many different definitions of leadership as there are persons who have attempted to define the concept." (Stogdil, pg. 11) (32) Based upon that statement, this *Desk Reference* is not going to define leadership. Instead it is going to provide ideas to small business owners on how to be recognized as a leader.

Leadership behavior

Any business owner or manager who wants to be seen by his or her staff as a leader, must:

- Understand he or she alone cannot perform every function or make every decision in the business,

o Be willing to hire people who have a desire to learn follow opportunities. Don't be defensive – support the growth of others. Take their advancement as a compliment to you for preparing them.

- Be consistent in treatment and interface with every person in the company.

- Emphasize the need for teamwork and openness between company management and staff without being tethered by organization structure.

- Remember they are perfect. Admit they have their own highs and lows, personal beliefs about life, about people, about motivation, and about trust.

- Remember that every other person they associate with has emotional highs and lows, good days, bad days, family concerns, etc.

- It is OK to project a "can do" attitude on the outside, while on the inside wonder, "Uh oh, what have I gotten myself into?" Manage personal behavior and emotions first, *then others.*

Leading others

A leader works to support their followers (employees) as much, if not more than they work for the company. A good leader is someone who can and will inspire others to do their best to support the business by being a motivated team member.

A motivated employee is involved in and enthusiastic about their work. They enjoy what they do and demonstrate consistent performance that supports their company and customer interests.

An unmotivated employee is usually a bored, unsupportive person. They are not involved in ongoing work and they will lower the morale of people around them. Their lack of productive participation can cost the company wasted effort, resources and morale.

Good leaders do not have to be clever, or even particularly smart. They DO however have to be honest, caring, focused, positive, and more than any other characteristic, authentic.

People recognized as leaders understand that most people want to do good work and be appreciated for doing it. Their followers need to feel they are understood, special, they belong, and that they have a chance to grow in their chosen career field.

Motivation is internal

Nobody can motivate another person. Motivation is internal and it is the driving force that triggers behavior and response within an individual. It is unique to each person. A person recognized as a high achiever is *motivated* internally by a belief in themselves, in their ability to reach the goal they are trying to achieve, and a willingness to take whatever action is required to accomplish their tasks.

Internal drivers support self-motivation that can keep a person focused on achieving their goal whether it is climbing a mountain, earning a college degree, being the best worker for a company, or simply crossing the street to reach the other side. The internal driver that supports motivation varies among individuals.

The *leadership* role of a small business owner is to see the people in the company as individuals, learn what motivates each person, and find a way to bring out the best in each person.

Basis for motivational differences

Every person has their own limited view of the world. Even though they may feel they have a broad range of experiences and are very open to new ideas and challenges, they are, never-the-less, limited by their exposure to the world.

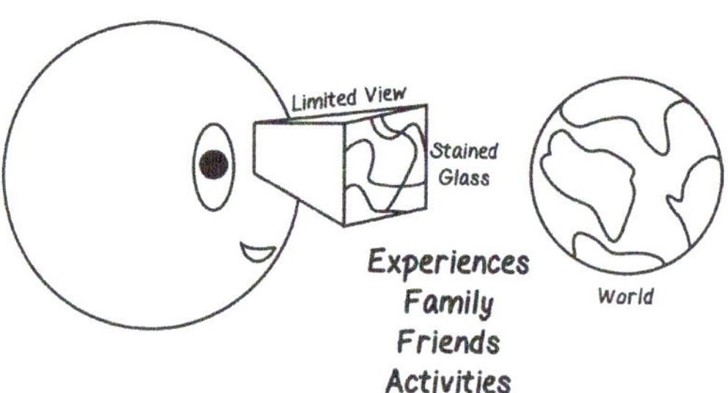

The view, or perspective each person has of the world around them can be thought of as looking through stained glass. It is almost but not quite clear. Everything they hear, see, feel, or think about is compared internally with something else they have experienced from their past. Their perspective on what they see is compared to what they have learned from prior experiences, family, friends, and activities.

When trying to lead others, or motivate them to take action, it is important to remember that each person has had different experiences than the person giving direction. As a result, each receiver interprets and follows directions in their own way.

Changing workforce

Many companies in business today are still operating with processes and organizational structures that were developed with values based on economic security, family, and workers supporting bosses. Over time, family life has changed. In many cases, both parents work during the day and children are more independent and take care of themselves.

Exposure to instant news coverage, demonstrations and activism, a constantly changing world of technology, and ongoing threats of violence in crowded settings, workers today have values bases on environmental issues, the women's movement, civil rights, and self-protection (lack of trust of some groups of people).

Today's workforce is far more diverse than any previous generation in terms of age, ethnic background, physical ability, marital relationships, education, and personal values. The workers of today are, and will continue to be, exciting to work with. They will support a company that accepts them as individuals and they will respect the leadership of people they feel are sincere, honest, and not locked up in their own self-interest.

New Manager Advice

As a company grows and begins to hire employees, many small business owners find themselves in a supervisory role for the first time. Even though they are probably very good at producing the products or service their company provides, they might not be sure how to conduct themselves with people reporting to them in the workplace.

Suggestions for a new manager:

- Don't let the new position of "the boss" change your behavior. Accept your role, but do NOT micro-manage. Allow new employees freedom to do the job they were hired to do.

O Decide to be a professional. Rather than be an employee's best friend, keep a line between yourself and social relationships with your employees. Remember your first responsibility as a supervisor is to keep ALL relationships with your staff and employees in your organization fair and equal.

O Stay in close contact with *all* employees. Make one-on-one contact with each employee during your first few weeks and into the future. Don't ignore or avoid anyone working for or with you.

The contacts can be brief stand-up conversations, coffee-break talks, or an invitation to talk things over; but make contact time equal for all employees.

Let the person know you appreciate him or her as an individual. It is *your responsibility to initiate the contact and build the relationship.*

Supervisor – Employee Relationships

Supervisor: According to the National Labor Relations Act (Section 2(11) "...a supervisor can hire, train, evaluate, promote, instruct, discipline, or terminate an employee." A small business owner by definition is a supervisor. (33)

Some people feel supervisors and employees can be close friends on and off the job and still have an effective working relationship. Whether or not that is true, is not as important as it is to avoid the appearance of favoritism (liking and being closer to some employees than to others).

A business owner should remain aware of potential concerns about boss/worker relationships, or the appearance of bias.

Consider *perception* first

Perception: an interpretation or impression; an opinion or belief.

Examples:

If Employee **A** feels the supervisor is too close to, or friendly with Employee **B**, it is probably true.

In the day-to-day contact of a typical work place, it is not only important to treat every employee equally, but it is considered *more important* to give the *impression* everyone is being treated the same.

If an employee sees something in the supervisor's treatment of another person that gives the impression of favoritism there is a good chance the supervisor IS giving favorable treatment. Even if this is not true, it can be interpreted and perceived as unequal treatment, and should be considered true.

It is very important for supervisors, managers, and business owners to avoid any action that could be interpreted or perceived as unequal or unfair.

Personal relationships

In any business, whether a small business with a few employees working in close proximity, or a large company with workers spread out over a wide geographical area, personal relationships should be considered important to the overall team orientation, workforce motivation, organization and productivity.

Supervisors and employees who *appear* to have a close personal relationship, whether true or not, can be perceived as engaging in favoritism. A work relationship involving favorable treatment of a particular employee, or category of employees has the potential of disrupting employee morale and making other employees feel less valued in their treatment, job assignments, compensation, and opportunity for advancement.

Suggestions

Business owners should remain aware of their relationship with other people in the company, and they should a clear employee relationship policy, especially for anyone promoted to a management position.

- Remember perception. If someone thinks the supervisor or owner is biased, then the supervisor or owner is doing something to show they ARE biased.

- Studies have shown, even though people think they are being objective, supervisors cannot be objective when they do the performance evaluation of a friend.

  - Supervisors should NOT establish close social friendships with employees. They should try to maintain a close WORKING relationship where they are comfortable spending time together.

  - The closer the supervisor/employee friendship, the greater likelihood the employee will feel free to disagree with their boss. A disagreement between the supervisor and a single employee can ripple through the company.

  - If a supervisor wants to maintain a friendship with one subordinate, then he or she must try to maintain friendship relations with all subordinates. Treat them all the same. Circulate throughout the work place and spend the same amount of time with each employee.

  - A supervisor should remain ethical, honest, and unbiased in their actions. It will affect the way employees see them. They should remember their gestures, expressions, and postures project more meaning to employees than words alone.

  - Observe body language of workers. The mood of a

company can become very evident to owners and customers that read these unspoken signs.

An effective leader has to try to understand what interests each individual, then find ways to support their particular skills, needs, or wants. This is like working with the differences in children in a family.

Employee rewards and celebrations

"If you have fun at your job, I think you're going to be more effective."

~ *Meg Whitman*

A major responsibility of any business owner or manager who wants a highly motivated and productive staff, is to make sure good work is recognized and appreciated. In other words, don't take the effort of any worker for granted. Be sure to thank them appropriately for doing their part as members of the team.

Recognize outstanding work, but don't ignore good performance. .

Author's experience:

> When the author of this *Desk Reference* left high school and began his first full time job in a manufacturing plant, he started with what some people today might refer to as a "no brainer" job. It was fairly simple, repetitious, and today *is* being performed by a robot – so maybe it was a no brainer.
>
> His first supervisor never referred to it as a simple task, and neither did his coworkers. At the end of each day his supervisor came by and said ,"Thank you for doing a great job today. I'll see you in the morning." That little sentence gave the new worker a feeling of pride and motivated him to believe in himself and want to do his part to help his company, his supervisor, and his work group.
>
> A simple and heartfelt "thanks" from the boss goes a very long way toward helping a person's self-esteem.

There is no one-size-fits-all reward system. Some people like company parties; others prefer to avoid company gatherings. Some people like gifts and awards; others are not interested in receiving gifts from the company. Some people like to work for employee-of-the-month, while others are not motivated by an award. There is no way to satisfy everyone with special recognition, so to be fair a company should establish procedures with more than one way to show appreciation for outstanding performance.

Keep it natural

While it is very important to recognize good work and highly productive employees, the appreciation must be timely, appropriate, and sincere to be effective. If people feel they are being ignored except for the "regularly scheduled recognition meeting," the boss's 'thank you' will probably be seen as insincere and not genuine.

To be effective, employee recognition should be given on a regular basis and in different ways. It can be given informally every day or so by simply making it a point to thank people for their work, or more importantly tell them how much you appreciate it when they go (even slightly) beyond normal expectations to help a customer or fellow employee.

Formal recognition can be done through monthly group meetings, or special celebrations. Even then, recognition should be timely. The manager or supervisor should thank workers right away for their extra effort and let them know their name will be submitted to the company-wide celebration.

Forms of recognition

Recognition of extra effort can be provided in many ways. Here are a few suggestions:

Low cost/quick response

Response time is from earned recognition to award presentation.

- Go to the person's work station and thank them personally.
- Take time during a regular staff meeting to acknowledge the special work of an employee.
- Email the employee thanking them for their special effort and let them know a copy of the email will be in their employee folder.
- Post notes praising an employee or group of employees on a work group bulletin board.
- Visit the work place unannounced and bring other top-level management.

Moderate cost/slower response

The cost is time away from the work.

- Call a special meeting to tell workers about the special effort of an individual or a work group.
- In the case of a work group with unusually high performance, consider bringing in catered food or paying for lunch together away from work.
- Give the high performance individual a partial day off of work.
- Provide a catalog of merchandise high achievers can select from. These are available through on-line companies. Search for 'employee gifts.'
- Give a gift card from a local retail outlet to a high achiever employee.

High cost/even slower response

- A company quarterly, semi-annual, or annual recognition meeting
- A special one-time monetary bonus for high performance
- Tuition reimbursement for completing off-hour training or graduating from college

"No act of kindness, or recognition of kindness, no matter how small, is ever wasted."

(Author unknown)

Conflict Resolution – Dealing with difficult people

If you as an individual, find yourself surrounded by people who are grumpy, hard to get along with, or generally not happy, the first place to look for a cause might be the mirror. If the majority of people you deal with are difficult it might be a response to the way YOU act or treat them.

Definition

There is no universally accepted definition of a *difficult* person. For example if you or someone working for you thinks person "A" is hard to get along with, then at least in your eyes, person "A" is a difficult person, even if most other people don't agree.

Difficult behavior in the work place is any behavior that hinders others in the performance of their tasks. In a working relationship, if anyone feels somebody else is causing them frustration or discomfort, then what they feel is true (at least from the perspective of the frustrated person) and will remain true until the cause is understood and dealt with.

Causes of difficult behavior

- feelings of insecurity about themselves and/or their ability
- putting protective barriers (emotionally or physically) to keep people from getting too close
- narrow focus, inability to recognize or accept options
- personality clashes and lack of willingness to get along
- a supervisor or manager's actions, or inaction
- different goals or different ideas on how to accomplish common goals

Behavior of difficult people

- They try to manipulate others without concern for other's feelings.
- They try to get a reaction rather than evaluate and respond.

Responding to difficult people

Ignoring the situation with a difficult person in the work place, is not a good solution. Difficulty in working relationships don't usually go away, but continues to get worse.

Suggestions for effective conflict management:

Spend time with them

Quite often misunderstandings occur because people have not made enough of an effort to get to know another person. They don't understand the concerns of another person. Spending time with others, especially new workers can help one learn what is important to them.

Identify motivating triggers

People tend to be motivated by different things, even if some interests are shared. Take the time to find out the values of other individuals, then support their interests.

Invest energy

Invest energy in a better relationship. Offer assistance and help them when others appear to be having a difficult time.

Chapter 10 – Communication

Does this make sense?

> *Our company through a network of orchestrated action items will transform multiple product mixes to effective functionalities using ubiquitous internal relationships while extending seamless front-end initiatives.*

Or this?

> *We will work together to review our production processes and where practical, improve performance by combining product lines.*

Both statements say the same thing – one is a little easier to understand.

Introduction

When asked about driving most people would say they are very good drivers. Ask a spouse or friend about a person's driving and the answer might differ. The same result if people are asked if they are good communicators. Most people would say they are, while some of their associates might not agree.

Human communication goes beyond speaking and writing. It is a means of sharing ideas and observations between people to create common understanding.

Note: Effective communication results in a common *understanding*, not necessarily *agreement* on ideas or opinions.

Communication can be formal or informal, verbal or written, through body movement and gestures, or a combination of these methods. The result will indicate whether the interchange was effective.

If an exchange accomplishes its intended purpose and the audience fully understands the message, it is probably effective communication.

This chapter contains suggestions to make communication effective in the business world, both internally in a company and externally with customers, suppliers, and the general public.

This chapter provides an overview of communication in business and professional settings in the context of shared meaning. It will address the role of communication in achieving organizational goals within new technology, diversification of the work force, and globalization of the customer base. The chapter will provide examples of communication skills including listening, writing and public speaking, verbal and nonverbal communication, group dynamics, and some strategies for problem solving, negotiating and conflict resolution.

Create an Elevator Speech

An elevator speech is a very short summary of what a company does, what product it sells or is developing, or what service it provides. It is called an elevator speech because it should last the average time of an elevator ride, which is around 90 seconds.

Any business owner should have an elevator speech in his or her memory which can be used in a social or business setting if someone asks what they do, or asks about their company. It is a quick or condensed explanation of the business that can be given at a moment's notice.

Situations that may require an elevator speech are Chamber of Commerce meetings, social gatherings, or introductions to potential customers. The elevator speech should be honest and presented enthusiastically, include the name of the business, the products or services it provides, and end with a business card and request to call them in a few days to schedule an appointment for a more detailed discussion.

Social and Business Communication

Social Communication

Social communication is the human interface people are involved with on a daily basis outside the business community.

> It can include interaction between co-workers, but not when directly tied to conducting business.

This is the sharing of ideas, interests, observations, and concerns between friends, acquaintances, relatives, and passers-by. It can be fairly deep, or in most cases very light and general in nature. It includes written, speaking, and non-verbal behaviors between a presenter and audience and usually has the goal of acknowledging the other person's close proximity, or sharing knowledge.

Business Communication

Business communication is the human interface between people engaged in producing or distributing (selling) products or services. Rather than *social communication,* business communication is the primary focus of this chapter.

It is usually directed at a specific business concern and (hopefully) relies more on *facts* then on *emotions.* It tends to be somewhat structured in the form of emails, published policies and procedures, internal memorandums, marketing media (advertising), meetings, and business related conferences.

Financial Loss from poor Business Communication

Poor communication in a business can waste time and effort due to misunderstanding instructions, reduce confidence and trust between coworkers, and damage customer and/or supplier relationships.

Examples of poor business communication, which could cause financial loss:

Poorly written instructions

Situation:

These written instructions were provided to an Administrative Assistant by a technician after installing a new office copier. They were intended to help the Administrative Assistant enter employee codes to control access to the machine.

Loss to company:

The poor quality of the written instructions caused an unesessary loss of paid time as the Administrative Assistant tried unsuccessfully to understand how to enter the codes. This was compounded when the Assistant shared the instrucions with other employees.

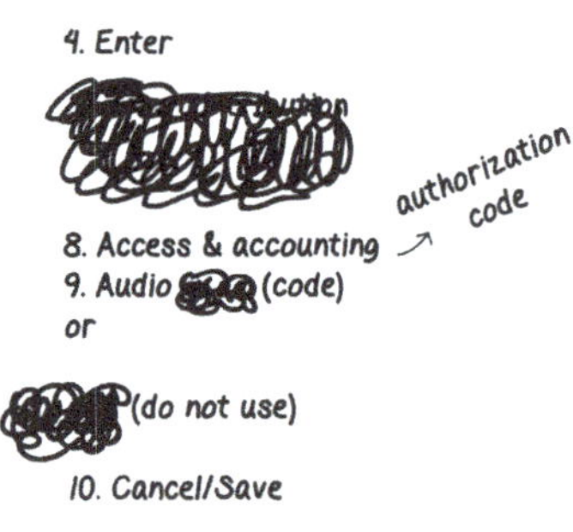

Written instructions and operating manuals are well known for explaining how a piece of equipment works and how many exciting features it has, but in many cases they do not do a good job of explaining

to a user or operator – how to make the "thing" function.

Written operating instructions should be short, easy to understand, and provide the user or operator with enough direction to perform their task adequately. If the operator is interested in the design specifications for a piece of equipment, they should have a different document or section to refer to – NOT the operating instructions.

Long, poorly planned meetings

Business meetings can be helpful, informative, and provide all particpants with a common understanding of company plans and directions – or – they can be long, dull, poorly planned, and generate confusion for attendees.

Situation:

> The work group gets together for their regularly scheduled *staff meeting*. It begins with the boss reading through paperwork on his or her desk, then occasionally looking at an individual in the group to discuss a specific problem from the desk paperwork. Other attendees have no interest in the topic so the meeting becomes a one-on-one discussion between the boss and a single individual. The other group members let their minds drift to private thoughts.
>
> 
>
> Eventually, the one-on-one discussion ends and the boss works the audience, asking each one individually if they have any concerns. Some do, and the others once again are excluded from the conversation. Others have decided not to bother with their concerns because they are losing valuable work time sitting in the staff meeting.
>
> The meeting concludes with a lot of frustration and people return to their workplaces.

Loss to company:

Ineffective meeting structure caused loss of paid work time for attendees who were not involved in the discussion. People attending the meeting were not able to do their regular work and might require overtime to catch up. There could also be a loss of customers due to the staff being unavailable to assist them during the meeting.

Poorly written email and/or memorandum

Situation:

Would you respond to this email?

Got your rquest for quote on a series 1.AAA-432 widget coupler ystrdy. We r short on them right now, cut should get some in in a week or two. When we do, they will be $575 each for up to 9, then $568 10 -29, and with higher numbers, we'll recalculate and let you know if you need more.

You also askd about 23.DRC-762 widget brackets. Plenty on hand for around $23 each – just need to know qty and we'll send a solid quote

Shipping and tax will be added later.

It is so full of errors a customer probably would not respond unless they were really desperate for a widget supplier. It certainly would not create a very professional image for the company sending the email.

This email responds to the same request for a quote:

Subject: Price estimate

Part number	Item	Quantity	Unit cost
1.AAA-432	Widget coupler	1-9	$575.00
		10-29	$568.00
23.DRC762	Widget bracket	---	$23.00

It would be more likely to result in a purchase from a customer.

Loss to company:

Poorly written emails that are full of errors or are not crisp with their wording are quite often misunderstood, and in many cases ignored by the addressee.

They can result in lost sales, wasted time trying to read and interpret them, or cause misunderstandings between coworkers, customers, and suppliers.

Distracted manager, or a manager who appears to be distracted

Situation:

If a manager does not make good eye contact with an employee while speaking with them, or if the manager appears to be distracted by someone or something trying to get their attention, it can be interpreted as not caring about employee concerns or opinions.

Loss to company:

If employees feel their boss or owner is not interested in listening to their ideas or concerns, the employees will stop communicating with management and morale among workers will decrease. Lower morale in the work place finds its way to potential customers, and eventually can result in a loss of business.

In addition, if employees are not comfortable talking with management, they will not provide ideas which could possibly improve production and profitability.

Through extensive studies of leadership the author of this *Desk Reference* feels:

"A true leader does not have time to *not* have time for their followers."

Generational differences

Situation:

Life in the workplace is changing. People working together in companies today represent a mix of several generations. Baby Boomers are retiring later so they can be better prepared for their senior years. These Boomers are working with a more diversified group of younger people referred to as Generation X, Generation Y, and the Millennium Generation.

Each of these generations has its own way of thinking and acting, and its own set of values. It is difficult for some people who do not think and act alike to perform happily in a team of associates.

Each generational cohort has a different perspective on changing technology, social networking during work time, and often, work ethic. Even though the value differences and expectations are understandable, they can be very disruptive to a small business environment.

Loss to the company

If coworkers do not understand and respect each other, it can lead to inappropriate comments and disputes, wasted work time, resentment among organization members, and a loss of company loyalty, which can in turn cause business losses.

Listening

Listening skills are very important to a successful business and pleasant social life. It is especially important to small business owners who make daily critical decisions and develop company strategic plans based on what they hear, or at least what they *think they hear.*

K. Timmons in the video *The power of listening* by Cornell University (CRM Films) is quoted saying: (34)

> "When a manager's listening abilities are poor, departmental performance is impaired and costly errors may result. American businesses lose an estimated one billion dollars daily due to poor listening skills that result in simple errors requiring rewritten messages, rescheduled appointments, or more complex errors leading to serious technological failures."

Some barriers to effective listening are fairly obvious and easy to correct. Others are more subtle and the listener may have to consciously practice new listening skills to improve their communication behavior.

Numerous academic studies have shown that the over 90% of human communication is non-verbal. People read body language, gestures, facial expressions, arm movement, etc. Texting and email are NOT total communication between humans.

Common barriers to effective listening

Environmental	A nearby conversation, construction noise, visual distractions, pre-conceived ideas about the message, and unplanned interruptions
Emotional	Personal concerns, prejudice, too much information (burying the point or message in detail)
Speaker relationship	Cultural differences, physical appearance, body language, vocabulary, status in relation to the listener
Physical	Tiredness, hunger, pain, daydreaming, time pressure, uncomfortable temperature (warm or cold)

Poor listening behavior

Imitation listening	Appear to be listening while letting the mind wander People imitating listening can look right at the speaker, smile when they should, and occasionally answer a question, but be ignoring the speaker's message because their mind is on something 'more' important.
Stage hog	Interested in what they (the listener) has to say They usually don't care what another person is saying.
Selective listening	It is fairly common to hear a family member accuse another person of selective listening – only paying attention to the speaker's comments that interest them and ignoring the rest.
Gap filler	Someone who only remembers part of what they hear, rather than taking in the full message. People who are gap fillers often make up information (sometimes subconsciously) to fill the gaps when they pass on the message or story. This poor listening trait is becoming more common as people text and multi-task. They don't take the time or effort to listen to an entire message.
Defensive listening	Someone who is insecure may only 'hear' personal attacks, or take things out of context.

Ambusher	These people listen carefully to gather information that can be used to attack what the speaker says either right away, or in the future. This is (sorry to say) a common listening technique for politicians and prosecuting attorneys.

Behavioral Noise in the workplace

In addition to physical noise (loud machines, traffic, crowds, etc.) there is another type of noise that can cause misinterpretation and misunderstandings. It is behavioral noise, sometimes referred to as *patterns of miscommunication.*

It is not always possible to prevent behavioral noise, but if a person is aware the causes of poor communication, they can try to improve their listening skills to minimize the potential damage caused by unclear messages.

Noise caused by jumping to conclusions

IUMRING TQ GONGIUSIQNS

The letters in the box might appear to say "jumping to conclusions." But by jumping to conclusions, the reader might miss the actual letters:

IUMRING TQ GONGIUSIQNS

By looking only at the top half of the letters, the readers mind will quite often misinterpret and fill in the missing portion. By typing capital letters,

C	on the top looks like	G
E	on the top looks like	F
H	on the top looks like	U

I	on the top looks like	J or L
R	on the top looks like	P or B
O	on the top looks like	Q
X	on the top looks like	Y

We hvae a tnedency to read and haer for thuoghts, rather than specific words and phrases. Our minds let us fill in blanks wihch may help us intrepret messages, but it can also get us in truoble if we do not intrepret correclty.

Our minds override misspelled words and let us think we see things that are not actually visible:

We have a tendency to read and hear for thoughts, rather than specific words and phrases. Our minds let us fill in blanks which may help us interpret messages, but it can also get us in trouble if we do not interpret correctly.

Another example:

Picture yourself looking for a parking space in a crowded shopping mall. You see a person with a full cart walking down an aisle of parked cars, so you follow the person, wait until they open the trunk, load packages – then shut the trunk and walk back to the mall.

You probably thought they were going to leave and you could use their parking spot. They did not leave and you might even become upset because you still need a parking space.

Explaining jumping to conclusions:

What we see, hear, or interpret may not be real. Our mind compares what we see, hear, smell, and feel with similar things we have experienced in the past and as a result, our mind lets us jump to conclusions about messages we receive. In most cases, it works out fine. In some cases, a misinterpretation can cause problems.

If we rush to judgment based upon what we hear or experience at a particular moment without taking into account the events leading up to what we are interpreting, we can reach a wrong conclusion and pass judgment on a situation, a comment, a gesture, etc. This can have devastating events in the business world.

Why people rush to judgment and don't seem to listen

In today's fast-moving world, many people feel they are under pressure to act now, instead of spending time thinking about the true facts.

Many people don't like to *think.*

They are too busy, so they just act, or react

It is VERY easy to reach the wrong conclusion when relying on reactions rather than thought. Does the conclusion make sense? The result can cause conflicts with other people, who have different conclusions from the same situation or message.

Any business owner operating in a fast business environment and feeling pressure needs to remember to make sure their actions and decisions are founded on *reality* (real and complete facts), not quick interpretations of partial facts.

If a business owner listens to the views of an employee, supplier, or customer, they need remember their reasoning is based upon their *interpretation of facts*, and all of the facts they are listening to necessarily might not be true.

President Ronald Reagan is quoted as saying:
"Trust, but verify."
It is OK to believe people, but in a critical situation, verify the facts.

Ideas to consider when interpreting facts:

1. Ask yourself, "Why do I think this is right?"
2. While considering your decision, ask yourself, "Did I make early assumptions, or only use a portion of the information I had available?"
3. Explain your reasoning to another person to help you clarify your decision making.

Noise caused from bypassing

Bypassing occurs when people are talking, and each person hears the same words but picks up a different meaning. People talk past each other which create noise.

Example:

The author of this *Desk Reference* passed a student at a study table. The student was looking at a schedule of classes for the next quarter and the author glanced over and said, "They never do seem to fit quite right do they?"

Bypassing – The author meant the class schedule

The student thought the author meant her clothes.

They both heard the words and interpreted them correctly, but the student and the author had different perceptions which resulted in mixed communication

Miscommunication through bypassing often results from multiple meanings of short messages. Each of the following sentences could be interpreted in more than one way, and each interpretation would probably be correct – in the mind of the listener:

"Did you bring it in?" - No firm definition of what "it" is

"Dog for sale: eats anything and is fond of children."

"Wanted. Person to take care of horse that does not smoke or drink."

"I'll be home soon."

"Illiterate? Write to us for help."

Mixed sources, author's unknown

To minimize misinterpretation through bypassing:

1. Be aware of the speaker and the listener. Think about how they are likely to interpret meaning and adjust the message if necessary.

2. If the message is considered critical, ask the listener to explain what they heard. ("Repeat that back to me.")

3. Watch the listener's reaction or behavior which results from the message.

Good listening habits

Do not interrupt — Let the speaker complete what they are saying. When a speaker is interrupted, the listener is inserting their own perception of what the speaker means and may miss the whole meaning of the message that was being sent.

A suggestion: If you have a tendency to interrupt other people during a one-on-one conversation, make yourself silently count to 5 or 10 before responding when the other person stops talking, Those seconds give you time to actually think about what they said. You might surprise them when they notice you ARE listening.

Listen to feelings and meaning behind the words, not just the words alone

Words provide content of the message but they do not always convey the feeling behind the message.

Test for understanding

Summarize the message you are receiving and ask the speaker if you are interpreting it correctly.

Automation and Communicating

Many people today drive home, hit a button to raise the garage door, then hit the button again to close it. They spend family time inside the house, often with windows covered, or in their back yard. They only see neighbors when they are mowing their front lawn, getting mail, or washing their car.

The same people often hide behind tinted windows in their cars so they cannot make eye contact or be identified by other drivers. They don't make eye contact in a store because they are too involved in a hand held telephone conversation. People are isolating themselves from other humans, even when they are in a crowd. They don't always know or trust their neighbors.

The same behavior is happening in a lot of businesses.

Workers do not make eye contact. In many cases they don't even know their co-workers names because they are separated by cubicle walls or even geography. Contact is by email or video conferencing. A lot of business transactions are done electronically with no in-person human contact involved. Even supplies, office mail, and cafeteria services are being handled more and more by robots in place of humans.

For younger workers, the loss of in-person communication begins in their school. Between classes, more and more students are busy texting and avoiding making eye contact with other passing students in a crowded hallway.

As humans go out of their way to avoid face-to-face contact, particularly eye contact, they lose their ability to acknowledge others as unique individuals – and they do not necessarily have to be nice to each other.

On the road, in a neighborhood, in a crowded mall, or business office segregated by cubicle walls, people can live in isolation and try to ignore others around them. It is different in a crowded sports stadium or on an airplane where people are forced to sit next to others they do not know. They have no choice but to make eye contact and react with them to events occurring on the playing field a nearby aisle. Total strangers trust strangers to pass peanuts, drinks and money hand to hand without concerns.

In our personal lives, many of us are awakened by an electronic device, and we use remote control to heat and cool homes, select entertainment, monitor our home and office security, lock our cars, and many other portions of life. We rely on technology (GPS) to tell us where we are, give us directions, find parking places and park our cars, and we count on applications (apps) to develop our shopping lists, schedule appointments, etc.

Due to our acceptance (and dependence) on apps and technical devices, we think we are improving communication, when in fact we are replacing effective human, face-to-face contact with electronic communication. We are raising a new workforce content to trust information found on the Internet. We rely on technology to pay our bills, do business on-line with strangers, and make critical decisions.

"Do not trust everything you see on the Internet"

President Abraham Lincoln

Technology is very helpful for many business functions, but, in the author's opinion, we should not rely entirely on robots and automated systems to control a business. There should still be a human mind 'looking over the shoulder' of the automated business system to keep it focused on customer expectations, monitor competition, and plan for the future.

Social Media Policy

Social media (blogs, message boards, chat rooms, electronic newsletters, social networking, etc.) is common in the everyday lives of many people today. It is a major part of how people communicate and stay in touch with friends, coworkers, family members, and others throughout the day both on and off the job. It is important for companies to establish clear and consistent policies to let every employee know when they can and cannot use company time and/or equipment for personal messaging.

Every small business owner should determine their social media policy and *publish it in their employee handbook.* Also, when it is published, make sure the social media policy is clearly explained to each employee.

Company social media policy should make it clear whether company computers can be used for shopping, on-line chatting with friends or co-workers, checking traffic, weather, or other online activities. It should state whether workers can use work time to check on family members or make personal calls, or if personal calls are limited to break time. It should include direction regarding the sharing of company proprietary information.

Considerations

Freedom of speech

The National Labor Relations Act protects all employees (including non-union). It is fairly tolerant toward employee use of personal social media accounts to discuss company business. Businesses with a policy preventing employees from sharing trade secrets or confidential business information should recognize that company personnel do have freedom-of-speech rights to discuss proprietary information among themselves.

Personal information or opinions

Employees using company social media to display personal opinions or personal information can have a negative impact on customer relations. Businesses developing a social media policy are not allowed to be selective about which personal matters or opinions can be sent online, so the policy should be clear: either every personal comment is allowed, or none are allowed.

Use common sense

Social media is evolving and along with the evolution, rules and interpretations are changing. Company social media should be considered common sense guidelines, not absolute and firm rules.

Technostress

You had a late night helping your son finish a school project that must be turned in to his teacher this morning. You also had a restless night due to concerns about a family member who is having medical problems and your car is making “funny” noises.

You arrive at work on time, but are not feeling rested or organized enough to dive right into the day’s challenges. You check your voice mail, turn on your computer and see a full screen of emails, most of them marked “urgent.” You know you should read and respond to them, but you are still preparing your presentation for a critical meeting that is scheduled to begin in two hours.

Your telephone rings and vibrates with a message telling you your presentation has been rescheduled and you will be expected to address a large audience in 45 minutes. You also receive a message on your speaker phone telling you your child left part of the school project on the kitchen counter and needs to have someone deliver it to the school right away.

The day has just begun and you are already being controlled by technology. Our day-to-day personal and work lives are constantly impacted by interrelated pagers, cell phones, day timers, and many other devices that will have become available by the time this *Desk Reference* is published.

Do you REALLY need all of the automated aid you have in order to get through the day? Or are the number of gadgets you deal with every day becoming overwhelming and running your life?

If you are tired, over worked, trying to do too much in a day, and find little time to relax, maybe it is time to unplug a few tools, avoid some apps, and take an occasional totally human day.

If your life is run by automated aids, and you are feeling a bit overwhelmed by the pace of activity in your life, you might be starting to feel ***technostress.***

<u>*Definition*</u>

Technostress is a term introduced in 1984 by Dr. Craig Brod in his book *Technostress: The human cost of the computer revolution* (pg. 16) (35) where he addresses the psychological impact on working people caused by rapidly growing automation in the work place. Since its introduction, the term *technostress* has been studied by several academic researchers and it has evolved through several definitions. For the purpose of this *Desk Reference*, it can be considered *a negative psychological relationship between people and rapidly changing technology.*

<u>*Types of technostress*</u>

Lack of human contact

Humans are social animals. Even though some people feel they might like to spend their life alone on an isolated island, away in a mountain cabin, or living alone in a small apartment, overall the majority of humans need and want regular interaction with other humans.

Most people want to see or be near people on a daily basis, even if their contact is limited to grocery shopping with other people around, or walking on a sidewalk near others. Our desire to be in close proximity to others is a natural behavior of our species and even though some alone time can be refreshing, too much alone time can cause loneliness, depression, and eventually illness.

Automated systems as basic as telephones, email, or digital cameras can provide human to human contact, but they do not support the basic human sociological need people have to be physically close to another person (at least part of the time).

To avoid technostress caused by *lack of human contact* companies should not have employees conduct *all* meetings by videoconferencing and share all written correspondence by email. They should require occasional face-to-face meetings and sharing of information.

> Colleges and universities teaching courses online to multiple locations or campuses usually require instructors to be on site and visit with students from each location or campus a few times each quarter or semester so they can spend time together in person.

Multitasking overload

Multitasking is a term that became common as computer technology advanced and machines proved they could perform several tasks at the same time. Computers do well with multitasking; humans do not do as well.

The human brain can jump from one task to another rapidly, but when it does, it keeps the previous task in a waiting line somewhere in its current memory. The more tasks a human brain tries to do at one time, the less efficient it becomes with each task in its current memory.

While a computer can handle several tasks simultaneously, the human brain is more limited. If a person is tasked with writing, answering several telephone lines, and prepare for an upcoming meeting, they will be less than 100% productive with each of their tasks because their mind has to constantly switch tasks. If they are given a few minutes at a time to concentrate on a specific task, the end result will be better quality and productivity with each task.

Information overload

Changing technology has provided, and continues to provide an ever-increasing amount of information for people to review, analyze, and react to in their daily lives. While having adequate information at our fingertips to make decisions, too much information can make decision-making far more difficult because of the time and effort required to sift through all of the data.

In an earlier time if a person was going to take a trip, they might ask their travel agent to reserve a hotel room for them in a particular city. In some cases, they might want to stay with a hotel chain they are familiar with, so the individual would call a hotel directly and make reservations.

Now, with decision-making tools at our fingertips, the travel reservation process is changing. We can go online to a website, answer a few questions about city, rates, budget, number of travelers, etc., then with the click of a button get a very long list of available rooms – sometimes an overwhelming list. Even still, we select what we "think" is just the right room. Click. Click. Our credit card is charged and we have a confirmed reservation.

Technology works well for some people, but not everyone. Some travelers might still want to talk with a human travel agent to learn about the hotel neighborhood safety, noise levels, and general information not available on advertising websites.

Signs of technostress

A small business owner should pay particular attention to their employees whenever a new system or automated device is being introduced into their work routine. Some people adapt quickly to changes in their daily routine, others take longer to adapt, and at times become highly agitated due to *technostress*. Assist the people who express frustration from new systems and provide additional training, or allow more time for full implementation of new automated systems or tools.

People suffering from *technostress* can become less productive and develop symptoms such as irritability, headaches, fatigue, panic, and general resistance to the change.

Suggestions to minimize stress:

- Be careful of how rapidly change is introduced.
- Provide adequate training for people affected by the change.
- Review and adjust the workload for people while they are adapting to new systems or processes.

- Avoid shortcuts and make sure any workplace hardware or software is reliable and user friendly.

Questions for business owners considering system changes

Is advanced technology always a good idea for the business?

Will a proposed system change pay for itself through improved productivity? Is the change being considered just because it is fun and new?

Do the workers want the proposed change, or are they being *pushed* into accepting it?

Should we keep updating to the latest systems, or maintain a moderate pace with new systems while emphasizing more human interaction between coworkers and customers?

Should all banking transactions be done through an ATM and online, or should some be with a bank teller to maintain personal contact with the bank?

Should we shift to more self-service or continue to offer personal service to customers?

It is good business and customer relations to allow call waiting interruptions when conducting business?

Should we encourage electronic communication, or insist on occasional face-to-face decision-making?

Public Speaking (Meeting Presentations)

According to a 2014 study by Chapman University (36) and several other academic studies, public speaking remains the top fear of Americans. It is followed by a fear of heights and then a fear of bugs. For some people, including many small business owners, public speaking, or making a presentation in a company meeting can be terrifying.

Like any stressful situation, the anxiety will usually diminish as the situation is repeated with a successful conclusion. In other words, if a nervous speaker has high anxiety during their first presentation, their level of stress will be reduced every time they repeat their presentation to a group. Eventually the nervousness and stage fright should become tolerable.

Overcoming public speaking stage fright

Most public speakers will admit to experiencing slight nervousness when they walk onto a stage or to a podium to address an audience. It tends to be minor for experienced speakers, but it is almost always there as they begin their presentation. They consider this a good thing as it keeps them very aware and alert as they begin and helps them tune in to the audience right away.

Suggestions to help overcome fear of public speaking:

- **Remember your fear or anxiety is internal.** Most audiences want to hear from you and would like you to do well. They are attending for a purpose and interested in what you are going to share with them. Think about the audience and try to help them instead of focusing on yourself and your presentation style.

- **Be well prepared.** This does not mean memorize the presentation. It *does* mean understand your topic and why you want to share information with the audience. Review information you think will be appropriate to the specific audience.

- **Remember the audience.** Any presentation should cover topics that the audience is interested in. Use language they are familiar with.

  Example: A Loan Officer would use a different approach and different terminology to discuss a loan application with a Loan Committee and with a person applying for a loan. A Medical Doctor would use a different style and vocabulary to discuss a patient's situation with a panel of doctors then he or she would use to talk with the patient.

A business owner speaking to a group about company expansion plans should have a different way of speaking to company employees, customers, investors, and the news media, even though the end result should be a similar understanding of the company plans.

- **Understand that the audience cannot see your nervousness.** If your voice quivers, or you feel like you are going to be sick, the audience won't notice. They are typically more focused on the message than the speaker. *Stand tall and look happy – even if you are not happy. Let them see a positive person.*

A hint about public speaking:

If a person has a flat sounding or somewhat dull voice they can improve voice quality by reading children's books out loud. It is almost impossible to read children's stories without changing voice pitch for different characters and animals in the book.

Things to DO during an oral presentation:

- Position yourself correctly. If possible, stand to the left of the audience, your right, when using a screen. *People are used to reading English from left to right, so their eye starts on the left side of a screen. If the speaker is on the left side where people are looking, they have better control of audience eye movement by being close to where the audience is looking.*
- Stand close to a visual display or screen. *By being close to the visuals, the speaker can gesture toward items and have better control of where the audience is looking.*

- Keep feet pointed toward the audience. *A person's body tends to follow the alignment of their feet. If the feet are toward the audience, rather than angled toward the side of a room, the body will face the audience, even as the speaker relaxes and doesn't think about their body movement.*

- Conduct all physical activity in silence. *If charts or displays have to be moved during a presentation, stop talking while doing these tasks. The movement can be distracting and the audience will not listen to important points.*

- *It helps the audience focus on presentation topics and changing slides.*

- Have someone else edit spelling and grammar of visual aids. *We cannot accurately edit our own work. We tend to overlook our own mistakes, so let someone else review our work before a formal audience.*

- Give accurate answers. If people ask questions, give correct answers. If the answer is not known, tell the individual asking the question you will find the answer. THEN BE SURE TO FOLLOW UP WITH THE ANSWER RIGHT AWAY.

Things to NOT DO during an oral presentation:

- Don't use a pointer unless it is really necessary. *Pointers can be distracting to an audience, especially if the speaker is fiddling with it to offset nerves. Laser pointers are also dangerous. They can blind a person for several weeks, or permanently if the laser beam hits the eye of an audience member.*

- Don't pace and rock. *Speakers who pace and move around a lot, or jiggle coins and keys in their pockets often appear nervous and unprepared or uncertain. They can lose credibility with their audience.*

- Don't lean on the lectern or podium. *A speaker can become very tense and may lose the effectiveness of their voice projection if they are locked into the lectern or podium. The majority of their presentation message is non-verbal, so don't hide behind a raised podium or table. Don't hide from the audience.*

- Don't overdo *PowerPoint.* *Too many slides or slides which are too busy can confuse the audience, distract them from your message, or sometimes, put audience members to sleep.*

A final suggestion: Whether presenting to one person or a room full of people, try to avoid scheduling a presentation right after lunch. A relaxed and full audience can be a sleepy audience.

Allow at least one hour for digestion and a return to work mode.

Benefits for Public Speakers

Whether a person speaking in front of a group is nervous or confident, there are some advantages to public speaking.

- Workers in general are always interested in hearing how *things are going* directly from the boss. Public speaking in this case shows the staff the boss cares about them and wants them to be informed.

- The individual speaking to the group is generally looked at as a leader of the group – always a good thing for a boss.

- Speaking directly to employees can go a long way toward offsetting rumors. The audience is more inclined to trust and believe a boss who will speak directly to them.

Communication mistakes

Not editing

Sending an email or processing instructions with errors can make a person, or company look lazy, or not interested in quality. Don't rely on automated spell checkers to correct all words that are not used correctly. Keep in mind, it is very difficult for anyone to edit their own work, so whenever it is practical, ask someone else to edit work before sending it.

Weak management

Avoid hiding from bad news with email. A manager who uses electronic media to deliver bad news about company downsizing, a personnel problem, etc. can appear weak and lose credibility. Bad news, as well as good news in a small business should be shared in person by the major decision maker and not delegated through subordinates.

Poor preparation

Any message or direction effecting employee or customer relations from a small business manager should be well thought out and evaluated before sending. Prepare and plan messages carefully, keeping in mind whom the audience will be and how the message might be interpreted.

Assuming clear understanding

It is helpful to remember that if a message can be misunderstood, it will be. Every audience member is coming from a different perspective than the sender, so never assume the receiver will hear and respond to any message exactly the way it was explained by the sender.

Final thoughts on communication in the work place

Be visible

Walk around the office and production area fairly often. Go to the work area; don't make people come to a private office to see the boss.

Walk around a different times and with different routes. Don't stay with a routine that lets everyone know when to expect the boss. If people know the boss will be nearby, they are less likely to stop work and stare when the owner comes by. They will just acknowledge his or her presence and continue with their work.

Don't play favorites

Say a casual hello to different people while passing by. Do not always visit the same person – it could be interpreted by others as favoritism.

Acknowledge the individual

If a worker has a picture, knick-knack, or unique artifact in their work place, comment on it and ask the person about it. It will demonstrate interest in the person as an individual, not just as a worker.

Keep it simple

When explaining something to an employee, remember to address them and use terms they expect and are comfortable with.

> Example: A person discussing an accounting problem would use different words when talking with a cashier, a bookkeeper, and an accounting supervisor. *Talk WITH the audience, NEVER DOWN to them.*

Listen with EYES and ears

Over 90% of human communication is non-verbal, so remember to observe the body language and expressions of other individuals, as well as the surroundings, conditions, and external conditions. Careful observation will go a long way toward hearing a total message.

Be honest

If you don't know the answer, say so, and follow-up.

Chapter 11 – Production and Operations

Introduction

Nearly any business, whether it produces a product or provides a service, is made up of furniture, fixtures, equipment, and people. The product is developed or the service is created through a relationship of work methods coordinated with a series of processes. Scheduling work assignments, committing delivery dates for customers, and managing the day-to-day functions of a business usually begins with an understanding of the relationship of all of the business processes and procedures that make the business function, or operate.

Designing Business Processes

It is probably safe to say every function in the world of Business Management relates to a *flow of work* – or steps in a *process.*

> A process can be defined as a series of actions, changes, or functions bringing about a result.

Or, to make it a more business-like definition:

> A process is a sequence of interdependent and linked procedures which at every stage, consume one or more resources (employee time, energy, machines, money) to convert inputs (data, material, parts, etc.) into outputs. These outputs then serve as inputs for the next stage until a final goal (product or service) is reached.

Or in plain English:

> A process requires coordination of people, time, machines, and materials to produce a product or service.

Every product or service has a starting point, then moves through a series of steps. A process flows until a customer is served, a product is produced, or an obligation is satisfied.

Production plant

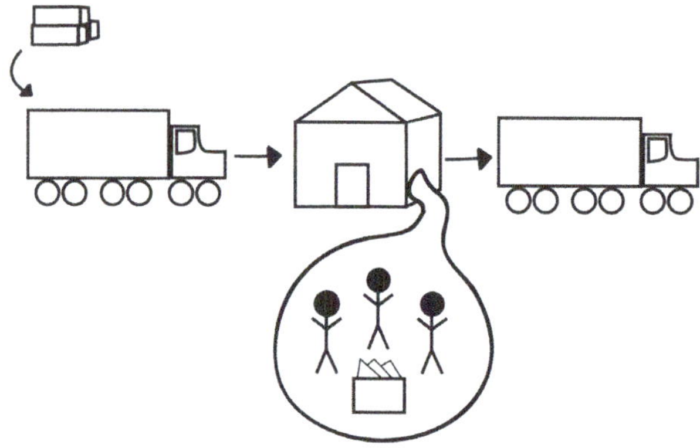

Production starts with a purchase order which *flows* through planning and operations to shipping and product delivery.

As materials arrive at the plant, they *flow* to the warehouse, are eventually pulled from shelves and follow a production process until they become finished parts.

Retail store

Finished goods arrive in a receiving area, are stored and eventually put on shelves in the retail space, where they move to the customer and on to a cashier.

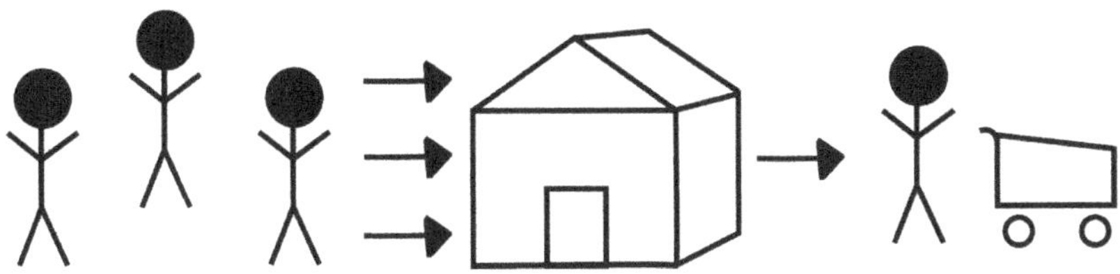

Customers arrive at the store, wander *(flow)* through the aisles and find themselves leaving the store with a full shopping cart.

Hospital

The *flow* occurs when a patient arrives for treatment, receives treatment and is discharged

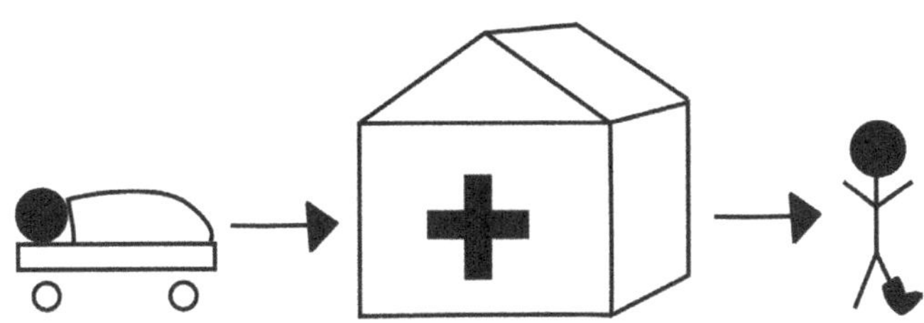

Restaurant

A customer *flow starts with a customer being seated,* reading a menu, ordering a meal, and concluding with payment to the cashier.

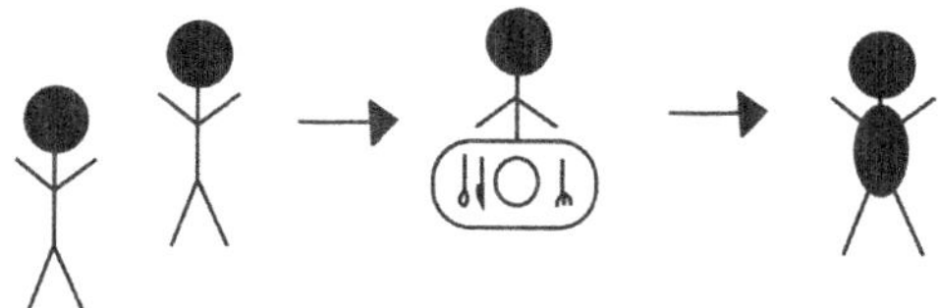

Another *flow* would start with the chef preparing a menu, ordering ingredients, receiving ingredients, preparing the ingredients to be ready for customer requests and then cooking meals.

The *flow of work, or process* relates to customers, as well as food being prepared and served.

Office

A *flow can* start with a letter arriving, a telephone call, an email, a customer arriving, or a scheduled meeting. In each case, the work flow process requires action to respond to the letter, telephone call, email, customer concern, or attend the meeting.

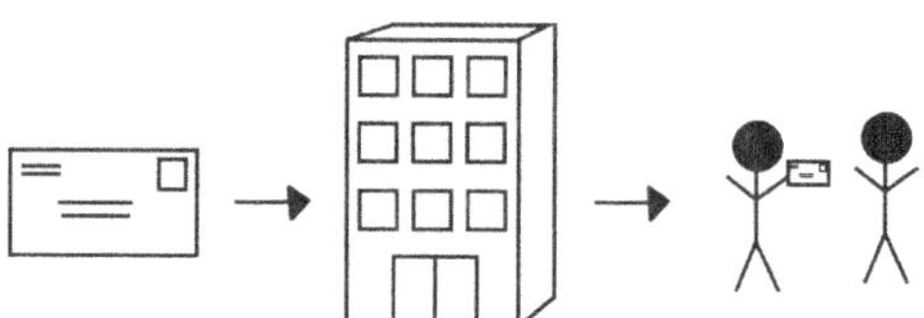

Whether a person is reviewing the processes and procedures of a manufacturing plant, an office, or a construction project, there is nearly always a *flow*, or sequence to the work which can be referred to as the *business process.*

When people shop they find a parking space, park their car, enter the store, go to the section they are interested in, check products, make their selection, and head to the cashier. *They are following a production sequence (a flow of work).*

A successful business owner or manager understands the FLOW of their products, services, and customers – and they design their business operations around those flows.

The first step in designing business operational flows is Business Process Analysis.

(BPA)

Performing Business Process Analysis (BPA)

Whenever a company is considering producing a new product or providing a new service, a logical first step is a Business Process Analysis. It becomes a communication tool to help other people in the organization understand how to build the product, or perform the new service.

Imagine the way through the new idea by performing a *flow analysis.* Sketch (draw) out the steps involved in the building the product, or performing the service. Create a road map.

Business Process Analysis of a new, or revised *product*

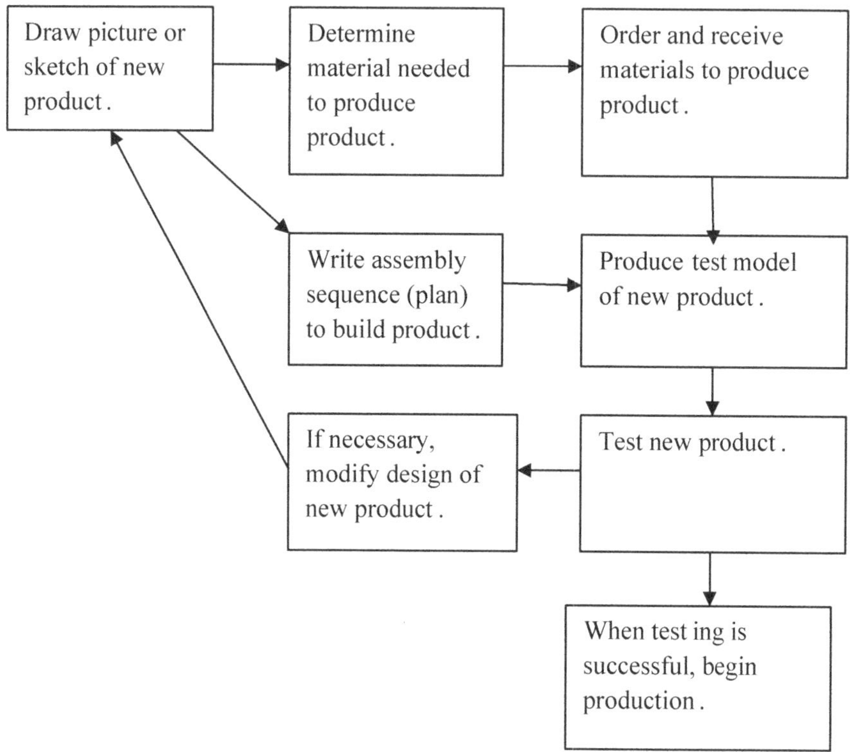

Business Process Analysis of a new, or revised service

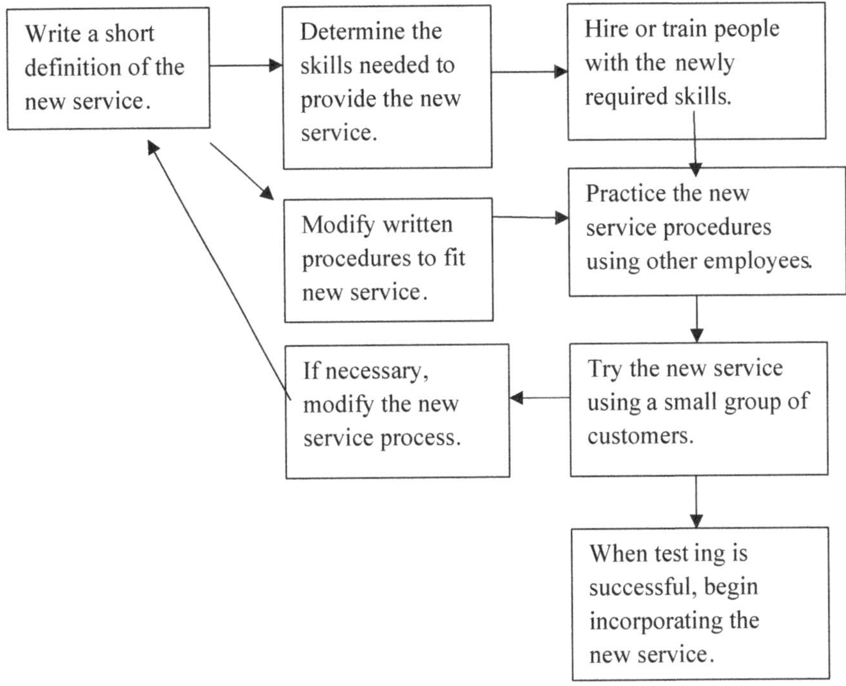

Performing a flow analysis (BPA) of an idea before implementing it will help the business owner or manager with the following tasks:

- Determine what material, supplies, equipment and new technology will be needed.
- Determine skill and staffing requirements.
- Determine if floor and work station changes are needed to perform the work.
- Develop cost estimates (parts, equipment, labor) to assist with pricing strategy.
- Evaluate production process changes on paper (drawings) to improve efficiency before physically moving anything.

Flow analysis forms the methodology for a business owner or manager to monitor performance of most job functions such as:

- hotel housekeeping
- delivery or maintenance service calls
- medical scheduling
- cashier duties
- restaurant customer service
- automobile maintenance and repair scheduling

By thinking about the steps required to produce a product or wait on a customer, a business owner is able to find and compare *value added* steps and *wasted, or unnecessary* steps in processes and reduce the cost throughout an operation. BPA can improve efficiency and save time required to prepare meals, get ready to study, drive a car, work in a garden, get ready to go to work, etc.

BPA provides a tool to look at each step in a production process and think about whether the step is *adding value* to the product or service, or is an unnecessary step that could be eliminated from the business day-to-day operations.

Bill of Material

Many items sold today require some assembly. The purchases generally come with packaged parts, drawings showing an assembly sequence, a drawing or picture of the finished product and sometimes, depending upon the complexity of the assembly, detailed written instructions. The list of packaged parts is referred to as a Bill of Material.

BPA analysis allows a business manager to think about, and list the material or parts that that will be required for each step of an operation. As the lists from each step in the process flow come together, they can be combined to create a Bill of Material" for each product or service being developed. For example, ingredients required for a menu item, material required to create a flower arrangement, or forms required to process a payment.

Tool and Equipment requirements

BPA also helps identify the tools and equipment needed to perform a task. Just like developing a Bill of Material for a process, list any tools and equipment that are needed in work stations and inventory.

Prepare operating procedures

Write the steps and/or tasks for a process as it is being done to create a procedure.

Business process, or flow analysis examples:

- The assembly sequence of an operation
- The order requirements for serving a customer
- prepare files and reference materials in the right order
- provide adequate equipment

When to perform BPA

Business processes, or work flow can – and should – be analyzed on a regular basis to be sure:

- All requirements are being satisfied and all required steps are performed.
- Time and resources are not being wasted through inefficiency or non-value-added steps.
- Procedures are being followed.

- Training is adequate to help people perform processes.
- The facility is organized in an effective manner with minimal movement of parts or people.

If business processes are analyzed regularly, operating methods can sometimes be improved by eliminating steps, simplifying forms, integrating tasks, and/or automating repetitive steps.

Production Process Options

During 1979, Robert H. Hayes and Steven C. Wheelwright wrote two articles which were published in the *Harvard Business Review* entitled "Link Manufacturing Process and Product Life Cycles" and "The Dynamics of Process-Product Life Cycles." Their writing introduced the idea of production design, which means developing the physical arrangement of a business to fit the product the company is planning to create. (37)

Hayes and Wheelwright discussed in the concept of work *flowing* through a facility and referred to the locations where product flowed as *a series of stages*. They argued that a production facility could achieve a high-level of efficiency and be most cost effective if the production stages were arranged according to production needs.

Project oriented floor arrangement

Used for large-scale, one-time, unique products which are customer specific and often too large to be moved.

Examples:

- Construction management office in a relocatable office building

- Band leaders platform used on a school football field
- Portable emergency equipment for fire crews

Job Shop floor arrangement

A job shop has specialized stations for each specific stage of a production process. Each location has equipment, inventory, and employee with expertise to work on a task. In a job shop, parts do not move in a straight line flow; instead, they move around a facility.

Examples:

Service station: gasoline pumps, tire repair bay, mechanical repair bay, car wash, and in our current environment, a small grocery outlet.

Grocery store: produce, meat, canned goods, etc., cashier checkout. Each customer might follow a different route though the store as they are following their shopping list.

Libraries: fiction, non-fiction, children's books, computers and reference. These could be considered job shops.

Hospitals: specialized wings such as cancer or pediatrics, and nursing stations.

A manufacturing company: lathes, mills, assembly, packing. Not all products follow the same order of processing, so part would move from station to station in a flow designed for each type of product category.

Batch work floor arrangement

A batch is a set of parts or services that move through a company in large quantities but not consistently. Batch arrangements are designed to repeat the same processing over and over, for high demand or time-specific events.

Examples:

- Moving lines of people into a stadium
- Loading an airplane at the passenger gate
- Baking donuts for morning commuter coffee customers
- Registering students for college classes
- Cooking for a banquet

Assembly Line floor arrangement

This arrangement is similar to *batch* processing, except it is for a high volume, almost never ending repeat processes.

Examples:

- Producing packaged foods
- Preparing and serving fast food
- Automobile manufacturing,
- Utilities such as electricity and water
- Agriculture harvesting
- Managing customers in an amusement park

Process Selection

When thinking about what kind of production process to design, a business owner or manager should think about the product or service they are planning to develop and work toward designing the right process.

Production Requirements	Process Design
One time, single location	Project
Multiple steps, not the same order for all products	Job Shop
Same steps for a large group of products, not all shifts	Batch
Same steps for a large group of products, all shifts	Assembly Line

Lean Production Systems

It is helpful for a small business owner to understand lean production systems, sometimes referred to as *pull systems*, or *Just-In-Time (JIT)*. If developed correctly, lean production systems help the company continually improve productivity, decrease waste, and increase operating profit – without having a negative impact on employee morale or customer relationships.

Some college textbooks define lean production systems as *operating systems that focus on the elimination of waste in all forms, and smooth, efficient flow of material and information throughout the value chain to obtain faster customer response, higher quality, and lower cost.*

Definition:

> Value chain: The process of organizing and connecting a group of activities that create **value** by producing goods or services from basic raw materials to a finished product.
>
> Each stage in a value chain (production process) should *add value* to the part, or be eliminated from the process.
>
> Examples:
>
> > When a contract is written, or modified, the contract has added *value* to the piece of paper
> >
> > When a contract is signed, the signature has added *value* to the contract.
> >
> > Wrapping a completed product for delivery, adds *value.*
> >
> > Painting a product adds *value.*
> >
> > *Most importantly,*
> >
> > When a cashier takes money from a customer and places it in a cash drawer, the act of placing money in the cash drawer has added *value* for the company.

The management theories that merged over time to create *lean production* began in America with a book called, *The principles of scientific management*, by Frederick Taylor in 1911, and later a series of consulting lectures by J. Edwards Deming in the 1950s.

<u>*Frederick Taylor, Scientific Management*</u> (38)

Frederick Taylor argued that companies in America were not competing adequately with other countries because of a lack of understanding by management and employees that created a culture of inefficiency. He said inefficiency in the workplace was caused by three major problems:

1. Fear that an increase in individual output resulting from improved processes or equipment would cause a large number of other people to lose jobs

2. No understanding or appreciation of efficient workmanship processes from management. Workers forced themselves to work slowly to maintain quality and protect their own self-interests.

3. On-the-job training without consistent procedures which a lot of wasted effort

Taylor's scientific management theory concentrated on helping management trust their workers and provide incentives for improved productivity, to prevent sweatshops. He used the science of Industrial Engineering to introduce these changes to production operations.

1. Study every job in a company in detail and break the job into *elements* with order, consistency, and reasonable estimates of the time required to perform them.

2. Develop consistent training for each job and see to it that each worker receives the training they need to perform their tasks efficiently.

3. Open up communication between management and employees and share ideas on process improvements.

4. Strive to assign an equal amount of work to all workers so no single person is overburdened.

Dr. W. Edwards Deming, The father of quality evolution (39)

"If you can't describe what you are doing as a process, you don't know what you're doing." (Deming)

Dr. Deming (1900-1993) was known for using statistics, systems thinking, and psychology to help business owners and managers improve production processes. He advocated training them to think of their entire company as an integrated system, rather than a lot of bits and pieces. He felt that, given the right culture in an organization, people working in different sections of a company could become team oriented and work toward product a common product or service, even if they were located in different functional areas of the company.

He tried unsuccessfully to share his ideas with American companies, so he went to Japanese export companies after World War II to help them. He introduced his theory of system thinking and taught them to produce quality goods more cheaply than in their past. The Japanese accepted his help and transformed their quality production of automobiles and electronic goods.

Applying Deming's theory to small business

Ideas from the Deming philosophy that are still helpful today include:

1. Always think beyond the next budget cycle.

2. Watch global competition, but do not forget local competition.

3. Develop a company culture of constant improvement. Do not stop improving.

4. Maintain honest and open communication between all members of a company, as well as suppliers and customers.

14 Principles of Management

Deming was never convinced that American companies understood his theories. He felt American owners are too focused on short term goals and maintaining the processes they developed, when they would be far more successful if they could think in the long term, develop a teamwork atmosphere within their company, and strive for ongoing improvement to work and production processes.

He developed "14 Principles of Management" which he believed could make any company successful – *but only if they applied all 14.*

1. Constancy of purpose: Continually improve products and services, allocate resources to provide for long range needs rather than short term profitability.

2. The new philosophy: Realize we are in an economic age that can no longer succeed with commonly accepted delays, mistakes, defective materials, and defective workmanship.

3. Stop dependence on mass inspections: Eliminate the need for constant inspection of every detail in a production process. Replace it with built-in quality and measurement of critical portions of production process, every step in the assembly process.

   An example would be installing the doors on a passenger elevator. The vertical edges of elevator doors that are hidden behind walls need to have space to move freely, but they do not have to be measured to an extreme tolerance.

On the other hand, the tolerance, or gap between the floor of a passenger elevator and the building floor is very critical and should be measured carefully. Any difference, no matter how slight, between the floor of a passenger elevator and the building floor a passenger steps on cannot have a ridge or people will trip.

4. Stop awarding contract awards based on price: In addition to price, require suppliers to include meaningful measures of quality. Improved quality of incoming parts will reduce production costs in the long run.

5. Constantly improve internal processes: Never stop improving product or service design, incoming materials, maintenance of facilities and equipment, machines and internal technology, supervision, training, and retraining.

6. Institute constant training: Keep learning modern methods for management to make better use of each employee.

7. Institute leadership: Help people do a better job by taking urgent action on any reports of material defects, maintenance requirements, poor tools, clumsy process (operation) procedures, and all conditions impacting quality.

8. Drive out fear: Encourage effective two-way communication.

9. Break down barriers: Eliminate barriers between departments, areas, and work teams.

10. Eliminate slogans: Eliminate slogans and posters, encouraging Zero Defects and productivity targets. They tend to create adversarial relationships and are useless without improved production tools or techniques.

11. Eliminate arbitrary numerical targets: Replace work quotas with helpful leadership.

12. Permit pride of workmanship: Award people for the quality of their work and not just the numbers of tasks completed, parts produced, or customers served.

13. Encourage education: Encourage self-improvement for everyone. An organization needs good people, who are committed to improvement.

14. Commit top management to action: Create a top management structure that will push every day on the preceding 13 points, and take action whenever and wherever it is necessary.

Womack, Jones, and Roos, Lean Thinking

In 1984, the Massachusetts Institute of Technology (MIT) provided James Womack, Daniel Jones and Daniel Roos a grant of $5 million to evaluate and compare the production processes between *American mass production,* relatively unchanged since Henry Ford and *Japanese production,* instituted by Deming and now referred to as *Lean Production.* (40)

The $5 million was funded by automobile manufactures, auto parts suppliers, and several governments, including Australia, Canada, Mexico, Taiwan, and Sweden. Manufacturers supporting the study included Peugeot, Fiat, Ford, Chrysler, General Motors and Saab.

After a 5 year study, they published their findings in a book, *The Machine that Changed the World, the story of Lean Production.*(41) The study found that companies functioning under the principles of *lean production* encouraged five traits.

- teamwork
- communication
- efficient use of resources
- elimination of waste
- continuous improvement

By comparing companies supporting *lean* production with companies emphasizing *mass* production they found that *lean production could reduce human effort, building space, planning hours, and production time by half.*

Their book, *The Machine that Changed the World,* was well received in manufacturing companies that produced parts , but not in office oriented service companies. A lot of readers were not able to relate the manufacturing style of *lean production* to their office or service work processes.

As a follow-on, in 1996, Womack and Jones published a second book explaining the results of their study, but oriented toward service companies. Their book *Lean thinking, banish waste and create wealth in your corporation* summarizes the primary principles of *lean production* in fairly generic terms:

- Specify the *value* of each product or service.
- Identify the *value stream* for each product or service.
- Make value *flow* without interruptions.
- Let the customer *pull* the value from the producer.
- Pursue *perfection.*

During several years of working with small business owners, the author of this *Desk Reference* has found a large number of managers who approach concepts like *lean production* with an attitude, "Just tell me the 5 steps I need to take. I'll force implement them, then our company will be efficient." Developing and maintaining a lean culture does not work that way. Lean production involves a long-term culture change – it is NOT a quick fix.

A quick fix mentality will not keep a company on top of their market for very long. The owner and all members of the organization MUST be constantly looking toward the long-range future and work together as a team to help their company improve.

Lean production is about people, dialog, threat free environments, positive reinforcement and, most importantly, common sense management. It can be incorporated into any small business by constantly remembering and reviewing these principles:

- Encourage (enforce) open communication (vertical and horizontal) throughout the company.
- Create a common vision. Share the company business plan often; don't file it away or just hang it on a pretty poster.
- Respond rapidly to ideas. Listen to all ideas and react with a very high priority.
- Encourage continuous improvement. Never be satisfied with the way things are. Processes can always be improved so encourage ongoing training.
- Create teamwork rather than foster competition within the work place.
- Maintain accurate inventory of raw materials and work-in-process.
- Use the A-B-C approach to inventory and production management. This will be explained in the Inventory Management chapter.
- Pre-stage work assignments. Don't start work on any project or process until all of the needed materials are in place.

Summary

Without a lot of theory, a *lean or well-designed* company operating system includes:

Open communication and Trust

Effective production or *operating efficiency* starts with the owner's leadership style. If the owner wants a smooth running, positive work place, he or she MUST share ideas with company employees and managers AND listen openly to all of their ideas.

Respond quickly to ideas

If an employee suggests a processing improvement idea, listen and react quickly. Do not place the idea in a pile to be reviewed by a committee on a monthly or quarterly basis. If an idea makes sense, try it. Show employees their suggestions matter.

Identify the value stream

Constantly review every production processing step in the company. Everything should add value in the eyes of the customer. If it does not add value , consider stopping or improving the process.

Pull, don't push work

Avoid building excess inventory by producing parts or provide services *when they are needed* -- not too soon, and never too late. Maintain schedules that anticipate demand and produce parts to support customer expectations.

Excess inventory can deteriorate, become obsolete, and cost money sitting on a shelf taking up space.

Practice continuous improvement

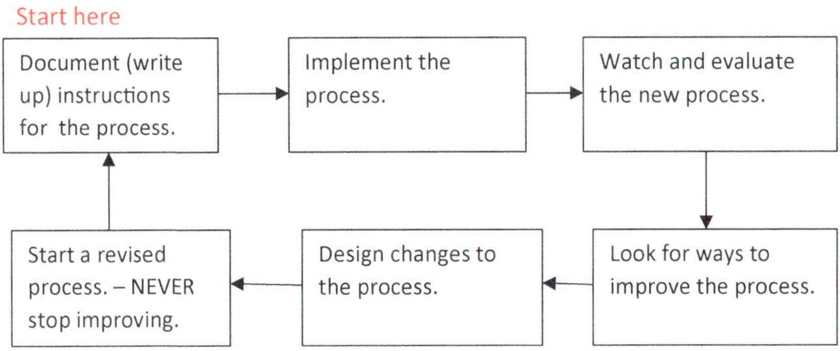

Start here

Document (write up) instructions for the process. → Implement the process. → Watch and evaluate the new process. → Look for ways to improve the process. → Design changes to the process. → Start a revised process. – NEVER stop improving. → (back to Document)

Chapter 12 – Facilities, Equipment, and Furnishings

The facilities are generally the largest and most expensive asset on the balance sheet for most companies. Facilities represent the most tangible element of a business system, and everyone involved in the business can relate to them.

Well planned facilities can be a competitive advantage that will support steady growth and changing needs. Poorly designed facilities can become a maintenance burden and negatively affect company profits.

Size and location considerations

Selecting a location for a new or existing company is one of the most critical decisions a small business owner can make, yet it is fairly common to choose a location based upon non-business criteria such as proximity to home or an existing relationship with the owner of a vacant property.

The right business location should satisfy the criteria in the company *Business Plan.* Start by reviewing the General Description of the business and develop size and location requirements to support the target customers, estimated production size, and future expansion.

Some criteria for a business location:

Visibility

This is not the same major consideration for a manufacturing company that it is for a retail company. The business should be easily seen by potential customers as they drive or walk by.

Be aware of the time of year when selecting a location. A building that is easy to see in winter might be hidden behind trees during spring and summer. A building with attractive landscaping during summer, may look drab and uninviting during fall and winter.

Signs

Sign are covered in detail in chapter 5, Sales, Marketing, and Pricing, but they should be considered when selecting a business location. Look at neighboring signs to determine whether they are attractive, visible from the street, and consistent in design. Put yourself in the role of a customer, consider whether the neighboring signs attract you to the business. Inquire about local signage regulations, or property management restrictions.

Windows and entrances (storefront)

Are they attractive and welcoming for customers? Will they support your business? Retail stores need large windows for display, while service businesses such as law offices need smaller windows. Can potential customers move easily from the parking area to the business entrance?

Cleanliness

Pay particular attention to the cleanliness and maintenance of the facility under consideration. Also look at the condition of immediate neighbors, the surrounding businesses, and the neighborhood in general.

As a rule of thumb, if a neighborhood is deteriorating (gathering litter and has poorly maintained businesses) or has several vacancies, potential customers will probably avoid it. It is generally a good idea to avoid a deteriorating area when selecting a new business location.

Expansion potential

Moving any company into a new location is a major expense as well as a disruption to production processes and services. Because of this, the business owner should try to choose a facility with room for growth. A rule of thumb is to estimate a size needed for about fifteen years of growth potential.

Neighboring businesses

Look around to see where the competition is. If you want a new espresso business and there are already four in the neighborhood, it is probably a good idea to avoid the location. On the other hand, if you want to open a specialty restaurant, you might want consider an area with other, specialty restaurants, but not the same specialty as yours.

The type of business being opened influences the location decision. Some retail clothing stores do well near others in a mall setting. Some businesses want to be near their suppliers (e.g. fish restaurant next to a fish market, manufacturing company near parts producers, pharmacy near a health clinic). Others do not want to be near suppliers (e.g. office supply store near a pulp mill due to odor concerns).

Available skills (labor force)

A business should be located near a large number of potential employees with the skills that will be required to produce the parts or service the company is going to offer.

Companies expecting short-term, high turnover employees, like fast food restaurants for example, do well when they are near large cities with plenty of high school or college students to apply.

Technical companies tend to be near each other, and quite often, colleges and universities with engineering and science programs.

Zoning regulations

It is very important to check with local authorities to be sure the location being considered is zoned for the type of business being planned. It is also a good idea to check with local planning agencies to find out if the city plans to change zoning designations in the future.

Safety

Check with local police agencies to find out about crime rates in the area.

Customer base

Look around the area and check with the local Chamber of Commerce or Planning Commission to find out if there are a large number of potential customers in the immediate area.

Floor arrangement (facility design)

Some businesses do not have an actual plan (schematic) for the arrangement of their office or production area. Their floor design just *evolves* over time as the company grows and generates congested areas. A well thought out floor design has many business advantages whether it is for a production facility, a retail store, a restaurant, or an administrative office.

From a business management perspective, a floor arrangement should:

- reduce or prevent bottlenecks of people and/or parts
- support governmental safety regulations

(OSHA, ADA, and other regulations are discussed in the Legal Concerns chapter of this *Desk Reference.*)

- make a natural flow for customers
- provide privacy and productive work spaces for employees

Using the concept of *continuous improvement*, a business owner should constantly evaluate their floor arrangement and consider improvements if they are justified enough to offset their cost and work disruption.

Typical reasons to consider a revised floor arrangement:

- Correcting a hazardous condition
- Introducing new products or processes
- Introducing new equipment or operating systems
- Expanding production rates
- Changing customer expectations

Basic types of floor layout (facility design)

The design of a production facility is usually grounded on the type and volume of parts being produced.

Continuous flow Linear arrangement

High volume and consistent products

The parts produced are the same; they move steadily throughout a process from start to finish.

Examples: candy bars, beer, milk, wire, paper rolls

Assembly line Linear arrangement

High volume with a variety of products

The parts are similar and move steadily from station to

station; the workers stay in place while the parts move by.

Examples: automobiles, toys, electronic assemblies, and (in the author's opinion), moving people through a TSA security screening in an airport

Batch processing Non-linear arrangement

Mid volume with a variety of products

Work stations (machines and operators) stay in place while the products move in batches (large groups) between work stations; all production parts do not follow the same route.

Examples: furniture (chairs, tables, etc.), cabinetry and counter tops; salon with sections for hair and nails

Job shop Non-linear arrangement

Low volume with a variety of products

Products move to a variety of specialty work stations as needed for specific needs.

Examples: automobile repair (brake department, lube department, tire area, etc.); medical facilities with X-ray, blood work, patient examination room, etc.

Project Non-linear arrangement

One of a kind, unique products; this is typically a temporary floor arrangement

Examples: office remodel or painting, installing new operating systems, creating space for auditors or consultants

Retail Non-linear arrangement

Moderate volume, unique products

Retail stores are usually arranged for customers to wander at their own pace throughout the public area.

Depending on what is being sold, customers may choose their items and bring their selections to a cashier, or they may go to a service counter to ask for product, such as high end auto parts or the pharmacy section of a drug store.

Warehouse Often linear

Moderate to high volume, consistent product types

These may be designed for long or short term storage of product which may be raw materials for a manufacturing company or packaged goods for a large retailer.

Office Non-linear

Prefabricated cubicles are a common choice for offices because they can be rearranged fairly easily to accommodate company needs.

Factories and warehouses

There is no perfect standard floor layout for a factory or warehouse, but there are general guidelines.

- Provide easy access for trucks, large equipment, and suppliers in a receiving or delivery area. Provide space for customers for merchandise pick-up, if appropriate. In a mid-size to large production company, it is usually better to separate the receiving area from the pick-up area since they access different storage areas.
- Include a quality inspection area for incoming parts and outgoing products. Depending on volume, the warehouse might need more than one inspection area.
- Include storage space for incoming materials, work-in-process parts, and completed products.

- Provide space for production machinery and equipment.
- Plan for any requirements for temperature-control or clean (dust free) rooms.
- Retail shops and manufacturing companies also need office space for administrative staff and management.
- A company may be large enough to provide a cafeteria, but even small companies need a break space. Consider space requirements for staff meetings.
- Allow for future expansion. hopefully the business will grow, so don't limit the floor space to current production needs.

Retail stores

Floor arrangement can be very important to retail stores. A welcoming, easy to understand floor arrangement can boost sales, while a confusing, or disorderly space can cause customers to leave without shopping.

General guidelines for retail stores:

- The majority of the available space should be devoted to attracting customers and generating sales.
- Work rooms and storage area should be easy for employees to access but hidden from customers.
- Entrances and aisle ways should be wide enough for a wheel chair, uncluttered, and welcoming for customers
- Lighting and interior temperature should be comfortable, adequate, and not a distraction.
- Racks or shelves should be arranged in a self-explanatory system. For example, clothing should be organized by

type, style, and size. Allow enough room for a customer to sort through items without feeling they are too tight or bunched up on the racks.

- Customers are usually content with a mix of right angles and grids in a retail store. Use straight aisles within grid sections such as canned goods and dairy products, hardware and parts, clothing by gender and style.
- When a customer enters a store, he or she will usually take a moment to take in their new environment. Use the entry area to place objects or decorations which create a desired atmosphere.
- At the end of the entrance area place a power display, large blocking display, or counter that forces buyers to stop, look, and change direction in order to proceed.
- Consider having an employee greet customers at the entrance to welcome them and to help them get a shopping cart or basket. If a customer has a cart with them, the buyers' impulse is much stronger since they have a way to carry several items. Additionally, most customers do not feel comfortable bringing only one item to check out in a cart or basket.
- Store aisles should have some directive purpose.
- Many customers, most typically male, head for the product they want, snatching it as they walk down the aisle, and then retreating out the same aisle. Locating major name brand items in the center of these aisles causes these shoppers to pass by a broad selection of products.
- Small floor tiles on strategic aisles produces the sensation of shopping carts moving more quickly, which in turn causes most shoppers to slow down. The obvious advantage is that shoppers to spend more time looking at products they are passing.

- Bring an impulse buy opportunity to every location where a customer might be waiting in a line: checkout areas, customer service counters or specialty areas.
  - Customers waiting in line can become bored. Arrange small items such as magazines and candy that they might not have planned to buy.

Author's hints:

Most customers in a retail store in the United States turn to the right as they enter a store if there is a counter, or display a short distance in front of the entry. If the store is trying to *push* a certain item the customer might otherwise overlook, place the item in a prominent display to the right of the entry. Most customers will see it as they enter the building and a large number will purchase it.

Place small baskets or carriers throughout the store so if a customer begins to pick up merchandise and they do not already have a cart, they can put their products in the newly found basket and have more room for additional shopping.

Offices

Office arrangements appear to be in a constant state of change. Several years ago offices were open areas with rows of desks or work stations visible to the office manager or supervisor at all times.

Later, companies transitioned to solid walls (many with glass on the upper half of interior walls) providing sound barriers to separate work groups within a large office facility.

Next came cubicles, sometimes very high, sometimes low enough to see over while standing, but not when sitting at a desk. Cubicles have the advantage of easy assembly so they can be rearranged to adapt to differing needs.

> **Warning – cubicle walls give a false sense of security. They do not reach a ceiling and are usually very thin – so they DO NOT prevent neighboring workers or passersby from hearing private conversations.**

It would be difficult to predict the next phase of office arrangements, but it is safe to say as technology advances and the flow of paperwork changes to electronic communication, office arrangements and worker expectations will continue to change.

General guidelines:

- Most office buildings were not designed to support a specific cubicle arrangement so every time a wall, no matter how small is added or relocated, it WILL affect the flow of heating and cooling, as well as lighting.
- Keep aisle ways, exits, entrances, and common areas open and uncluttered to provide easy movement in the event of an emergency.
- Provide ample electronic capability to support current system needs, as well as support future growth. (This is difficult to plan for with constantly changing office systems.)

Locating departments (Floor design process)

Deciding where to place departments, work groups, storage areas, customer service areas, etc. in a new building can be somewhat haphazard and experimental, or it can be pre-planned using a few structured steps. The recommended floor design process is described below.

Step one - Estimate company growth plans

As you go through the floor design process, don't limit your planning to current needs which can become crowded if the company grows. Think about the size you expect the company to be in 15 years. Plan to accommodate new technology, and personnel growth.

Step two - Identify departments or work groups

Prepare a list of departments or work groups that will be located in the new facility.

Do NOT pay attention (at this stage) to how many people are in any work group, or how much floor space each group will need.

(Identifying departments or work groups:

This example uses the cafeteria for the imaginary Sun Spot Resort which is mentioned throughout this Reference Guide. The Sun Spot Resort business plan is included at the end of this Guide.

The Sun Spot Resort

Sun Spot Resort – Cafeteria

A 20 table restaurant serving basic native cuisine (fresh from the sea or nearby plantations). The restaurant is open seven days a week serving breakfast, lunch, and dinner.

Work Groups/Functional Areas

Dining

Cashier/Reception

Kitchen

Food Storage

Food Preparation

Dishwashing

Dining Room Storage

Kitchen Storage (pots, pans, etc.)

Step three – Develop department or work group relationships

Consider each department or work group in relationship to every other group.

Functional relationships are generally identified by the letters A, I, O, U, X.

A	*absolutely* necessary to place next to each other
I	*important* but not critical to place next to each other,
O	closeness is OK, but not vital
U	*unimportant* if they are close
X	*undesirable* to place next to each other

Enter the relationship rating into a chart, like the one shown below.

Sun Spot Resort Cafeteria

Relationship Diagram

	Dining	Cashier	Kitchen	Food Storage	Food Prep.	Dishwashing	Dining Rm Storage	Kitchen Storage.
Dining	--	O	A	U	U	X	A	X
Cashier	--	--	U	X	X	X	U	X
Kitchen	--	--	--	A	A	O	U	A
Food Store	--	--	--	--	A	X	X	I
Food Prep.	--	--	--	--	--	X	X	A
Dishwash.	--	--	--	--	--	--	X	A
Dng Rom St.	--	--	--	--	--	--	--	X
Kitch. Store.	--	--	--	--	--	--	--	--

Step four – Estimate square footage

Roughly estimate the square footage required for each work station. Then add the number of work stations for each department or work group to create a rough estimate of square footage for each department.

> Remember to include space for a worker or operator with each work station. For example, a typical computer work station has a surface of 2' x 5', or 10 square feet.
>
> Be sure to allow additional space for a worker's chair, access to drawers, and possibly file cabinets, and space for guest chairs. The actual estimate for a an office work station is closer to
>
> 5' x 5', or 25 square feet per worker.
>
> Add 10 – 15% for aisles and potential growth.

Step five – paper cut outs

Draw paper squares or rectangles representing the estimated total size of each department or work group.

For interior design, the usual scale is ¼" on the drawing = 1 foot on the building sketch.

Cut out the drawing to create a scale size square footage diagram for each department or work group.

Example:

Sun Spot Resort Cafeteria

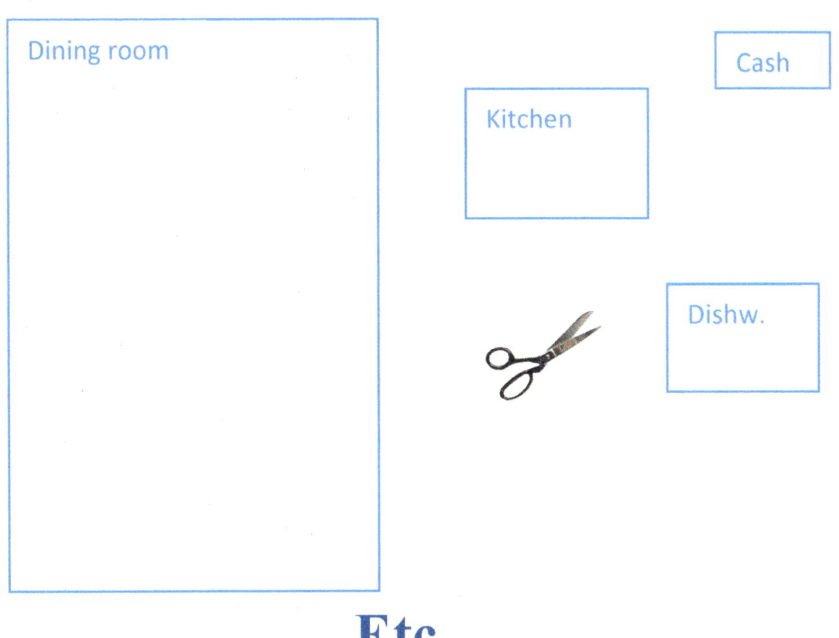

Etc.

Step five – Arrange on floor layout diagram

This step should be done in a group setting with all key members of the company involved to share ideas and generate acceptance for the final layout.

Using a scale floor drawing of the proposed building, arrange the department or work group scale cutouts in a setting so that they fit – and support the relationship diagram from step three. This may take several tries.

Additional thoughts on facility planning

Ideas to consider when developing departmental, or work group relationships:

Restaurants:

- Keep dishwashing and cleaning supplies away from food preparation to minimize risk of contamination
- Keep customers away from kitchen and storage areas to minimize background noise
- Dishwashing should be near food preparation and kitchen storage areas.

Factories/Warehouses:

- Keep painting space and clean areas away from grinding, lathes, and other equipment which can send dust or debris into the air.
- Do not place temperature sensitive equipment on the southern side of a North American building because summer heat can affect some equipment settings.

- Do not locate sensitive or delicate equipment near an external wall that is close to to railroad tracks or heavy vehicle traffic areas.

Offices:

- Locate groups close to each other if they tend to work closely with the flow of information. For examples, insurance records should be close to Claims. Planning should be near Scheduling.

Grocery Stores:

- Place common shopping items (dairy, meat, bakery, delicatessen, etc.) on the side and back walls. Customers will go to these destinations, and quite often pick up impulse items in the aisles as they go to their destination.
- Display produce near the entrance. Well displayed produce can be very effective for impulse buying.

Equipment lists

Suggestions for starter equipment requirements are available from many office furniture, restaurant supply, and other industry unique sales companies. Partial examples of equipment lists are shown below.

Bar/cocktail lounge check list:

Coolers & Refrigeration

- Wine Cooler
- Keg storage
- Beer taps

Equipment

- Cash registers
- Entertainment System
- Ice machine
- Ice Scoop (Never leave scoop in the bin.)
- Liquor well
- Blenders
- Frozen drink machine
- Soda gun
- Cocktail shakers and strainers

Kitchen checklist:

Range Oven Grill Deep-fryer Walk-in cooler Sauté pans Sauce pans Baking sheets Spatulas

Author's suggestion:

> Based upon personal experience, the author has found it is a good idea to look at used restaurant, office equipment, machine shop, retail display stores before buying new. There are some excellent pieces of used equipment available that have been refurbished to a commercial grade condition.

Telecommuting (Working from Home)

Telecommuting is discussed in the chapter on Legal Concerns in this *Desk Reference*. The bottom line is that the same safety and liability issues that apply in the company buildings apply in the home while a person is conducting company business.

Before agreeing to have employees work from home, a business owner should familiarize themselves with the legal constraints that apply.

Depreciation

According to the Internal Revenue Service (IRS) Small Business/ Self Employed Web site dated March 4, 2015 "…depreciation is an income tax deduction that allows a taxpayer (business owner) to recover the cost of certain property. It is an annual allowance for the wear and tear, deterioration, or obsolescence of the property."

For a business, most types of **tangible property,** except land, are depreciable. The list includes, but is not necessarily limited to buildings, machinery, vehicles, furniture, equipment, and some capital improvements to the property.

In addition, businesses can sometimes depreciate **intangible property** such as patents, copyrights, and software.

In order to be allowed depreciation for tax reporting purposes, the property to be depreciated must meet ALL of the following IRS requirements: (41)

- The taxpayer must own the property.
- The taxpayer must use the property for an income-producing activity. If a taxpayer uses a property for business AND personal purposes, they taxpayer can

only deduct depreciation based on business use of the property.

- The property must have a determinable useful life of more than one year.

There several rules covering rates of depreciation, how depreciation can be reported, and some limitations. A small business owner should consult with a professional tax advisor to learn how to establish records and account for depreciation of their property.

Further IRS information is available on-line by reading IRS Publication 946, How to Depreciate Property. (42)

Chapter 13 – Procedures and Audits

The audits referred to in this chapter are *NOT* audits performed by regulatory agencies such the Health Department or the Internal Revenue Service. In this *Desk Reference*, audits are reviews of the business processes by the owner or staff to be sure that the company is consistently following company procedures, operating efficiently and economically, and using company resources to meet organizational objectives.

Company Operating Procedures

You can start confusing people by what you say at the top of the procedure.

Purpose of operating procedures

Regardless of what they are called, desk procedures, standard operating procedures (SOP), unit instructions, standard practices, the purpose is the same. In this chapter, they will be referred to as operating procedures. They are written instructions describing the actions or steps that are required to complete tasks (operations) within the company.

They provide consistency in job functions. Every company has some processes which are unique the organization, which hopefully make it successful in its business. If a business had unique or proprietary processes, the written *operating procedure* is the tool to ensure consistency.

Importance to company

Some people consider writing operating procedures to tell a person how to perform their daily task a tedious waste of time. To others, it is an essential part of developing and maintaining an efficient production environment.

> As a young supervisor, the author of this *Desk Reference* was in the category that considered writing operating procedures a waste of time. He thought that as long as experienced workers knew how to do their job and they could explain job functions to newer co-workers, written procedures did not add value.
>
> Then he matured a little one day. He lost an experienced worker due to a medical emergency on their way home. He learned quickly that nobody in the work place knew how to perform some critical tasks in the department. There were no written operating procedures to refer to.

Protecting the company

Written operating procedures, approved by the owner, can provide:

- efficient use of resources, waste reduction, improved profit
- compliance with regulatory agencies
- protection against liability or human resource complaints
- fewer production errors
- troubleshooting tool

Operating procedure topics

Not every process in a company needs to be documented in an operating procedure, but critical steps, rules, and functions should be. The level of detail involved is usually at the discretion of the owner or department manager.

Examples of typical operating procedure titles:

Administration

Employee/Management time keeping and payroll

Billing and accounts receivable

Accounts payable

Audit procedure and review schedule

Staffing (Human Resources)

Job descriptions

Salary and compensation

Employee training and orientation

Social Media policy

Use of company resources for personal reasons

Smoking and safety

Production (Operations)

Production (primary and/or critical processes)

Equipment operations

Equipment maintenance and inspection

Material receiving and storage (inventory record keeping)

Product inspection, storage, delivery

Sales and Marketing

External communication, press release, social media policy

Warranty and refund/exchange policy

Product or service pricing policy

Product or service estimating authority

Preparing operating procedures

Operating procedures are usually for people who understand their major job functions, but for consistency within the company, need to have a reference source to perform specific tasks according to established standards.

Example:

A cook in a fast food restaurant may know how to prepare a hamburger for a customer, but each chain or franchise has a slightly different target market. By following the written operating procedure, the cook will be able to provide what the customer expects.

The same idea can apply to nearly any industry. Customers have expectations when they walk into a business and the written operating procedure will help the business owner train employees to ensure the customer receives what they expect.

Suggestion – When assigning people to write operating instructions, be careful of mixing cultures or primary languages. In other words, it usually helps if a person with the primary language of French writes instructions for French workers, a Spanish person writes instructions for Spanish people, and a person with the primary language of English writes instructions for English speaking people.

The following sample instructions explain how to take care of a new oven. The instructions were written by an apartment owner in Ho Chi Min City, Viet Nam who though he/she was writing in clear understandable English:

Maters needing attention

1. **Avoids the fuel gas stove spatial fever, in order to avoid damages to this product.**
2. **Correctly selects washes the thing, by prevents the flaking product surface the painting.**
3. **Lampblack confidential regular clean, wipes off is attached to superficial the moist true oil share. (Switch, Electrical part and so on electric motor must prevent the water.)**
4. **When clean is careful and the metal part margin wound, best puts on the rubber glove.**
5. **Invites below application method 25W the light bulb illumination, please.**

A question to you, the reader –Could you maintain the oven using those user instructions?

Level of detail

Operating procedures should provide instructions for important (critical), or complex processes, but not every function in the company. They should tell a person how to proceed with their task in plain, easy to understand language.

Working people want useful information in an operating procedure, without a lot of fluff.

The writing process

Writing effective operating procedures begins with an understanding that all documentation follows a *process* .

Analyze

Think about the purpose of the writing, what the procedure should accomplish and what type of information should be provided.

Consider the target audience. The writing should address their specific needs and expectations.

Arrange the content

Operating procedures usually begin with a descriptive title followed by a sentence or two explaining the process.

Writers should think of themselves as a reader, or user. How will a person use the writing? What would they look for? What kind of help do they need?

Begin with a rough outline, or index. Group, or sort the available information (documents to be used for reference while writing) in the same order as the rough outline.

Test the new procedures

New or revised operating procedures should be tested on several users before being considered final and distributed.

Procedure writing

One of the easiest and most understandable techniques for procedure writing, or preparing operating instructions, is through flow oriented *procedures.* The technique uses job analysis, or *process flow charting* to follow work steps and write directions. Flow charts can be developed for any form of work, whether it is performed in an office environment, a production facility, or on the road.

Chapter 11, Production and Operations of this *Desk Reference stated:*

"Every product or service has a starting point – then it moves through a series of steps (it flows) in a process until a customer is served, a product is produced, or an obligation is satisfied."

A flow oriented procedure follows the same logic. It describes the *flow* of work in a series of written steps that are numbered and can be referred to by workers trying to perform a task.

A fairly typical non- flow operating procedure for a cashier might look like this:

RINGING UP AN ORDER

1. Leave the customer's money on counter until you have given him/her change.

2. Do not use the decimal key. Enter dollars and cents, last 2 digits will be cents.

3. Enter the amount circled for each type of item, and then press

"ENTER".

4. After all items are entered, press "SUB TOTAL".

5. Enter amount received and then press "AMT TEND/CASH". The register will display the customer's change, and the money drawer will open.

6. Give customer receipt, make change, and place his/her money in drawer.

ERRORS

1. If you haven't pressed "ENTER" yet, then press "CLEAR".

2. If you have pressed "ENTER", press "VOID".

3. If you're entering another item, complete the order as if the customer has paid the exact amount. (Press "SUBTOTAL", enter exact amount, and press "AMT TEND/CASH". Then, close the drawer, press "JNL FEED" to advance the journal tape a few lines, open tape cover, write "VOID" on journal (right) tape, and sign your name. Tear off receipt, write "VOID", sign your name again, and place in drawer. Enter the customer's order again.

4. If the register beeps, you've hit the wrong key. Press "CLEAR" to clear the error, and continue. (Remember, don't use the decimal key. Press "SUBTOTAL", before you enter amount received.)

The same procedure written in a flow format:

Cashier: **Ringing up a Payment**

1. Place cash on register shelf

2. Enter amounts without using the decimal key.

3. Enter amount circled for each item.

4. Press " ENTER."
5. Enter amount from customer.
6. Press "AMT TEND/CASH."
7. Give customer change and receipt.
8. Place cash in register drawer and close it.

Cashier: **Correcting cash register Errors**

If "ENTER" *not* pressed:

1. Press "CLEAR."
2. Re-enter amount circled for item(s).

If "ENTER" *was* pressed:

1. Press "VOID."
2. Re-enter the correct amount and *continue entering amount for circled items.*
3. Press "SUBTOTAL."
4. Press "AMT TEND/CASH."
5. Close drawer and press "JNL FEED" to advance the register tape.
6. Write "VOID" on the register tape and *sign your name.*
7. Press "CLEAR."
8. Re-ring the customer's order.

Flow oriented operating procedures or work instructions are based on the assumption that all job functions have a *starting* point (telephone ringing, visitor entering, form arriving, email opened, receipt of material, scheduled meeting time, etc.), a series of steps or actions, and an *end* point (complete telephone call, visitor leaves, etc.).

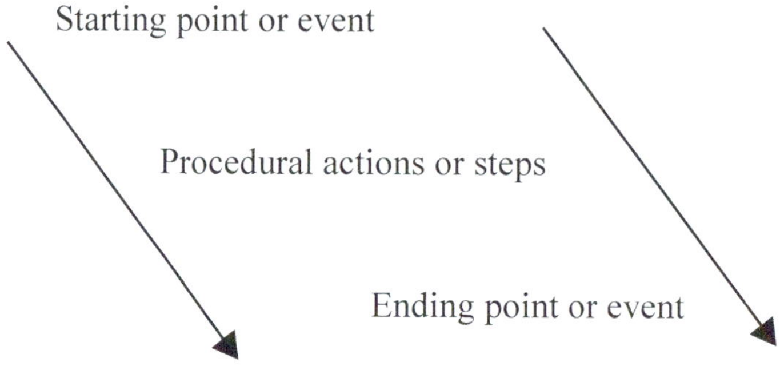

When a job process begins with the *start* point, it requires a series of tasks to be performed until the job is *completed.*

Auditing company processes

Introduction

Every small business should review the systems and procedures on a regular basis by conducting an *Operational Audit.* The audit can be conducted by the owner, his or her management staff, or by an outside firm.

Definition

The Institute of Internal Auditors (IIA) (43) defines Operational Audit as a" systematic process of evaluating an organization's effectiveness, efficiency and economy of operations under management's control and reporting to appropriate persons the results of the evaluation along with recommendations for improvement."

External and Internal Audits

There are usually two types of audit. One type is external and conducted by an outside agency monitoring the small business for compliance to financial record keeping, health and safety regulations, zoning requirements, etc.

The other type is an *internal audit* conducted by company staff or hired consultants. It is not reported to outside auditors, but is used by owners and management to help them improve efficiency and effectiveness of their own operating functions.

External Auditing

External operational audits are usually done by public accounting firms. These professionals are not otherwise associated with the businesses they audit so they can provide a fairly objective opinion. Some business owners prefer using outside consultants to avoid potential bias in their findings. External audits, due to the overhead costs related to their firms tend to be more expensive than internal audits.

Internal Auditing

Some business owners perform their own operational audits, or assign them to a person working inside the company due to cost limitations as well as possible concerns about protecting proprietary information. Sometimes manager perform audits on an ongoing basis moving from department to department in order to provide a continuous picture of what's going on in the business.

Many mid-sized companies with a few hundred employees

conduct several small internal audits each year to keep procedures innovative and revenue high. Although most employees are honest and objective, some are not. There can be a risk those employees who audit their friends or co-workers might minimize errors to hide problems.

Purpose

An thorough operational audit will test company policies and procedures for efficiency and effectiveness, expose real or potential ethical concerns in the company, and keep the owner aware of potential operational risks.

Advantages

If operations are reviewed regularly, a company should be able to maintain production efficiency and function more profitably over the long run. They are a good tool for business owners and management to evaluate and offset the potential of future risks.

Disadvantages

Conducting and reacting to operational audits can be very time consuming and costly. When employees work with the auditor, they are taken away from their regular duties which might cause delays in some services. To minimize disruption avoid rush periods or high seasonal demand times when scheduling operational audits.

Fraud Protection

Most people are honest, want to enjoy their work, and are not prone to fraud or theft. Some people are curious and with a child's innocence will look at files, or get into things in the work place that are not part of their job and are off limits. Confidentiality restrictions apply to data such as personnel records, proprietary information related to product development, and company financial records.

Sometimes minor curiosity can carry a person deeper and deeper into their search and eventually, if not stopped it can result in fraud or theft.

Fraud, according to the U.S. Government Accountability Office (GAO) (44) is: "conduct involving bad faith, dishonesty, a lack of integrity, or moral turpitude. It is a type of illegal act of obtaining something of value through willful misrepresentation."

Minimizing risk (risk avoidance)

The risk of theft or dishonesty can be minimized by encouraging a culture of teamwork, honesty, and mutual support.

Encourage these practices:

- ongoing emphasis toward improving safety and quality
- ongoing effort to ensure ethical conduct by all members of the company
- procedural controls to minimize the opportunity for fraudulent practices
- regular audits of operations and financial transactions for consistency and honesty

Business owner role

To minimize the risk of loss:

> Act in a way that emphasizes risk awareness and encourage others to report their concerns.
>
> Act with honesty and high ethical personal standards as an example for employees, customers, and suppliers.
>
> Develop and implement procedural controls to identify risks, and prevent reoccurrence and future damage.

Fraud Triangle

A fraud triangle is a concept used by auditors and fraud examiners developing or reviewing processes.

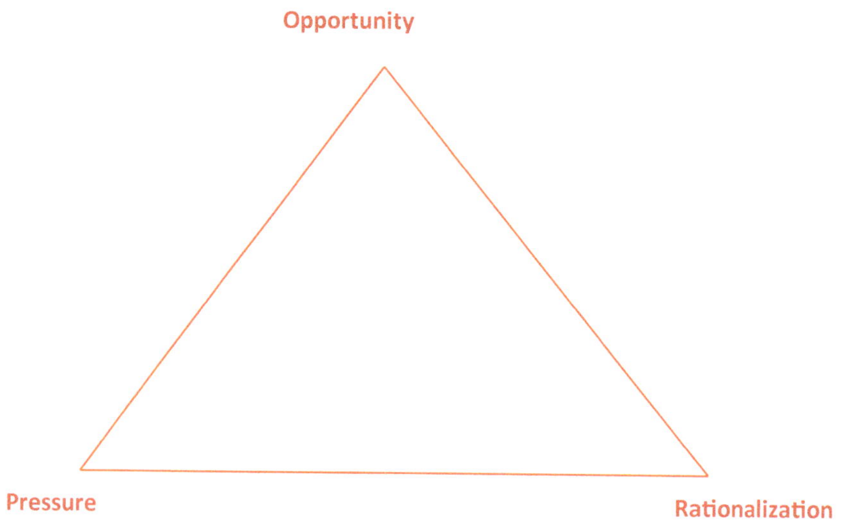

Opportunity Generally comes from a weakness in internal controls.

Some examples:

- Inadequate supervision and review of work
- Work separated by specialization and often independent of co-worker assignments
- Lack of controls or quality review

Pressure Workers can feel pressure from a variety of concerns.

- Personal financial problems
- Personal behavioral problems (e.g. gambling, drugs, etc.)
- Unrealistic work deadlines and performance goals

Rationalization This form of self-talk comes from internal justification of dishonesty. Some examples of rationalization statements:

- "I really need this little bit of cash and I'll put it back as soon as I get paid."
- "I'd rather have the company after me than the IRS."
- "I just can't afford to lose everything I've worked so hard to get."
- "Nobody could finish this project on time without cutting corners a little."

Rationalization and opportunity can open the door to risk. Keep the *fraud triangle* in mind when developing operating processes and procedures. Establish controls to minimize opportunities.

Chapter 14 – Scheduling and Time Management

Project Management

Most companies from time to time get involved in special projects which are one-time, non-routine operations coordinated in a team effort to accomplish a single goal or end result.

Examples:

Moving departments or the entire company to a new location

Installing a new software operating system

Developing a new product

Planning a company celebration or holiday gathering

Projects are NOT 'business as usual' and they typically require a team made up of people who don't usually work together. Team members may be from different organizations, or similar organizations but different geographic locations.

Projects have a beginning and an end, quite often with a fixed or designated completion date. Because projects are not business as usual, they can be confusing to manage. Large projects can involve a complex structure of people, machines, equipment, supplies, money, and time all trying to work together to achieve a goal on schedule. The relationships of all segments of a project can be overwhelming at times, unless the project is broken down into reasonable manageable job assignments, or tasks.

> A manageable work element or task is considered (by an unwritten rule) to be a job or work assignment that can be accomplished in no less than 8 or no more than 80 labor hours.

One of the best tools to help manage company project is is a Work Breakdown Structure

Work Breakdown Structure (WBS)

A WBS is a hierarchical plan indicating what must be done and who is responsible for each job assignment or task in order to achieve a goal on schedule and within budget. WBS breaks down large, complicated processes into workable, manageable assignments for team members.

WBS Step one

A WBS, or *project management plan* begins with a description of the end result, or final goal of the project.

Examples:

Project — Moving departments or the entire company to a new location

End result *All departments in place and functioning as planned*

Project — Installing a new software operating system

End result — New system fully tested and operating efficiently with trained staff members.

Project	Developing a new product
End result	New product designed, produced, tested, and available for sale

Project	Planning a company celebration or holiday gathering
End result	Celebration successfully completed, facility cleaned and put back in order, and (hopefully) all participants happy with the result

WBS Step two

When the goal, or end result of the project is clearly defined and all team members understand what the project goal is, the next step is to think about all of the tasks, or activities that must be finished to complete the total project. The team should hold a meeting, or series of meetings to brainstorm tasks to be accomplished, including any necessary testing or training.

For each task, or work assignment, assign an individual to be in charge of it. If necessary, with a small group of co-workers, develop a list of activities that must be completed.

Plans for large projects are often shown on a WBS chart to help all team members know how their assignment fits into the total project, as well as let management know who is responsible for each portion of the project.

Project	**Developing a new product**
End result	New product designed, produced, tested, and available for sale

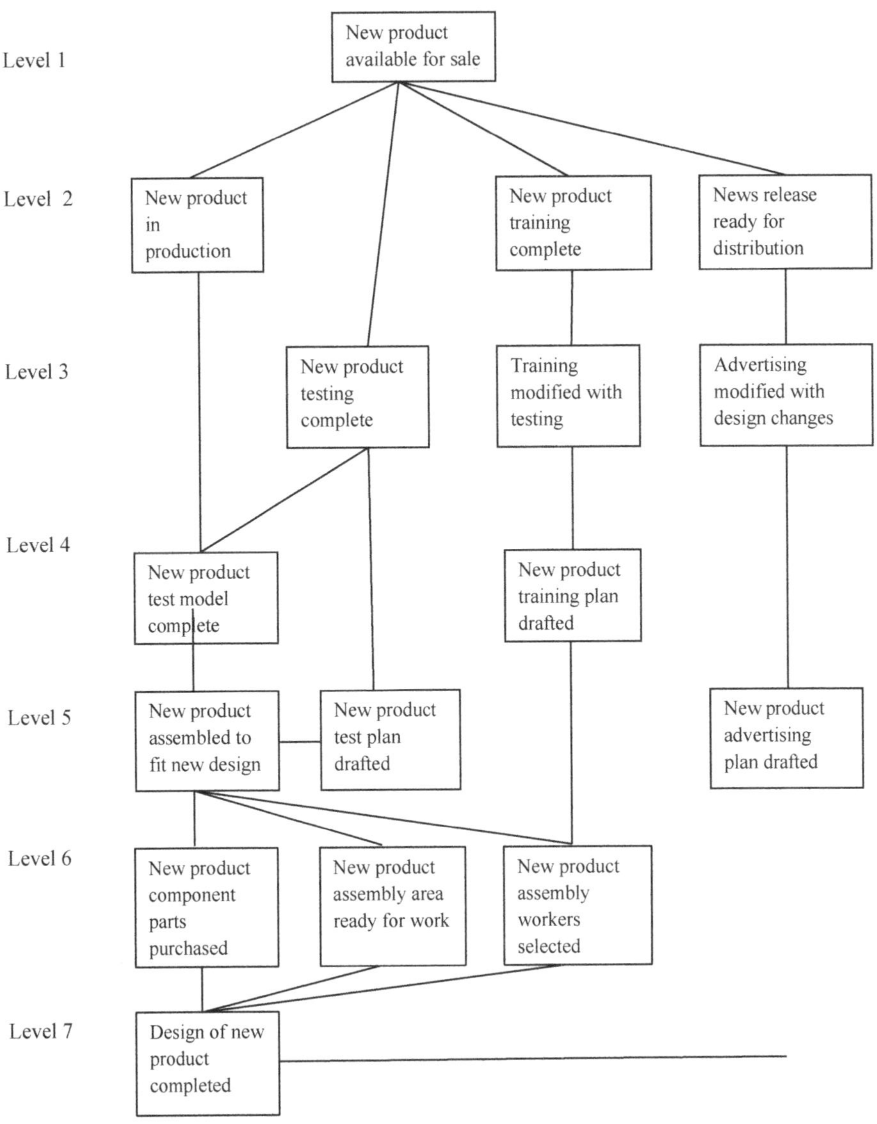

A WBS chart can look a little busy, but when viewed from the top down it will show on the lowest level what has to be accomplished, and in what order, to complete the project.

The lowest levels on a WBS chart are the *manageable* work assignments.

Another example:

This one does not require a WBS chart, but it does show how to break down work assignments to a manageable level.

Project	Planning a company celebration or holiday gathering
End result	Celebration successfully completed, facility cleaned and put back in order, and (hopefully) all participants happy with the result

More specifically for this example the "end result, or goal" is:

On June 24, we will have a picnic for all company employees at the community beach using a maximum budget of $450.00.

It cannot just *happen* without some planning. Breaking the project (the company picnic) into manageable tasks, using a WBS.

A WBS is, by definition, a hierarchy. It has levels of jobs or tasks to be performed.

Level 1

Have a company picnic

A single level WBS is too general to tell anyone what they are supposed to do to make the picnic happen. It needs more detail, or more specific work assignments defined. The planning needs to go to another level in the WBS hierarchy.

Level 1 Have a company picnic

Level 2 Bring food and beverages

Prepare picnic area

Provide entertainment

Notify company employees

It still does not tell people what their assignment is. Add a WBS level 3 to the "prepare picnic area" branch.

Level 3 Cleaning & litter pickup

Tables, signs, tents, etc.

Permits and reservations

In this example, the WBS hierarchy is complete. People can understand what they have to do, when it must be done, and how they will know when their task is complete.

WBS considerations

Suggestions to consider when developing a project WBS:

Level of Detail (8/80 rule)

Don't make the WBS too detailed. Don't create a MIS plan with built in micro management. Leave enough freedom to allow team members to perform their portion of the project without someone constantly looking over their shoulder.

Don't make the assignments so broad they cannot be monitored effectively.

Use the 8/80 rule. Break work assignments into elements, or tasks that can be accomplished in no less than 8 labor hours, or no more than 80 work hours.

WBS is not a Schedule

The WBS cannot be used as a replacement for a project schedule. A WBS does not have to be in any time sequence. It is simply a visual breakdown of job assignments.

WBS changes can cause scope creep

The WBS should be considered a fixed project document. Any changes should be considered very carefully as they are likely to change the scope of the project. Scope creep happens when a project grows beyond an acceptable budget or deadline.

WBS is not a company organization chart

The WBS and company organization chart are not expected to be the same. To some people, they may look the same, but they are not.

The company organization chart shows chain of command and lines of communication while the WBS is only meant for a single project.

Project Scheduling

Building on the definition of a project which is "…a one-time, non-routine operation coordinated in a team effort to accomplish a single goal, or end result," a project schedule can be developed from a WBS breakdown.

For each task or work assignment on the WBS:

Estimate how long it will take to accomplish.

Identify what work assignment if any, must be completed before it can begin.

List the work assignments in order with starting with the first one which must be completed before any others can start, then follow with the next one than can be started, and so on until they are all listed. If more than one can be started anytime without having to wait on a different one, include it with the first work assignment.

Using the company picnic example:

Getting permits and reserving the picnic area could be listed as a starting task since it does not rely on other activities. Developing table plans, signs, tents, and decorations can also be done independently of other tasks.

Cleaning and litter pickup are listed last.

Enter the task list on the left side of a schedule chart and with a date strip across the top, draw in a time estimate for accomplishing each task:

Company picnic

ACTIVITY	Week 1	2	3	4	5	6	7	8	9
Determine date of picnic									
Obtain permits and reservations									
Plan menu and refreshment list									
Notify employees and staff									
Purchase menu items & beverages									
Pick up food and beverages									
Plan entertainment									
Arrange entertainment									
Develop table & tent arrangements									
Prepare signs and directions									
Set up tables, tents, signs									
Clean up after picnic									

Managing the owner's personal time

Of all the resources available to a small business owner and every other person,

TIME is most valuable in terms of its limitations – *it cannot be replaced.*

Time should be savored, enjoyed, used effectively, and treated with respect.

Once used, it will never return.

This section is written on a more personal basis to the business owner, or any other individual looking for some ideas on organizing their time.

Habits and Time

As a business owner, how did you start your workday? Did you unlock the door of the building or office and look around briefly to see if anything appears to be in its place? Did you turn lights on, and your computer? Did you say hello to people nearby, or possibly stop to ask them how they are doing? Did you prepare or get a cup of coffee?

Begin reading email messages? Etc.

However it starts, most people start their day the same way. People are creatures of habit. We like orderliness, or at least a steady routine. However, we can easily slide time wasting activities or bad habits. Habits can eat into valuable time, leaving the day filled with confusion, unfinished tasks, and a lot of frustration.

Time wasting habits can be changed, or at least reduced with a little objective self-reflection. Every once in a while, people need to look at how they spend their time, consider changing their routine, break out of their comfort zone, and see whether their time is being managed efficiently.

Telephone:

Do you stop what you are doing and answer the telephone every time it rings? Do you look to see who is calling and then decide whether to answer right away? In either case, you are taking time away from another task and letting the telephone prioritize your *time.*

Suggestion: If the telephone rings, unless you are a customer service representative or in a supporting administrative role and are expected to answer the telephone and take messages, ignore it. Most companies have voice mail or an individual assigned to take messages. Your *time* in most cases is better served by completing what you are doing, then responding to the telephone caller when you can give them your full attention.

Calendar or scheduled meetings:

Do you have so many meetings or scheduled calendar events that you cannot get enough *time* to work on problems that are raised during the meeting? Do you feel like you are constantly going to meetings without enough preparation? If your day is full of meetings and your calendar is too crowded to allow you time to perform management duties, your *time* is probably disorganized, somewhat sporadic, and not being used efficiently.

Suggestion: Review your calendar and prioritize your meetings. Maybe you don't need to appear in person for every meeting you are scheduled to attend. Maybe you can delegate more of your responsibility and decision making to someone else. Maybe you need to *freeze* a few hours for yourself – and refuse meetings during them.

When the author of this *Reference Manual* was responsible for a large organization with a lot of scheduled meetings, he added a few to his published calendar for Conference Room 4B. In reality, there was no Conference Room 4B, but it froze times on his calendar for working without interruption. Meetings held in Conference Room 8R were code that meant his staff could see him with concerns, but people outside his organization would assumed he was not free during those times.

Daily staff meeting:

Some people in smaller organizations can waste a lot of work *time* during the day telling coworkers on an individual basis about personal events and sharing company gossip. This can be disruptive to others if they are expected to listen to the gossiper when they should be working on company business.

Suggestion: Start each work shift with a short group meeting and encourage everyone to share the events in their lives they want to talk about, as well as ask about company rumors they have heard. When the personal discussion is finished, respond to rumors and let them know about critical, or high priority work assignments for the shift. If people can count on sharing their concerns at the start of each shift, they will be more likely to concentrate on work related issues during their scheduled work time.

Multitasking:

Many people believe they can be totally productive while they are multitasking, or working on several things at the same time.

Example:

You are finishing a major report that is due to be completed in one hour and it has a long way to go. A coworker stops by to ask you for immediate help with a problem. A customer drops by unexpectedly and is waiting in the lobby to see you. A piece of critical equipment is broken and you are the only person in the area that knows how to fix it. You are hungry and know you will not have time to eat when you go to discuss the major report.

Suggestion: Admit you are human and you cannot do a good job on anything if you try to do too many at one time. Prioritize quickly.

Work on the major report. Tell the coworker you will be available when the report is turned in. Send a message to the customer expressing appreciation for the visit but you are expected in a meeting. Their visit was unexpected anyway. Offer to reschedule. The broken equipment might override the major report IF it is stopping production for several people. If not, let it wait until the report is finished. Hungry? Eat something simple while working on the report.

Many recent studies have shown that while computers and modern technology can work on several tasks at the same time, the human brain cannot. It just thinks it can.

Multitasking and the Brain

Think about walking down the sidewalk sorting mail, listening to a recording on ear buds, texting a friend, and watching for a pedestrian light to show you can cross the street. Since you are texting and sorting mail, and you have your ear buds entertaining you, the light may have just turned so you step into the street – oops – the driver who was making a phone call and looking at their GPS map entered the crosswalk just as the light turned and did not see you – ouch!

Both the pedestrian and the driver would believe they were totally aware of everything around them, but the fact is neither one would have been in control of their situation or watching out for their own safety and the safety of others.

The author is not suggesting he is a neuroscientist, but he has reviewed many studies of brain function and human behavior during his years of doctoral research and as a faculty member of several universities. A consistent result of studies related to multitasking indicates the human brain has limitations which can impact busy lifestyles.

When a person needs to focus on a particular problem, they utilize the front portion of the brain called the prefrontal cortex. It covers the right and left sides of the brain and helps the brain focus on the task at hand. If a person is working on two tasks at the same time, the brain will share both sides and give both tasks equal treatment. If there is a third task, problems arise. The brain can handle two tasks well, but with a third, there is a tendency to lose concentration on all three and the chance of errors will increase dramatically.

This is an over simplified discussion of brain activity during multi-tasking, but it is only intended to suggest to a person that if they try to do too many things at once, they are less likely to do a quality job on any of them. If they decrease the number of things they are trying to do at one time, they will probably find better quality results and less frustration in the scheduling of their *time.*

Final thoughts on time management

Just say NO

If a person is feeling overwhelmed by the number of tasks they are trying to do at the same time, they probably need to learn to say no.

If person feels they have taken on all they can handle, then it is time to say NO. True friends will understand, and a boss should be able to understand when a worker has reached their work limit.

Remember the family

Most busy business owners and managers are very aware of their children's education and learning activities. They usually make sure to schedule time on their calendar to attend important games, plays, or other events for their children, even though they have to be away from the work place. Remember the big picture and priorities. When all is said and done, is it be more important to make a few extras dollars or to appreciate the accomplishments of family members?

Chapter 15 – Inventory Management

Accounting for depreciation of *fixed assets* (furniture, fixtures, computer equipment, etc.) is discussed in chapter 12 – Facilities, Equipment, and Furnishings.

This chapter addresses *managing* Inventory – having it available for production needs.

Empty Shelves	**Full Shelves**

No inventory = no sales. **Available inventory = potential sales.**

It sounds pretty simple but the process of managing company inventory needs to be well thought through and planned (managed).

Inventory can refer to office supplies such as pencils, pens, staples, and paper, or to larger items like vehicles, special equipment, and specialized tools.

Health care providers maintain an inventory of drugs, surgical supplies, and specialized equipment. Grocery stores require a controlled inventory of produce, meat products, bakery items, canned and packaged goods, frozen foods, and sometimes household supplies. Specialty stores need an inventory of their product line.

All inventory, no matter what it is, requires up front money from the company. This chapter will share several ideas on how a business can balance sufficient inventory to operate with control of their operating capital.

Objective

Support production and customer needs by providing adequate inventory in all categories without creating over-stock conditions or storing obsolete material and creating an adverse effect on company cash flow.

The inventory management challenge for a small business owner is to have enough products on hand to without having tying up operating capital on parts that are gathering dust, or tying up valuable display space.

Inventory is Evil

Not really, but if a small business manager can keep the phrase "inventory is evil" in mind, it might help keep them aware of problems associated with poorly managed inventory.

Concerns about holding inventory:

- It ties up money and does not add any value to the company bottom line while it is being stored.
- Too much inventory can hide production problems.
    - Damaged parts might go unnoticed if there is always enough inventory to replace the damaged parts. The parts may have to be scrapped (thrown out) and the problem which caused the damage does not get fixed.
    - Valuable material or parts might be susceptible to pilferage (stealing) if an employee feels there is always plenty on hand.
    - Late delivery from suppliers can be a sign of problems that should be addressed before missed deliveries become critical. Too much inventory might obscure supplier problems until they is too late to correct.

Safety stock

Inventory may be "evil" but is it a necessary evil. There will be occasional loss due to damage, missed deliveries, , and possibly even minor theft. For these situations, the company should keep a small store of extra inventory which is referred to as safety stock. The recommended amount of safety stock will vary by industry and individual company, but it should be considered in the design of an inventory management system. Later portions of this chapter will give ideas on how to develop an estimate of required safety stock.

Considerations for Inventory Management

In addition to *safety stock*, a well-planned inventory management system should involve:

- categories or classifications by type, size and date (perishable items in a grocery store)
- calculations of order cost, storage cost, and inventory shortage cost (the opportunity cost to the business when it runs out of something), and the cost of inventory obsolescence
- delivery lead times
- market (customer interest) forecast to estimate demand

Categories of inventory

Maintaining accurate records of available inventory can be overwhelming if it is all counted and monitored continually. It can be managed effectively with less stress if it is categorized with each type of inventory controlled in a way that is appropriate for the category.

Types of inventory normally found in a small business:

Raw material	Manufacturer -- metal, wood, composite material, paint... Jeweler – gold, silver, gemstones, solder… Bakery – flour, spices, grains, butter, milk…
Purchased parts	Manufacturer – nuts, bolts, brackets, small components… Jeweler – chains, clasps… Bakery – cub cake holders, decorative figures…
Work in process	Manufacturer – partially finished parts and assemblies Jeweler – ring needing stone, or bracelet without clasp mounted Bakery – baked goods in the oven or unseparated on baking sheet
Finished goods	Manufacturer – parts completed and ready for shipment Jeweler – jewelry in display case ready for sale Bakery – baked goods ready for sale to customers
Replacement	Finished goods stored to replace damaged or worn finished goods

This category can also include partially completed goods (work in process) stored in case needed to repair or replace damaged goods.

Inventory Management Systems

ABC Inventory System

An ABC Inventory System is used to help maintain adequate inventory without an unreasonable amount of time and personnel to count stored items. Resources are allocated by criticality, or importance to production and sales.

Using an ABC system, the company rates each item in their inventory based upon usage, criticality to production, and cost. Each item in the company is classified as an **A** part, a **B** part, or a **C** part.

<u>ABC classifications</u>

A parts and supplies

High value, expensive parts

Critical parts (A shortage would stop or seriously impact production.)

Difficult parts to obtain (long reorder lead time or no longer available)

Very important by particular owner criteria

Usually only 10 -20% of total company inventory

B parts and suppliers

Mid-level value (not the most expensive, or least expensive parts)

Important, but not critical to production

Not difficult to replace

Usually about 50% of total company inventory

C parts and supplies

Low cost items

Not critical to production, needed, easy to get replacements

Usually about 30% of total company inventory

ABC Controls

A parts and suppliers should be controlled carefully in fairly secure storage, counted frequently, and have a well-designed and monitored inventory accountability process.

B parts and supplies should be monitored carefully, but not as extensively as **A** parts. While **A** parts might need daily counting, **B** parts can generally be controlled adequately if they are counted monthly, or in some cases, even quarterly.

C parts and supplies should not need frequent counting. They are low value and so easily replaced, it makes more financial sense to reorder them as needed and not spend the resources to monitor them frequently. For accounting purposes, an annual count would probably be adequate. **C** parts are typically controlled by a *two box* or *reorder flag* system, both of which are explained below.

Assigning ABC Classification

In a small business the owner usually designates the criteria for inventory. Larger companies may require input from the owner, the company purchasing agent, the production manager, and the company accountant. Every part or item purchased for production or sales should be rated as an **A** item, a **B** item, or a **C** item, then managed accordingly.

Counting, monitoring techniques

There are several methods of counting and keeping track of inventory items. Some are time consuming, labor intensive and expensive; some are automated, but need to be verified manually at times; some are inexpensive and easy to do, but not necessarily as accurate as manual counts.

The inventory monitoring method(s) chosen by a company should relate directly to the ABC classification, or criticality of the parts. **A** parts should have more labor intensive monitoring, while **C** parts do not need a high-level of monitoring.

Physical Counting of Inventory

Physical counting is just what it sounds like: labor intensive, repetitious, and usually not a favorite task. On the good side, it does not have to be done often, usually once a year, depending upon recommendations of the company Accountant and possibly insurance agent.

The process is also just what the name implies. People touch or at least look at everything the company considers inventory and verify the accuracy of the inventory records. Then records are adjusted to match the physical count.

A small business owner should *trust* their inventory records,

but at least once a year, *verify* by physically counting.

Since physical counting is *verifying* inventory records, this section is going to explain some other inventory monitoring processes that will support many businesses. These systems can be trusted, but they all need to be checked (verified) occasionally. No system is perfect.

Planning a physical count

Most employees do not like doing a physical count of inventory. It is not what they consider themselves hired to do, and it can be time consuming and a bit tedious. Understanding this should not stop it from being performed. These ideas are intended to minimize the negative aspects of a 100% physical count of company inventory.

Schedule	Let people know well in advance when they will be expected to participate in the physical count. It generally requires about a full day, so physical counts are often scheduled for a time when the company is closed to regular business. Letting them know in advance can help people schedule baby sitters, prepare mentally for the task, and be more supportive than if they are asked to do a surprise inventory count.
Staffing the count	It is usually not a good idea to have people count items in their own area of responsibility. A supervisor or lead should be in the area to help identify types of parts, but the count should not be done by people normally assigned to the area. People counting in their own area might not see everything because they are too used to what they see every day. It is similar to people trying to edit their own writing. We tend to overlook mistakes we made ourselves. Another consideration is theft

	detection. If people have been stealing inventory they are not likely to report any shortages. For a large inventory, consider contracting with a firm that performs inventory counts for businesses.
Freeze transactions	Stop all business that could move inventory or impact inventory quantities while the physical count is in progress. Any movement of inventory during the count could result in inaccuracy.
Celebrate the end	Celebrate the end with a small party for participants.

Cycle Counting

Cycle Counting is frequent and regular counting of critical or high value inventory (**A** classification. Since a shortage of **A** parts can potentially stop production, or have a negative financial impact, it is important to always know they are available.

While a 100% physical inventory count will usually stop company operations for at least a day, cycle counting is less disruptive to production. The process involves a fairly quick count of critical inventory (usually daily) and can be done before or after regular work shifts without disrupting operations. Cycle counting can be a scheduled activity at the beginning or after any shift work.

If a physical cycle count of inventory does not agree with an inventory management system printed count, adjust the printed count to accurately reflect the physical, or actual quantity of parts available. Then take immediate action to find out why the quantities differed and correct the problem.

Perpetual Inventory System

This is generally part of an automated point-of-sale system with bar codes. Every **A** or **B** item in inventory has a bar code attached to it. When an item is received the bar code is scanned and the computer adds it to available inventory. When the item is sold or shipped out of the company, the bar code is scanned and the computer deletes the item from available inventory. The bar code, point-of-sale system is able to maintain a real time perpetual count of available inventory.

Physical counts verify against the computer perpetual inventory.

Differences between computer printed inventory and physical counting can result from several causes such as:

- parts or material damaged during production
- loss due to theft or pilferage
- a computer entry error
- failure to enter material received or shipped into the computer system

Two Box System

A Two Box System is a common method of controlling "**C**" classified items (low value, high quantity, easy to replace item such as nuts and bolts for a machine shop, spices for a kitchen, or latex gloves for a health care facility.

The first requirement of a two box system is to know how long it takes from the time an item is ordered from a supplier until it is typically on the company shelf. This is referred to as reorder lead time (ROLT).

Using the example of nuts for a machine shop:

> If the ROLT for nuts is one week, the quantity of nuts on the production inventory shelves should be the amount workers will need to perform their tasks plus another quantity that can support production needs for at least one week.
>
> The nuts would be stored on shelves in at least two boxes, or bins. Each box should hold enough nuts to take care of production needs for slightly longer than one week (ROLT). One box should remain closed until the other is empty.

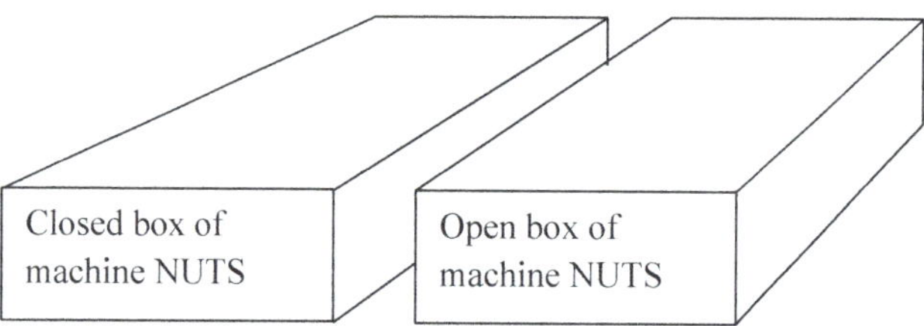

> Workers draw from the open box or bin. When the open box is empty, it is moved to another location or turned upside down; and the production workers begin taking nuts from the box that had been closed.

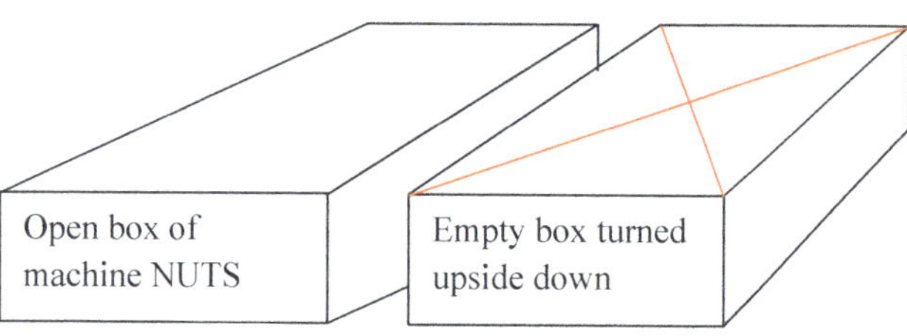

The person responsible for maintaining inventory and ordering replacement part should check **C** parts storage areas regularly (at least once a week) and when they find an empty box or bin which is stored in a Two Box System area, order replacement parts.

When the new parts arrive, keep their box closed, place them next to the open box being used by production workers – and the result is a new ROLT flagging indicator.

Flag Inventory System

This system is similar to the Two Box System, except it does not require extra storage bins or boxes. It is common to see reorder flags in racks of greeting cards and sales racks in retail sales racks with a large quantity of small parts (e.g. craft stores, hardware stores with nuts, bolts, etc., kitchen ware outlets, etc.).

This system, like the Two Box System, requires the company to know the minimum quantity of each item (the reorder point) to have on hand so they will not run out of stock while a replacement order is in process. Based upon the reorder point, they place a card or flag in the supplies directly in front of the minimum number of stored parts they want to have when it is time to reorder.

When people draw parts from the front of the storage area, they will eventually come to the flag. The flag should be removed and placed where purchasing will get it and place an order for replacements.

Bar coding/Point-of-sale

As technology advances, it is getting more common to sell goods with binary coding on the packaging. In some cases, the binary code is on the product when it arrives at a retail store. In other cases, the binary code is placed on the product by the retail store staff before it is displayed for customers.

The same concept works in industries outside of retail sales. Furniture and equipment often has a binary code sticker so it can be identified in the capital asset inventory. Binary coding an also be found on hospital supplies, attached to parts in a manufacturing process, and nearly any situation where quantity counts are important to the business.

Rather than spend a lot of space explaining bar code, or binary code inventory tracking system, the author of this *Reference Guide* recommends using the Internet to research bar code systems available for your type of business. There are far too many systems available today and new one being added to give them fair treatment in this *Guide.*

The end result is that a business lets their information system count and track incoming inventory using a binary code reader and deduct inventory by scanning a binary code when inventory is sold, or moves between locations.

Calculating the reorder point

When should the company place an order be sure they have enough stock on hand, but not too much? (Remember, "Inventory is evil.")

How long will take to receive parts or merchandise after the order is placed? This is referred to as reorder lead time (ROLT).

The reorder point is the term which identifies the minimum quantity in storage when replacement items need to be ordered to maintain the production or sales needs. There are three variables to consider when establishing a reorder point.

Lead time	The number of days from the time an order is placed until the item is received and available to work with or place on sales shelves.
Daily usage	Average quantity of an inventory item the business uses each day. Be sure to allow for fluctuations during holiday sales, or seasonal differences.

Reorder point formula for each inventory item, or class of inventory:

Reorder point = Lead time x Daily usage

Example:

A retail company selling shirts expects to sell 350 shirts per day and the shirts usually take 7 days to arrive from the time an order is placed.

The reorder point for shirts

= 7 days x 350 = 2450 shirts on hand.

When their shirt inventory reaches 2450, it is to reorder.

This may sound OK, but it does not provide any protection for delays in receiving the new order of shirts, or problems with the shirts they do receive. In order to maintain customer relations and be sure to have inventory on hand, a company should consider maintaining a slightly higher than needed inventory – or *safety stock.*

Safety stock	The minimum quantity, or level of an item the company should keep on hand while waiting for replacement parts or merchandise to be delivered.

If the company selling shirts decides to keep at least two days' worth of shirts to sell at all times, their safety stock for shirts would be a 2 day inventory. Selling 350 shirts a day would mean their planned safety stock would be 2 x 350, or 700, so they would adjust their reorder point to be sure they always had at least 700 shirts on hand for customers to select from.

Reorder point formula for each inventory item, or class of inventory *including safety stock*:

Reorder point = Lead time x Daily usage + level of Safety Stock

Including an allowance for *safety stock, t*he reorder point for shirts would be:

Reorder point = 7 days x 350 = 2450 **+ 700 = 3150**

By including Safety Stock, when their shirt inventory reaches 3150, it is time to reorder.

Economic Order Quantity (EOQ)

How much inventory does the business need to maintain to function properly?

How much (what quantity) should the company purchase when it places an order?

Definition:

> *Economic Order Quantity (EOQ) is the amount (quantity) of an inventory item that should be purchased when placing an order for new or replacement items to minimize the cost of holding the part in inventory.*

Or

> EOQ is how many pieces of an inventory item should be ordered to support the needs of the company at the lowest cost.

To calculating the EOQ of any inventory item, or class of item consider these factors.

Inventory costs

The cost of inventory for a business is calculated in two broad categories: ordering costs and carrying or holding costs.

Ordering costs

Placing the order

Transporting the merchandise

Processing receiving paperwork

Inspecting the merchandise

Processing the payment

Shown graphically

Ordering cost (When the quantity on hand reaches a reorder point)

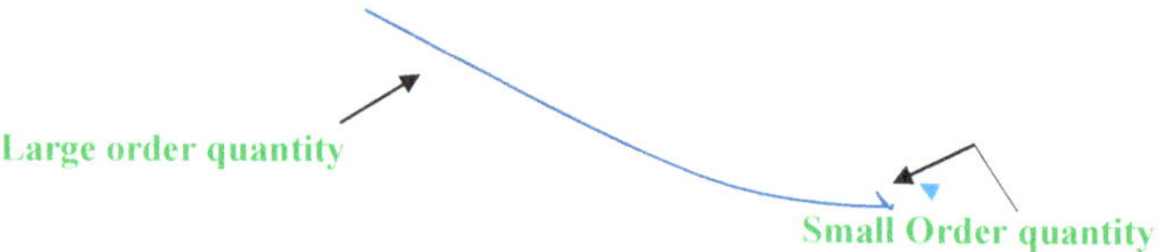

Carrying or holding costs

Storage space (rent, insurance, maintenance, etc.)

Money tied up in stored inventory (lost interest or opportunities)

Damage or spoilage to inventory

Potential obsolescence of stored parts or material

Salaries of staff responsible for maintaining inventory

Inspecting the merchandise

Processing the payment

Shown graphically

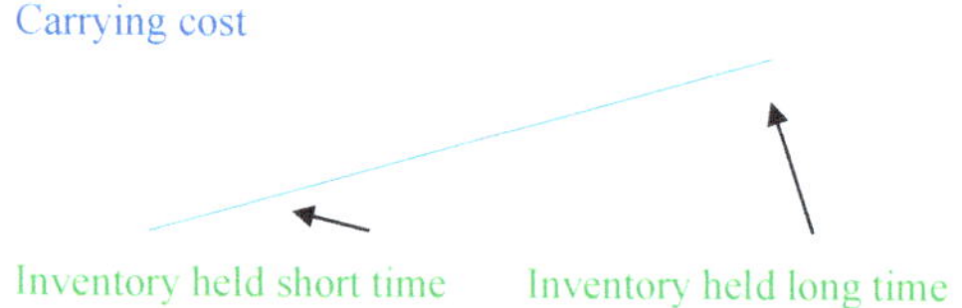

Shown graphically

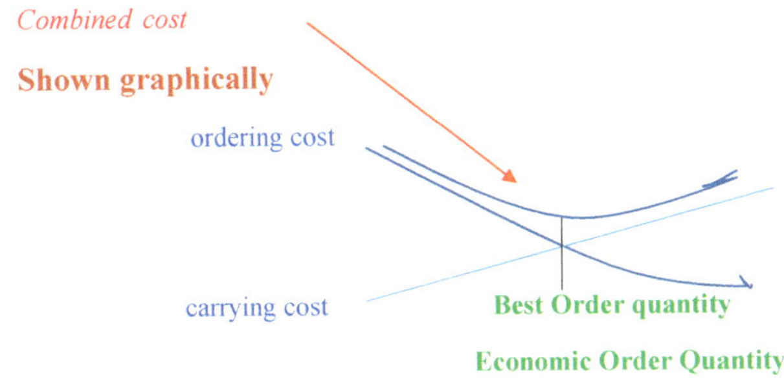

EOQ = where annual ordering and carrying costs cross

A company can *reduce ordering costs* by placing fewer, but larger orders which will increase holding costs.

A company can *reduce holding costs* by placing smaller orders more often which will increase ordering costs.

A company can minimize both *ordering and holding* costs by calculating and working with the Economic Order Quantity.

EOQ is developed by calculating the relationship among:

- total annual inventory cost of an item, or classification of items
- price paid per item
- number of items (pieces) purchased per year
- annual holding cost for an item
- number of pieces of an item ordered with each purchase
- fixed cost of processing each order (labor and paperwork)

Useful hint for small business owners:

> **Use the Internet to find appropriate inventory management software that includes an EOQ calculating feature.**

Just in time (JIT) Inventory

As mentioned earlier, having too much inventory on hand can be very expensive to a company, as well as hide production problems.

If a worker damages a part and has to throw it out and begin another, the financial loss might not show if the company maintains has a large inventory of replacement parts. By not seeing the lost or damaged production part, the business owner might not know there is a production problem related to machine defects, poor worker training, faulty procedures, etc.

Ship at sea

There is a well-known drawing in several textbooks of a ship sailing on top of the sea.

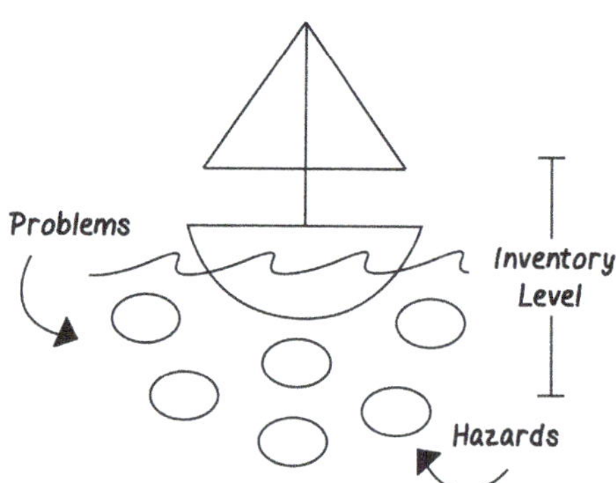

The height of the sea is the amount of inventory on hand, including *excess inventory*. The ship represents the company production, while the *sea of inventory* is full of operational problems that look like rocks.

Rocks, or problems hidden by the *sea of inventory*:

Lack of or poor training for workers

Poor product or process design – prone to mistakes by workers

Missed schedule dates for ordered supplies

Poor supplier quality causing returned parts

Equipment breakdowns slowing production

Unreliable suppliers

The message in the picture:

> If the company maintains too much inventory, the ship will stay above the rocks and never hit them resulting in wasted inventory holding costs which are hiding potential problems that will not be corrected.

Work with suppliers

The Toyota system works with their suppliers to order small batches of parts frequently. They coordinate scheduled deliveries in time to support production needs, but not so early that they will have to carry a large amount of excess inventory.

JIT systems use a small number of suppliers to provide all of the company inventory needs. They communicate production schedules and work out frequent deliveries so the purchasing company does not have to pay for the inventory until it is *almost* needed.

The result will be less holding cost and fresher inventory items in stock. It also supports a stable buyer/supplier relationship where the supplier can become almost an extension of the small business.

Strategic thinking

Always think ahead when considering Inventory Management.

Be aware of potential labor issues. If a supplier has a union contract about to expire, consider buying inventory ahead in case there is strike. If planning ahead brings some inventory in early and there is no strike, consider it safety stock and let the on-hand inventory run down some before placing a new order.

Be aware of long range weather forecasts if the business is seasonal. It the business relies on heavy snow and a mild winter is forecast, adjust purchases to minimize excess inventory. If the business relies on a hot summer and the forecast is for a mild summer, again, adjust inventory orders.

Be aware of customer trends and adjust ordering to support the predicted trend.

Chapter 16 – Quality Management

Introduction

A quality product or service reliably and consistently meets or exceeds customer expectations. It means customers get what they expect for what they paid. Quality means no returns or repairs and a pleasant, reliable service.

Quality of a product or service is reliant on the quality in the design of the process that provides the product or service

(Reference, Chapter 11 – Production and Operations)

David Garvin of the Harvard Business School, in the November 1987 issue of the *Harvard Business Review* listed what he referred to as "Eight Dimensions of Quality." (46)

1. Performance or operating characteristics
2. Features or product characteristics
3. Reliability of a product, of probability of failure
4. Conformance to specifications or design requirements
5. Durability or expected product life
6. Serviceability, or ease and cost of repair
7. Aesthetics or ability to please a customer
8. Perceived quality or value to a customer

The take away message for a small business owner is that *quality* in a product or service has many dimensions. It is far broader than a lot of business people realize and customer perception is everything. If the customer is satisfied with the *quality* of a product or service, it is a good sign. If they are dissatisfied, then the product or service has a problem, no matter how proud of it the company is.

The phrase "the customer is right" certainly applies to quality. A small business owner should never get complacent with quality – it can always be improved, no matter which dimension is being considered.

Cost of poor quality

Specific costs directly resulting from quality concerns are categorized as:

Internal failure costs	Resulting from defective material or workmanship before a product or service reaches the customer, costs include throwing out damaged goods, problem solving time, and rework.
External failure costs	Resulting from delivering goods or unacceptable services to customers, costs include warranty repairs, loss of customer goodwill, rework costs, and possible regulatory penalties.
Appraisal costs	Accumulated during production from, appraisal costs include specialized inspection equipment and labor and interruptions to production while inspection is being performed.
Prevention costs	Resulting from actions taken to prevent quality problems, costs include training, designing and implementing robust systems to improve safety and product life expectancy.

Total Quality Management (TQM)

The approach to managing quality of products and services in companies has evolved over several years using terms and acronyms like Quality Control, Quality Assurance, TQM, ISO 9000, and Six Sigma. Whatever name or terminology is used, a small business owner should do all he or she can to manage quality:

- provide quality products and services that meet or exceed customer expectations
- remember they have direct responsibility for continually improving quality
- perform systematic analysis and improvement (BPA) of work processes
- emphasize quality improvement throughout the company

The *American Society for Quality* (47) refers to Total Quality Management (TQM) as "...a management approach to long-term success through customer satisfaction. TQM is based on all members of an organization participating in improving processes, products, services and the culture in which they work."

Committing to TQM

If a company is going to commit to Total Quality Management, the owner and managers must:

- Commit to providing customer satisfaction
- Commit to continually improve production processes
- Commit to ongoing employee training
- Commit to open and honest communication

- Commit to making data driven decisions

In summary, a company commitment to Total Quality Management is not just a process of working to make presentable finished goods; it is a way of life for the business.

Quality Management Tools

There are several tools used by companies to monitor production quality and to evaluate quality problems. The following pages provide examples of the most common tools. Additional ideas can be found using the Internet and searching for "seven basic quality tools."

Check Sheet

A check sheet is a form used to collect and analyzing data. It is considered a generic tool that can be used for a wide variety of uses.

When to Use a Check Sheet

- When data can be observed and collected repeatedly by the same person or at the same location
- When collecting data on the frequency of events, problems, or defects
- When collecting data to monitor a production process

How to use a Check Sheet

1. Decide what event or problem will be observed.
2. Decide when data will be collected and for how long.
3. Design the form so that data can be recorded simply by making check marks in an appropriate space.
4. Test the check sheet to be sure it collects the appropriate data and is easy to use.
5. Each time the problem occurs, record data on the check sheet.

Example:

This Check Sheet was used by the author to determine department locations in a company that was moving to a new facility. Each department was listed on the check sheet. Over a period of a few weeks, every time any individual in the company went to a different department they put a check mark on the sheet. The resulting tabulation was used to design the floor plan so that departments were placed close to the ones they had the most contact with.

Recording Department:	**Claim Processing**
Department visited:	Recorded visits:
Accounting	𝍸 ||
Underwriting	𝍸 𝍸 𝍸
Files/Records	𝍸 𝍸 𝍸 𝍸
Human Resources	||
Sales	𝍸

A second example:

Concern: **Interruptions from work**

<table>
<tr><th></th><th>Mon</th><th>Tues</th><th>Wed</th><th>Thurs</th><th>Fri</th><th>Total</th></tr>
<tr><td>Information request</td><td>|||</td><td>||</td><td>||||</td><td>|||</td><td>|</td><td>13</td></tr>
<tr><td>Incorrect telephone #</td><td>卌</td><td>卌</td><td>|</td><td></td><td></td><td>11</td></tr>
<tr><td>Research missing data</td><td>卌 卌</td><td>|||</td><td>卌</td><td></td><td></td><td>18</td></tr>
<tr><td>Parts missing</td><td>||</td><td></td><td>卌</td><td></td><td>卌</td><td>12</td></tr>
<tr><td></td><td></td><td></td><td></td><td></td><td></td><td>54</td></tr>
</table>

Fishbone Diagram

A cause and effect diagram commonly referred to as a fishbone diagram because of its shape, identifies possible causes of a quality problem and provides a structure to break a problem into small easy-to-evaluate causes.

When to Use a Fishbone Diagram

- When identifying possible causes for a problem
- When people are having trouble breaking a problem into manageable parts

How to use a Fishbone Diagram

1. Draw a straight horizontal line and write the problem at the right of the line.

____________________________________Cold coffee

2. Draw 3 slanted (rear facing) lines off of the horizontal line on top and 3 on the bottom. It should look like a fishbone, or a three-headed arrow.

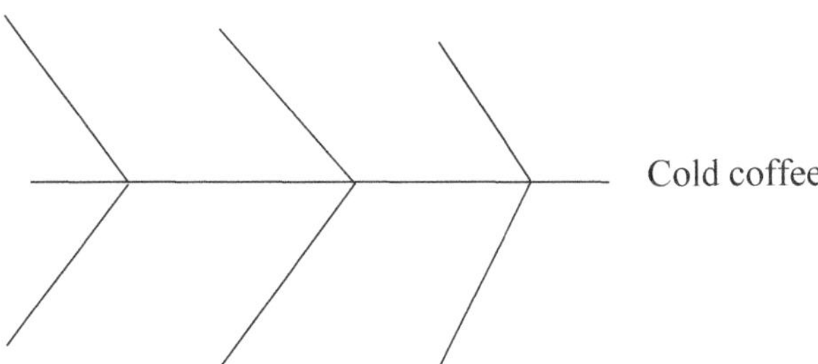

3. Label each slanted line

- Methods
- Machines (equipment)
- People
- Materials
- Measurement
- Environment

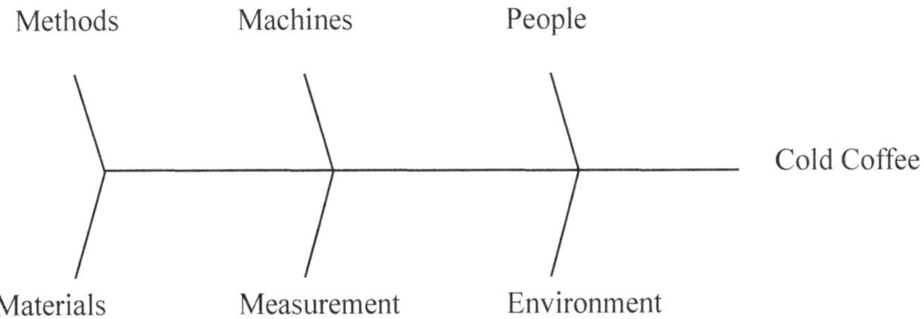

4. In a group discussion, concentrate on just one category at a time and think of all of the things that could be causing the problem.

Methods	Forgetting to turn on the coffee brewing machine
	Not allowing enough time for the coffee brewing machine to heat up properly
Machines	Coffee brewing machine burner not functioning
	Electricity not getting to the coffee brewing machine
	Coffee brewer turns off too quickly
People	Poor (or no) training to use coffee maker
	Coffee maker not aware of coffee temperature
Materials	None (Might apply if the concern is coffee flavor.)
Measurement	None (Might apply if the concern is coffee flavor.)
Environment	Using a non-insulated cup outside in a snow storm (May fall into People category)
	Coffee sits too long in a cold room

5. Based upon the group discussion, develop plans to correct the problem areas.

Control Chart

A control chart is a graph showing how processes change over time. Data is plotted by time. The chart has a central line for average or normal range, an upper line for the upper acceptable limit, and a lower line for the least acceptable limit.

Examples of when to use a control chart

- To monitor service time for customers at a check out station to see if service is within acceptable time limits, or is changing over time.
- To monitor the temperature of an office, an oven, etc. to see is the temperature is staying constant or changing to unacceptable ranges.
- To monitor the fit of tight tolerance machinery to see if blades or other critical pieces of machinery are wearing and getting out of tolerance.

How to use a Control Chart

1. Decide what should be monitored to be sure performance is within standards

    Example: Monitor wait in a restaurant from the time a customer is shown to a table until a server has placed their order for a drink or meal.

2. Establish target time limits.

    Example: Target time - 4 minutes
    Too short - 1 minute (customer feels rushed)
    Too long - 10 minutes (customer becomes impatient)

3. Prepare the control chart.

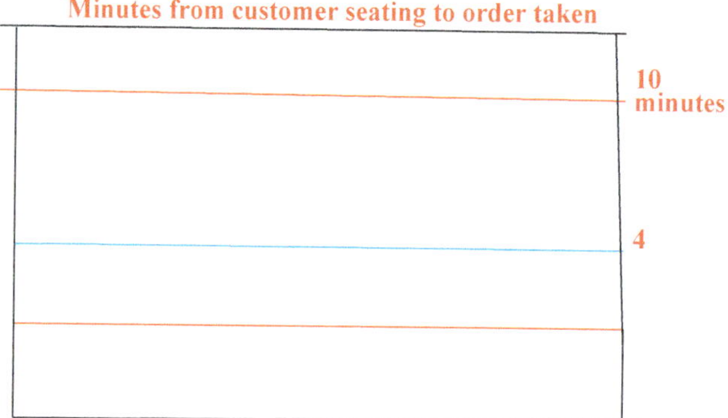

4. Time a sampling of customers. **4 minutes**

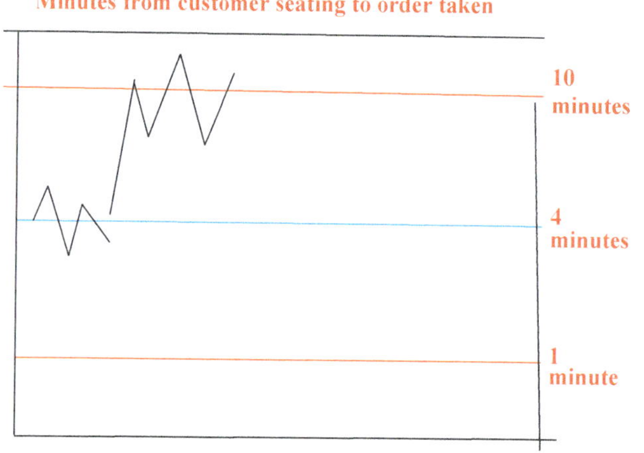

5. Monitor the trend and if it appears to be drifting out of acceptable levels, investigate (possibly using a fishbone chart) to find and correct the cause.

As mentioned at the beginning of this section, there are several tools used by companies to monitor production quality and to evaluate the cause of quality problems. These were only a few examples of some of the most common tools.

Chapter 17 – Legal Considerations

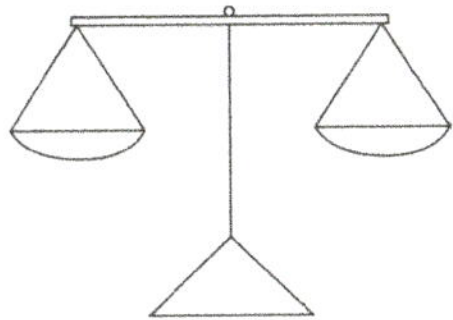

Owning and managing a business requires a more than average awareness of the law and its effect on the workplace. It can be confusing at times, and possibly a bit overwhelming; but overall, if a person registers for proper licenses with the government, operates with fairness and high ethical standards, and treats employees, customers, and suppliers with respect, there should be no legal concern. This chapter is included in the *Desk Reference* to provide some suggestions and insight to help small business owner's remain aware of laws related to their company.

> ***Disclaimer:*** *The author of this Desk Reference is not a trained or licensed attorney. Information shown in this chapter is written from a layman's view. It is based upon several years of business work experience and academic research. Nothing in this chapter is intended to be viewed as legal advice. It is simply suggestions for a small business owner to consider during the planning and operation of their company.*

Business Size and the Law

There are a wide variety of federal, state, and local laws directed toward business practices. Most laws or sets of regulations state whether they apply to all companies or to companies with a certain number of employees (e.g. 5, 15, 20, or 50). Smaller businesses may be exempt from certain regulations.

Employee vs. Independent Contractor

Some small business owners may think that people they hire and pay a salary are employee. Maybe they are and maybe they aren't. According to the Internal Revenue Service *(IRS) Small Business and Self-Employed Website* it is not quite that simple, but it is important to know whether a person working for a company fits the criteria for an employee.

The IRS says "…it is critical that business owners correctly determine whether the individuals providing services are employees or independent contractors." (48)

The reason:

> If the person providing services is an employee, the company MUST withhold and pay FICA (Social Security and Medicare) taxes, withhold income tax, and pay unemployment tax on wages paid to an employee.
>
> If the person providing services is an independent contractor, the company generally does not have to withhold or pay any taxes from the individual.

IRS Definition: Employee

"Under common-laws rules, anyone who performs services for another is their employee ***if the hiring person can control what will be done and how it will be done.*** This is so even when the hiring person gives the employee freedom of action. What matters is that the hiring person has the right to control the details of how the services are performed."

IRS Definition: Independent Contractor

An individual is an independent contractor if the payer has the right to control or direct only the result of the work and not what will be done and how it will be done. The earnings of an independent contractor are subject to Self-Employment Tax.

A person is NOT an independent contractor if he or she performs services that can be controlled by an employer (what will be done and how it will be done). This applies even if they are given freedom of action. What matters (to the IRS) is that the employer has the legal right to control the details of how services are performed.

IRS Statutory Employees

Some workers are independent contractors, but due to certain IRS defined conditions, must be treated as employees *for federal tax purposes.* They are referred to as statutory employees.

Workers typically found in the category of independent contractor are:

- Drivers distributing beverages (other than mill), meat, vegetables, and bakery products
- Full-time life insurance sales agents
- At-home worker using materials or goods supplied by the hiring company and returning the finished goods to the hiring company per their specifications
- Full-time salesperson working on behalf of the company.

"Social Security and Medicare taxes MUST be withheld for Statutory Employees IF all three of the following conditions apply:

- The service contract states or implies that substantially all the services are to be performed personally by the individual.
- The individual does not have a substantial investment in the equipment or property used to perform the services (other than an investment in transportation facilities).

- The services are performed on a continuing basis for the same payer."

At-will Employment

Under federal law and some state, or local laws, individuals can be refused employment, disciplined, or fired for many reasons, or in some cases for no reason unless they are covered by specific statutes, employment contracts, or collective bargaining agreements. (49)

At-will employment which allows employers or employees to terminate their relationship without cause or explanation appears to be a result of the United States respect for freedom of contract, employer deference, and both employers and employees favoring an at-will relationship over job security.

There are exceptions to the at-will option: civic duty, referred to as *whistle blowing,* employees called to National Guard active duty, and employees who refuse to perform an act prohibited by law.

Federal Work Place Laws

A small business owner should be aware of federal work place laws, even if they are unlikely to violate them. A summary of the current federal work place laws is shown below:

Antidiscrimination	Civil Rights Act of 1964 prevents work place discrimination based on race, sex, religion, national origin, color, age 40 or older, disabilities, and sexual preference.
Wages and hours of work	Fair Labor Standards Act requires employers to pay a minimum wage rate per hour and to pay 1

½ times the regular rate for each hour over 40 worked during any given workweek. It also imposes restrictions on employment of children under the age of 18.

Equal Pay Act requires employers to pay equal wages to male and female persons performing equivalent work.

Pensions and Retirement

The Employment Retirement Income Security Act (ERISA) establishes eligibility for company pension plans as well as controlling Individual Retirement Accounts (IRA) and workplace annuity participation (e.g. 401K, 403B, etc.).

Union-Management Relations

The National Labor Relations Act requires employers to engage in collective bargaining with unions if formally requested by the majority of their employees.

Workplace Safety

The Occupational Safety and Health Act (OSHA) establishes standards and controls for workplace safety for equipment, work areas, training, etc. OSHA regulations related to employer liability for workers in a home office are explained below under the heading **Home Office Liability.**

Immigrant Workers	The Immigration Reform and Control Act (at the time of this writing) prohibits United States companies from hiring illegal aliens. It requires employers to verify the eligibility of individuals to work in the United States, and it prevents discrimination directed toward legal immigrants.
Returning Military	The Uniformed Services Employment and Reemployment Rights Act of 1994 requires employers to reinstate employees who left to serve in the United States military when they return from active duty.
Family Medical Leave	The Family and Medical Leave Act requires employers to grant up to 12 weeks (this may be changing) for the birth or adoption of a child, an employee's serious health condition, or to care for a seriously ill close relative (spouse, parent, or child).
Health Insurance	The Affordable Care Act (referred to by some as Obama Care) appears to be in transition at the time of this writing. A small business owner should investigate this act through their insurance provider or legal advisor to be sure they comply with the Act as it becomes better defined.

Layoff Notices

The Worker Adjustment and Retraining Notification Act (WARN) requires an employer to give 60 days' notice if it appears they may be laid off due to a business downturn or plant closure. When written, this act was only directed at large companies (defined by the number of employees) so unless it is, or has been revised, it may not apply to small businesses.

This summary only applied to business oriented federal law. It does not include a discussion of state or local regulations that may override the federal law in a specific regional area.

Bona Fide Occupational Qualification (BFOQ)

BFOQ was discussed in Chapter 8, Staffing (Human Relations)

It is so important that it is included in this chapter so it is not overlooked.

BFOQ is a legal reference for qualifications (skills, experience, or attributes) a person must have in order to perform a specific job function. It means if an employer requires a job applicant to have certain abilities in order to be hired, those *abilities or qualifications* MUST be an actual requirement of the job.

If the job requirements include age restrictions, or require a specific religion, race, gender, etc. the business could be violating the law *unless* they can prove the required religion, race, etc. is necessary to perform the job.

When advertising to fill a job opening or when screening job applicants, it is essential that any selection criteria must be a true requirement to perform the job.

Employer-Provided Cell Phones

According to the IRS Notice 2011-72, "...the IRS will consider all use of an employer-provided cell phone as a non-taxable fringe benefit so long as the cell phone is provided *primarily for non-compensatory business reasons.* The IRS included the following explanations: (50)

1. The term *cell phone* includes cellular telephones or other similar telecommunication equipment such as iPhones and Blackberries.

2. The notice eliminates the need for employers and/or employees to maintain records showing how much cell phone time is used for business and for personal reasons.

3. There is still a requirement for records indicating the cell phone is:

   a. Used to contact the employee at all times for work-related emergencies.

   b. Available for the employee to speak to clients at times when the employee is away from their workplace.

   c. Available for the employee to speak to clients in other time zones outside the employee's normal work hours.

A cell phone, according to the IRS is NOT a valid non-compensatory business expense if it:

1. Is provided as extra compensation for the employee.

2. Is provided to promote employee good will or improve relationships.

3. Is provided to attract a prospective employee (as part of their

compensation).

Employer liability – Employee car accident

Based upon recent court decisions, if an employee varies their normal route while going to or coming from work to provide an "incidental benefit" to the employer (pick something up, run a short errand, etc.), and the employee is involve in an accident, the employer can be held liable for the damages. The same employer liability can apply if an employee is involved in an accident in a company vehicle, even if they are doing personal business on non-work time.

Recommendation

To the extent possible, employers should avoid situations where an employee uses their personal vehicle during the work day, including commuting to and from work, to perform any work-related activities unless it is absolutely necessary.

Companies should avoid providing a company vehicle to employees unless it is absolutely necessary. If an employee is involved in an accident while in a company vehicle, the company will have a very good chance of being held liable for damages.

Home Office Liability

Telecommuting, or working from home can sound very good on the surface, but employers need to be aware of liability concerns. There are many people who would argue working from home helps employee productivity and creativity through increases morale. It can save fuel, family time lost to commuting, and do good things for the environment.

It all sounds positive, but from a business perspective, a small business owner should remain aware that he or she is required by laws and regulations to *carefully protect employees against liabilities* in their place of work whether it is a business office, or their own home. With the rise in telecommuting, courts have been treating the hazards an employee is exposed to while working from home in the same manner as the hazards they would be exposed to in their company work place.

Examples:

State Compensation Insurance Fund v. W.C.A.B./Kinnon, 45 Cal. Comp. 253 (1980)

> A professor preparing class notes at home slipped on the papers he left lying on the floor and was injured. The court awarded him workers' compensation benefits.

Sandberg v. J.C. Penney, WCB No. 0702441, CA 140276 (June 1, 2011)

> An employee working from home was injured when she tripped on her dog on the way to look for some company fabric samples in her garage. She was awarded worker's compensation benefits.

<u>The concern</u>

Based upon apparent trends by the courts, employers should assume that the courts will treat hazards in the home in the same way they would in the business work place while the employee is working. If the company does not have a clear and written policy for the employee working from home, they could be held responsible for an injury to an employee if they fell on some stairs while getting up in the middle of the night to get a drink of water and decided to check on their company email while they were up. That could be considered work time since the person was "doing company business."

<u>Recommendation</u>

Include a written telecommuting (working from home) policy in the employee handbook and make sure the employee understands the policy before authorizing any work-at-home activity.

The policy should address:

- Expected work hours (while at home)
- Designated area of the home for the employee to work in, and if the employer feels it is necessary, access for the employer to inspect the area for safety and ergonomic considerations
- Required periodic breaks
- Clear description of work done at home

Be sure the employee understands that telecommuting is a privilege, not a right or compensation benefit.

OSHA Home-Based Worksites

The following information is provided by the U.S. Department of Labor, Occupational Safety and Health Administration (OSHA): (51)

Directive number: CPL 2-0.125, Effective: February 25, 2000

Subject: Home-Based Worksites

Purpose: |To provide guidance to OSHA's compliance personnel about inspection policies and procedures concerning worksites in an employee's home.

Program Change: States are expected to have enforcement policies and procedures which are at least as effective as those of Federal OSHA.

Definitions:

Home based worksite The area of an employee's personal

	residence where the employee performs work for the employer.
Home office	Office work activities in a home based worksite (e.g. filing, keyboarding, computer research, reading, writing). Such activities may include the use of office equipment (e.g. telephone, facsimile machine, computer, scanner, copy machine, desk, file cabinet).

Policy: OSHA will only conduct inspections of home based worksites such as manufacturing operations when OSHA receives a complaint or referral that indicates a violation of a safety or health standard threatens physical harm, or there is an imminent danger, including reports of a work-related fatality.

The scope of the inspection in an employee's home will be limited to the employee's work activities. The OSHA Act does not apply to an employee's house or furnishings.

Employers are responsible for hazards caused by materials, equipment, or work processes which the employer provides or requires to be used in the employee's home.

Workers' Compensation Insurance

Most states require companies to purchase workers' compensation insurance for their employees. It covers employee's medical expenses and some of their lost wages if they are injured while working on their job.

Like many other types of insurance, the cost or premiums to employers is related to how hazardous their business is and how many claims are filed. It is advantageous to the business to maintain a safe operation with few, or no claims – including work-at-home accidents.

Required Records (Record Keeping)

The Internal Revenue Service (IRS) Small Business/Self Employed Web Site dated March 31, 2015, addresses the small business owners' question: (52)

"What kind of records should I keep?"

The IRS response:

A business may choose any recordkeeping system that is suited to the business as long as it *clearly* shows the business income and expenses. The recordkeeping system should show a summary of business transactions in an orderly manner. The books must show gross income, as well as deductions and credits.

> For a small business, the business checking account is acceptable as the main source for entries into business books.

According to the IRS, some businesses choose to use electronic accounting programs and they are acceptable provided they meet the same basic recordkeeping principles as recommended for manual systems. All IRS hand written, or hard copy recordkeeping rules and regulations apply to electronic recordkeeping systems.

The IRS recommends reading on-line IRS Publication 583, Starting a Business and Keeping Records. (53)

Types of required business documents

According to the IRS, businesses should generate and save supporting documents for all purchases, sales, payroll, and other transactions involved in the business. They should be kept in an orderly and safe location and organized for easy retrieval, for example, filed by year and type of income or expense.

The IRS recommends keeping:

Gross receipts	Cash register tapes
	Deposit information (cash and credit sales)
	Receipt books
	Invoices
	Forms 1099-MISC
Purchases	Cancelled checks or other documents that identify payee, amount, and proof of funds transferred.
	Cash register tape receipts
	Credit card receipts and statements
	Invoices
Expenses	Cancelled checks or other documents that identify the payee, amount, and proof of funds transferred
	Cash register tapes
	Account statements
	Credit card receipts and statements
	Invoices
	Petty cash slips for small cash payments
Travel, Entertainment, Gifts, Car	Deductions for travel, entertainment, gifts, and car expenses are somewhat restrictive. Specific information can be found by reading IRS *Publication 463, Travel, Entertainment, Gift and Car Expenses.* (54)
Assets	Any records required to establish

	a value to be used for depreciation should include the following:
	When and how the asset was acquired
	Purchase price
	Cost of any improvements to the asset
	Amount of any deduction taken
	Deductions for depreciation
	Deductions for casualties (e.g. fire or storm)
	How the asset was used for the business
	When and how the asset was disposed of
	Selling price
	Expenses involved in selling the asset.
	<u>Typical documents satisfying the requirements:</u>
	Purchase and sales invoices
	Real estate closing statements
	Cancelled checks that identify the payee, amount, and proof of funds transferred
Employment taxes	All employment records must be kept for at least 4 years. Additional information related to employment tax records can be found in IRS Publication 15, Circular E, Employers Tax Guide. (55)

Conclusion

The legal considerations can appear to be a bit overwhelming to a person trying to operate a small business. This chapter was not intended to make people nervous about running their business; but only to make them aware of some of the regulations they should adhere to.

The recommendation of the author to any small business owner is to protect your business and yourself.

- Keep relationships with employees professional. You will spend a large amount of time together in and around the workplace, but always remember, you are working with another professional, not necessarily your best friend. If relationships can stay professional, it will be much easier on all parties to handle instruction, performance reviews, and if necessary, discipline.

- Give all employees respect as participating individuals and a reasonable amount of time for them to take care of medical and family concerns. Respect their privacy when they need it.

- Be sure any employee treated or considered exempt really is exempt according to the legal description. (Refer to the Staffing chapter if necessary.)

- Be careful to avoid sexual harassment; but if it, or other discriminatory practices are evident in the company, take quick action to correct it.

- Follow the steps of talking, writing, corrective action, etc. before terminating an employee.

- Develop and practice a fair compensation policy. Be objective and job related with performance reviews.

- Give proper training to all workers, including managers.

- Publish and explain a company ethics policy for all employers and managers.

- Publish and explain a company Internet policy letting all employers and managers know email messages sent or received on company time or equipment are company property. Be clear about company policy related to using the Internet for company business, personal business, ordering suppliers, sharing passwords, etc.

Appendix A – Personal Financial Statements

This appendix includes the U.S. Small Business Administration (SBA) application form which is required for an SBA loan. Applicants must provide personal finance information, independent of the company financial statements. The form is available on the SBA website and is in PDF format.

OMB APPROVAL NO.: 3245-0188
EXPIRATION DATE: 01/31/2018

PERSONAL FINANCIAL STATEMENT
7(a) / 504 LOANS AND SURETY BONDS

U.S. SMALL BUSINESS ADMINISTRATION **As of ______________, _______**

SBA uses the information required by this Form 413 as one of a number of data sources in analyzing the repayment ability and creditworthiness of an application for an SBA guaranteed 7(a) or 504 loan or a guaranteed surety.

Complete this form for: (1) each proprietor; (2) general partner; (3) managing member of a limited liability company (LLC); (4) each owner of 20% or more of the equity of the Applicant (including the assets of the owner's spouse and any minor children); and (5) any person providing a guaranty on the loan

Return completed form to:
For 7(a) loans: the lender processing the application for SBA guaranty
For 504 loans: the Certified Development Company (CDC) processing the application for SBA guaranty
For Surety Bonds: the Surety Company or Agent processing the application for surety bond guaranty

Name	**Business Phone**
Home Address	**Home Phone**
City, State, & Zip Code	
Business Name of Applicant	

ASSETS (Omit Cents)		**LIABILITIES** (Omit Cents)	
Cash on Hand & in banks	$	Accounts Payable	$
Savings Accounts	$	Notes Payable to Banks and Others (Describe in Section 2)	$
IRA or Other Retirement Account (Describe in Section 5)	$	Installment Account (Auto)	$
Accounts & Notes Receivable (Describe in Section 5)	$	Mo. Payments	$
Life Insurance – Cash Surrender Value Only (Describe in Section 8)	$	Installment Account (Other)	$
Stocks and Bonds (Describe in Section 3)	$	Mo. Payments	$
Real Estate (Describe in Section 4)	$	Loan(s) Against Life Insurance	$
Automobiles (Describe in Section 5, and include Year/Make/Model)	$	Mortgages on Real Estate (Describe in Section 4)	$
Other Personal Property (Describe in Section 5)	$	Unpaid Taxes (Describe in Section 6)	$
Other Assets (Describe in Section 5)	$	Other Liabilities (Describe in Section 7)	$
		Total Liabilities	$
		Net Worth	$
Total	$ 0	**Total** *Must equal total in assets column.	$ 0

Section 1. Source of Income.		**Contingent Liabilities**	
Salary	$	As Endorser or Co-Maker	$
Net Investment Income	$	Legal Claims & Judgments	$
Real Estate Income	$	Provision for Federal Income Tax	$
Other Income (Describe below)*	$	Other Special Debt	$

Description of Other Income in Section 1.

*Alimony or child support payments should not be disclosed in "Other Income" unless it is desired to have such payments counted toward total income

SBA Form 413 (7a/504/SBG) (09-14) **Previous Editions Obsolete** **Page 1**

Section 2. Notes Payable to Banks and Others. (Use attachments if necessary. Each attachment must be identified as part of this statement and signed.)

Names and Addresses of Noteholder(s)	Original Balance	Current Balance	Payment Amount	Frequency (monthly, etc.)	How Secured or Endorsed Type of Collateral

Section 3. Stocks and Bonds. (Use attachments if necessary. Each attachment must be identified as part of this statement and signed.)

Number of Shares	Name of Securities	Cost	Market Value Quotation/Exchange	Date of Quotation/Exchange	Total Value

Section 4. Real Estate Owned. (List each parcel separately. Use attachment if necessary. Each attachment must be identified as a part of this statement and signed.)

	Property A	Property B	Property C
Type of Real Estate (e.g. Primary Residence, Other Residence, Rental Property, Land, etc.)			
Address			
Date Purchased			
Original Cost			
Present Market Value			
Name & Address of Mortgage Holder			
Mortgage Account Number			
Mortgage Balance			
Amount of Payment per Month/Year			
Status of Mortgage			

Section 5. Other Personal Property and Other Assets. (Describe, and, if any is pledged as security, state name and address of lien holder, amount of lien, terms of payment and, if delinquent, describe delinquency.)

Section 6. Unpaid Taxes. (Describe in detail as to type, to whom payable, when due, amount, and to what property, if any, a tax lien attaches.)

Section 7. Other Liabilities. (Describe in detail.)

SBA Form 413 (7a/504/SBG) (09-14) **Previous Editions Obsolete** Page 2

Section 8. Life Insurance Held. (Give face amount and cash surrender value of policies – name of insurance company and Beneficiaries.)

I authorize the SBA/Lender/Surety Company to make inquiries as necessary to verify the accuracy of the statements made and to determine my creditworthiness.

CERTIFICATION: (to be completed by each person submitting the information requested on this form)

By signing this form, I certify under penalty of criminal prosecution that all information on this form and any additional supporting information submitted with this form is true and complete to the best of my knowledge. I understand that SBA or its participating Lenders or Certified Development Companies or Surety Companies will rely on this information when making decisions regarding an application for a loan or a surety bond. I further certify that I have read the attached statements required by law and executive order.

Signature ______________________ Date ______________

Print Name ______________________ Social Security No. ______________

Signature ______________________ Date ______________

Print Name ______________________ Social Security No. ______________

NOTICE TO LOAN AND SURETY BOND APPLICANTS: CRIMINAL PENALITIES AND ADMINISTRATIVE REMEDIES FOR FALSE STATEMENTS:

Knowingly making a false statement on this form is a violation of Federal law and could result in criminal prosecution, significant civil penalties, and a denial of your loan or surety bond application. A false statement is punishable under 18 U.S.C. §§ 1001 and 3571 by imprisonment of not more than five years and/or a fine of up to $250,000; under 15 U.S.C. § 645 by imprisonment of not more than two years and/or a fine of not more than $5,000; and, if submitted to a Federally-insured institution, a false statement is punishable under 18 U.S.C. § 1014 by imprisonment of not more than thirty years and/or a fine of not more than $1,000,000. Additionally, false statements can lead to treble damages and civil penalties under the False Claims Act, 31 U.S.C. § 3729, and other administrative remedies including suspension and debarment.

PLEASE NOTE: The estimated average burden hours for the completion of this form is 1.5 hours per response. If you have questions or comments concerning this estimate or any other aspect of this information, please contact Chief, Administrative Branch, U.S. Small Business Administration, Washington, D.C. 20416, and Clearance officer, paper Reduction Project (3245-0188), Office of Management and Budget, Washington, D.C. 20503. PLEASE DO NOT SEND FORMS TO OMB.

SBA Form 413 (7a/504/SBG) (09-14) **Previous Editions Obsolete** Page 3

PLEASE READ, DETACH, AND RETAIN FOR YOUR RECORDS

STATEMENTS REQUIRED BY LAW AND EXECUTIVE ORDER

SBA is required to withhold or limit financial assistance, to impose special conditions on approved loans, to provide special notices to applicants or borrowers and to require special reports and data from borrowers in order to comply with legislation passed by the Congress and Executive Orders issued by the President and by the provisions of various inter-agency agreements. SBA has issued regulations and procedures that implement these laws and executive orders. These are contained in Parts 112, 113, and 117 of Title 13 of the Code of Federal Regulations and in Standard Operating Procedures.

Privacy Act (5 U.S.C. 552a)
Any person can request to see or get copies of any personal information that SBA has in his or her file when that file is retrieved by individual identifiers such as name or social security numbers. Requests for information about another party may be denied unless SBA has the written permission of the individual to release the information to the requestor or unless the information is subject to disclosure under the Freedom of Information Act.

Under the provisions of the Privacy Act, you are not required to provide your social security number. Failure to provide your social security number may not affect any right, benefit or privilege to which you are entitled. Disclosures of name and other personal identifiers are, however, required for a benefit, as SBA requires an individual seeking assistance from SBA to provide it with sufficient information for it to make a character determination. In determining whether an individual is of good character, SBA considers the person's integrity, candor, and disposition toward criminal actions. Additionally, SBA is specifically authorized to verify your criminal history, or lack thereof, pursuant to section 7(a)(1)(B), 15 USC Section 636(a)(1)(B) of the Small Business Act (the Act). Further, for all forms of assistance, SBA is authorized to make all investigations necessary to ensure that a person has not engaged in acts that violate or will violate the Act or the Small Business Investment Act, 15 USC Sections 634(b)(11) and 687(b)(a), respectively. For these purposes, you are asked to voluntarily provide your social security number to assist SBA in making a character determination and to distinguish you from other individuals with the same or similar name or other personal identifier.

The Privacy Act authorizes SBA to make certain "routine uses" of information protected by that Act. One such routine use is the disclosure of information maintained in SBA's investigative files system of records when this information indicates a violation or potential violation of law, whether civil, criminal, or administrative in nature. Specifically, SBA may refer the information to the appropriate agency, whether Federal, State, local or foreign, charged with responsibility for, or otherwise involved in investigation, prosecution, enforcement or prevention of such violations. Another routine use is disclosure to other Federal agencies conducting background checks; only to the extent the information is relevant to the requesting agencies' function. See, 74 F.R. 14890 (2009), and as amended from time to time for additional background and other routine uses.

Right to Financial Privacy Act of 1978 (12 U.S.C. 3401) -- This is notice to you as required by the Right to Financial Privacy Act of 1978, of SBA's access rights to financial records held by financial institutions that are or have been doing business with you or your business, including any financial institutions participating in a loan or loan guaranty. The law provides that SBA shall have a right of access to your financial records in connection with its consideration or administration of assistance to you in the form of a Government guaranteed loan. SBA is required to provide a certificate of its compliance with the Act to a financial institution in connection with its first request for access to your financial records, after which no further certification is required for subsequent accesses. The law also provides that SBA's access rights continue for the term of any approved loan guaranty agreement. No further notice to you of SBA's access rights is required during the term of any such agreement. The law also authorizes SBA to transfer to another Government authority any financial records included in a application for a loan, or concerning an approved loan or loan guarantee, as necessary to process, service or foreclose on a loan guaranty or collect on a defaulted loan guaranty.

Freedom of Information Act (5 U.S.C. 552)
This law provides, with some exceptions, that SBA must supply information reflected in agency files and records to a person requesting it. Information about approved loans that will be automatically released includes, among other things, statistics on our loan programs (individual borrowers are not identified in the statistics) and other information such as the names of the borrowers (and their officers, directors, stockholders or partners), the collateral pledged to secure the loan, the amount of the loan, its purpose in general terms and the maturity. Proprietary data on a borrower would not routinely be made available to third parties. All requests under this Act are to be addressed to the nearest SBA office and be identified as a Freedom of Information request.

Flood Disaster Protection Act (42 U.S.C. 4011) -- Regulations have been issued by the Federal Insurance Administration (FIA) and by SBA implementing this Act and its amendments. These regulations prohibit SBA from making certain loans in an FIA designated floodplain unless Federal Flood insurance is purchased as a condition of the loan. Failure to maintain the required level of flood insurance makes the applicant ineligible for any financial assistance from SBA, including disaster assistance.

SBA Form 413 (7a/504/SBG) (09-14) **Previous Editions Obsolete** **Page 4**

Executive Orders -- Floodplain Management and Wetland Protection (42 F.R. 26951 and 42 F.R. 26961) – SBA discourages settlement in or development of a floodplain or a wetland. This statement is to notify all SBA loan applicants that such actions are hazardous to both life and property and should be avoided. The additional cost of flood preventive construction must be considered in addition to the possible loss of all assets and investments due to a future flood.

Occupational Safety and Health Act (15 U.S.C. 651 et seq.) -- This legislation authorizes the Occupational Safety and Health Administration in the Department of Labor to require businesses to modify facilities and procedures to protect employees or pay penalty fees. Businesses can be forced to cease operations or be prevented from starting operations in a new facility. Therefore, SBA may require additional information from an applicant to determine whether the business will be in compliance with OSHA regulations and allowed to operate its facility after the loan is approved and disbursed. Signing this form as an applicant is certification that the OSHA requirements that apply to the applicant business have been determined and that the applicant, to the best of its knowledge, is in compliance. Furthermore, applicant certifies that it will remain in compliance during the life of the loan.

Civil Rights Legislation -- All businesses receiving SBA financial assistance must agree not to discriminate in any business practice, including employment practices and services to the public on the basis of categories cited in 13 C.F.R., Parts 112, 113, and 117 of SBA Regulations. This includes making their goods and services available to handicapped clients or customers. All business borrowers will be required to display the "Equal Employment Opportunity Poster" prescribed by SBA.

Equal Credit Opportunity Act (15 U.S.C. 1691) -- The Federal Equal Credit Opportunity Act prohibits creditors from discriminating against credit applicants on the basis of race, color, religion, national origin, sex, marital status or age (provided the applicant has the capacity to enter into a binding contract); because all or part of the applicant's income derives from any public assistance program, or because the applicant has in good faith exercised any right under the Consumer Credit Protection Act.

Executive Order 11738 -- Environmental Protection (38 F.R. 251621) -- The Executive Order charges SBA with administering its loan programs in a manner that will result in effective enforcement of the Clean Air Act, the Federal Water Pollution Act and other environment protection legislation.

Debt Collection Act of 1982, Deficit Reduction Act of 1984 (31 U.S.C. 3701 et seq. and other titles) -- These laws require SBA to collect aggressively any loan payments which become delinquent. SBA must obtain your taxpayer identification number when you apply for a loan. If you receive a loan, and do not make payments as they come due, SBA may take one or more of the following actions: (1) report the status of your loan(s) to credit bureaus, (2) hire a collection agency to collect your loan, (3) offset your income tax refund or other amounts due to you from the Federal Government, (4) suspend or debar you or your company from doing business with the Federal Government, (5) refer your loan to the Department of Justice or other attorneys for litigation, or (6) foreclose on collateral or take other action permitted in the loan instruments.

Immigration Reform and Control Act of 1986 (Pub. L. 99-603) -- If you are an alien who was in this country illegally since before January 1, 1982, you may have been granted lawful temporary resident status by the United States Immigration and Naturalization Service pursuant to the Immigration Reform and Control Act of 1986. For five years from the date you are granted such status, you are not eligible for financial assistance from the SBA in the form of a loan guaranty under Section 7(a) of the Small Business Act unless you are disabled or a Cuban or Haitian entrant. When you sign this document, you are making the certification that the Immigration Reform and Control Act of 1986 does not apply to you, or if it does apply, more than five years have elapsed since you have been granted lawful temporary resident status pursuant to such 1986 legislation.

Lead-Based Paint Poisoning Prevention Act (42 U.S.C. 4821 et seq.)
Borrowers using SBA funds for the construction or rehabilitation of a residential structure are prohibited from using lead-based paint (as defined in SBA regulations) on all interior surfaces, whether accessible or not, and exterior surfaces, such as stairs, decks, porches, railings, windows and doors, which are readily accessible to children under 7 years of age. A "residential structure" is any home, apartment, hotel, motel, orphanage, boarding school, dormitory, day care center, extended care facility, college or other school housing, hospital, group practice or community facility and all other residential or institutional structures where persons reside.

Executive Order 12549, Debarment and Suspension 2 CFR 2700
1. The borrower or contractor certifies, by submission of its application for an SBA loan or bond guarantee, that neither it nor its principals are presently debarred, suspended, proposed for debarment, declared ineligible, or voluntarily excluded from participation in this transaction by any Federal department or agency.
2. Where the prospective lower tier participant is unable to certify to any of the statements in this certification, such prospective participants shall attach an explanation to the application.

SBA Form 413 (7a/504/SBG) (09-14) **Previous Editions Obsolete** **Page 5**

Appendix B – Startup or Expansion Estimates

The author of this Desk Reference is not an accountant, financial advisor, or legal consultant. Information provided in this appendix is based upon many years of business experience and academic research. It is intended to provide suggestions to a small business owner to help them when they visit a legal or financial advisor to discuss current regulations and company budget estimates.

Worksheet available

There is an Excel worksheet available online to help develop an estimate of the financial cost to start a new business, or expand an existing business. The form is available on the SCORE section of the U.S. Small Business Administration (SBA) Web site.

Introduction

Anyone about to start a new business, or expand an existing business should develop a budget and determine how the project will be financed before committing to a business change. Questions to consider during the planning process include:

How much money will be needed?

How was the cost estimate developed?

How will the money be used?

Where will the money come from?

Seed Money

When developing an estimate of startup or expansion costs, include detailed amounts. Remember to estimate the cost of legal support, insurance and some allowance for unknown contingencies and seed money.

Seed money is used to:

- conduct business for the first few months (typically 6-18).
- cover one-time start-up costs.
- feed the owner's family before the company generates a profit.

Startup Tax Deductions

According to the SBA (*Startup cost tax deductions – how to write off the expense of starting your business*, Dated January 9, 2012, author: Caron Beesley), there are some startup expenses that can be written off against the business as"…as soon as you are operational."

Beesley's information bulletin quotes the IRS which defines startup costs as deductible expenses that are used to pay for:

1. The cost of investing the creation or acquisition of an active trade or business, which includes costs incurred investigating markets and competition, product analysis, labor supply analysis, visiting potential business locations, and similar expenses.

2. The cost of getting a business ready to operate (before the doors are opened or the business starts generating income). Examples include employee training and wages, consultant fees, advertising, and travel costs associated with locating suppliers, distributors, and customers.(56)

Limitations

The startup expenses *cannot be deducted* unless the business becomes operational.

Warning

Any small business owner considering deducting expenses incurred before the business is operational should consult with an accountant and *keep good records.*

Appendix C – Cash Flow Projections

Worksheet available

It is a generic worksheet, designed to help a wide range of businesses. Because it is generic, it can appear to be pretty detailed for some small business owners. The author of this *Desk Reference* recommends using the worksheet to get some idea of the information a business needs for accurate cash flow projections, and then modifying it to fit their particular company.

Importance

Whether a business is applying for a loan, or planning to operate without a loan, developing an annual cash flow projection is a very important part of business management. The business, even if it is a non-profit enterprise, is expected to generate enough income to keep the doors open and provide products or services to customers. The cash flow projection is a tool to help a small business owner make changes if necessary.

It is considered one of the most important documents given to a potential lender. Lenders will usually review cash flow estimates very carefully before granting a loan to decide whether the estimates appear to be realistic.

Appendix D - Sample Business Plan for Sun Spot Resort

This is an example of a *business plan* for a fictitious company to show the reader what a plan might look like. It is not the only format for a business plan and it might not fit the needs of all small business owners. The *Sun Spot Resort* is an imaginary resort located on a yet-to-be-discovered land called Magic Island in the South Sea.

The Sun Spot Resort

Business Plan -- January 8, 2015

Owners: **Sam and Martha Washburn**

Address: Magic Island, South Pacific

Telephone: 1-18-234-993-2994

Fax: 1-18-234-993-3339

Email: Sunspot@nowhere.com

EXECUTIVE SUMMARY

The Sun Spot is a mid-sized resort located on the shores of Magic Island, far out in the South Pacific. It is considered a comfortable location where middle class couples and families can visit, stay a short time, and spend a relaxing time together. T*arget* customers include couples with small children and retired couples visiting without their grown kids. The resort tries to provide an environment that will keep customers returning year after year – and so far, it has been successful.

The Sun Spot has grown steadily since it began in 1998, under the direction of Sam and Martha Washburn. The current staff varies between 150 and 200 people, depending upon the season.

The owners feel it is time to consider expanding the resort to support an increased customer base, while maintaining the mid-size feel and customer oriented culture established throughout the company history. The resort is becoming very popular and they would like to expand by adding 20 villas, a combination pool and beach front cafeteria with a swim up bar for mid-day meals, and a new hotel wing.

This business plan explains the expansion plans of Sam and Martha Washburn.

GENERAL COMPANY DESCRIPTION

The Sun Spot is a mid-size resort located on the shores of Magic Island, far out in the South Pacific. The resort includes:

- A 70 suite hotel. Each suite includes one or two bedrooms, a sitting room, and a patio or deck facing the ocean.
- 30 villas located throughout the resort grounds. Each villa (small cabin) includes two or three bedrooms, a sitting room, a small kitchen, and a private patio.
- A 20 table restaurant serving native cuisine fresh from the sea and nearby plantations. The restaurant is open seven days a week serving breakfast, lunch, and dinner.
- A small gift shop located in the breezeway between the hotel lobby and the restaurant.
- A small marina which provides water craft rentals, private docks for registered guests, a concession area for fishing charters and parasailing. It does *not* include fuel or repair services.
- 4 outdoor recreation areas with tennis courts, volley ball courts, and swimming pools.
- A walking/jogging trail with picnic and sitting areas situated along the shoreline.

In support of their desire to keep the customers happy, the owners are very careful when hiring staff. They prefer to hire local high school and college students to work as receptionists, restaurant wait staff, and gift shop attendants during the busy tourist season because the students seem to get along with young children visiting the resort.

MANAGEMENT TEAM

The owners, Sam and Martha Washburn, are the primary operators (General Managers) of the resort. They share functional responsibility with Sam spending most of his time with the guest rooms, marina, and grounds and Martha actively in charge of the restaurant and gift shop.

There are only two positions other than Sam and Martha that could be considered management:

Kitchen Chef, Pierre de Sol

Pierre began as a dishwasher in a Los Angeles cafeteria, where he watched cooks prepare numerous delicacies over his 5 years tenure in the position. Later he moved on to the *Hardened Artery* restaurant in Baconsville where he earned the coveted Trans Fat award from the community. He left the *Hardened Artery* and moved to the *Sun Spo*t when the *Hardened Artery* had to close as its customer base diminished.

Maintenance Manager, Ole Dole

The head maintenance person with responsibility for all resort infrastructures (gardening, plumbing, electrical, etc.) Ole began learning his trade as a store greeter for a big box home repair center talking with contractors and home hand persons. He was with the big box store for 12 years before moving on to a landscaping job on Wisteria Lane. After some awkward moments with the residents of Wisteria Lane, he moved to the South Seas to accept his position with the *Sun Spot*.

LOCATION AND FACILITIES

The Sun Spot Resort is located on Magic Island, a sister island to Bali High (made famous in the movie and stage play South Pacific). It is accessible by boat or seaplane with regularly scheduled travel from Bora Bora.

The island, it is said, was once the home of pirates, conquistadors, and resident natives. The mystery and adventure still attracts tourists as they wander in search of treasures buried in the white sandy beaches.

ACCOMMODATIONS

Each guest room has been custom-designed to resemble a privately-owned cottage or condominium suite. They are decorated in bright, soothing hues that create a sunny atmosphere and relaxing experience. Amenities in each guest room include:

- Plush king or queen bed arrangements
- Balcony or patio with ocean view
- Bathrooms with separate basins and dressing areas
- Coffee maker
- Microwave
- Hair dryer
- In-room safe

DINING

The restaurant is a casual dining venue. It provides moderately-priced contemporary specialties in a comfortable setting. The menu varies from tasty burgers to fresh seafood caught the same day it is offered in the restaurant.

MARINA

The marina offers a large fleet of rental boats and watercraft. The fleet includes a variety of boat sizes and prices to meet the needs of nearly every guest. The inventory ranges from pontoon party boats to jet skis and open bow luxury boats.

STAFFING AND TRAINING

Employees are encouraged to bring friends and family members to apply for positions with *The Sun Spot.* Sam and Martha have been very satisfied with the applicants they have talked with over the years. They feel there is a sense of community since the students they hire know each other from school.

All employees from guest registration to housekeeping, restaurant, marina and resort maintenance staff, are taught through on-the-job training.

MARKETING STRATEGY

The primary marketing of *The Sun Spot Resort* will continue by word-of-mouth and general reputation. The resort will be sending survey questionnaires to guests after they leave and they will be asked to send comments to social medial sites such as Facebook.

LEGAL CONSIDERATIONS

The resort is in compliance with all appropriate local and national laws and regulations including, but not limited to, business licensing, Health Department licensing for the restaurants, fish and game registration, and marine safety inspection.

The business is registered as a partnership, but it will change to a Limited Liability Corporation (LLC) before expansion begins.

FINANCIAL PLAN

Personal financial statements will be made available to any potential lender using whatever format they require, or suggest.

This expansion budget is a request for a credit line in the amount of $2.5 million. It is supported by attached construction estimates for new lodgings, restaurants, and a new software operating system.

Bibliography

Chapter 1

1. Peter, L.J., & Hull, R. (2009). *The peter principle, why things always go wrong.* New York, NY: Harper Collins.

2. Ibid

3. Bolles, R.N. (1981). *The Three Boxes of Life and How to Get Out of Them*. Berkeley, CA: Ten Speed Press.

4. Holmes, T.H., & Rahe (1967). The social readjustment rating scale. *Journal of Psychosomatic Research,* 11(2), 213-221.

5. Carroll, P. (2010). *Win forever, live, work, and play like a champion.* London, England: Penguin Books (Portfolio).

Chapter 2

6. Https://www.SBA.gov.

Chapter 3

7. Https://www.SBA.gov.

8. Https:www.SCORE.org.

9. Diamond, L.E., & Diamond, H. (2007). *Teambuilding that gets results* (pg. 7). Naperville, IL: Sourcebooks.

10. Berry, T. (Date unknown). *Lean business plans to get what you want from your business.* Retrieved February 2, 2015 from Timberry.bpPlans.com.

Chapter 4

11. Blanchard, K.H., & Johnson, S. (1982). *The one minute manager.* New York, NY: William Morris and Company.

Chapter 5

12. Dillman, D.A. (1978). *Mail and telephone surveys the total design method.* New York, NY: John Wiley and Sons.

13. Http://www.J.D. Power.com.

14. Http://www.KFC.com.

Chapter 6

15. Https://www.SBA.gov.

16. Https://www.SCORE.org.

17. Https://www.SBA.gov.

18. ibid

19. Http://www.MercyCorps.org.

20. Http://www.IRS.gov.

Chapter 7

21. Https://www.SBA.gov.

22. Berra, Y. (2002). *When you come to a fork in the road, take it.* New York, NY: Hyperion Books

23. Facebook Fan Page: *Alan Mulally*

Chapter 8

24. Scott, M., & Bruce, R. (1987). *Five stages of growth in small business. Long Range Planning* 20 (3), 45-52.

25. Http://www.dol.gov.whd/flsa/.

26. Http://www.dol.gov.

27. Http://www.dol.gov.whd/flsa/.

28. Ibid

29. Http://www.IRS.gov.

Chapter 9

30. Maxwell, J. C. (2001). *Developing the leader within you.* Nashville, TN: Nelson Impact.

31. Bass, B. M. (1990). *Bass & Stodgdill's Handbook of Leadership (3rd ed.). New York, NY: The Free Press. (page 7).*

32. Ibid (page 11).

33. Http://www.NLRB.gov.

Chapter 10

34. CRM Productions (1978). *The power of* listening. New York, NY: McGraw-Hill Films

35. Brod, D. (1984). *Technostress the human cost of the computer revolution.* Menlo Park, CA: Addison-Wesley. (page 16).

36. Garber, R.I. (2014, October 27). *What do the most Americans fear most?* Retrieved Blog post April 29, 2015.

Chapter 11

37. Hayes, R.H. & Wheelwright S. C. (March, 1979). *Link manufacturing process and product life cycles* and *The dynamics of process-product life cycles.* Harvard Business Review. Product 79107-PDF-ENG.

38. Taylor, F.W. (1998, 1st ed. 1911). *The principles of scientific management.* Norcross, GA: Engineering and Management Press.

39. Http://www.deming.org.

40. Womack, J. P., & Jones, D.T. (2003). *Lean thinking banish waste and create wealth in your corporation.* New York, NY: Simon & Schuster.

41. Womack, J. P., & Jones, D.T., & Roose, D. (1991). *The machine that changed the world.* New York, NY: Harper Collins.

Chapter 12

42. Http://WWW.IRS.gov.

Chapter 13

43. Http://www.theIIA.org.

44. Http://www.GAO.gov.

Chapter 14

Chapter 15

45. Womack, J. P., & Jones, D.T. (2003). *Lean thinking banish waste and create wealth in your corporation.* New York, NY: Simon & Schuster.

Chapter 16

46. Garvin, D. (1987, November). Competing on the eight dimensions of quality. *Harvard Business Review.*

47. Http://www.ASQ.org.

Chapter 17

48. Http://www.IRS.gov.

49. Stein, R.A., Executive Director, (1997). *The American bar association guide to workplace law.* New York, NY: Three Rivers Press.

50. Http://www.IRS.gov.

51. Http://www.DOL.gov.

52. Http://www.IRS.gov/smallbusiness/selfemployed/.

53. Http://www.IRS.gov/publications/p583/.

54. Http://www.IRS.gov/publications/p463/.

55. Http://www.IRS.gov/publications/p15/.

Appendix A

Appendix B

57. Http://www.SBA.gov/howtowriteoff/.

Index

F

G

H

I

J

L

M

About the author

Richard (Dick) Larkin, M.B.A., Ed. D. is a SCORE Counselor and Certified Mentor with the U.S. Small Business Administration. He began his business experience as a production worker with The Boeing Company where he worked his way through a variety of commercial and military positions including Project Management, Quality Assurance, Finance, Procurement, and Supply Chain Coordination.

In addition to Boeing, his career has included extensive industrial engineering experience with an international insurance company, a construction industry trust fund administration, several machine shops, and an electronic assembly company. He has owned and operated a bookstore, a coffee shop, and a management consulting service.

Dick has been a professor with the Business Department of several colleges and universities located in Washington, Maryland, and Germany. He has written textbooks and taught a variety of courses including Management Information Systems, Operations Management, Principles of Management, Human Relations, and Human Resource Management.

CPSIA information can be obtained
at www.ICGtesting.com
Printed in the USA
FSOW03n2341151215
14288FS

9 781943 955725